Spirituality in Practice - SiP

A Collection of Essays

Exploration for peace and harmony within
as well as collaboration and cohesiveness
with all that surrounds us.

Dr. Krishnamoorthy (Subbu) Subramanian

Table of Contents

Dedication

This book is dedicated to all my teachers.

They include teachers from elementary school, my Sanskrit
teacher in High School, my advisers in college, Swami
Chinmayananda, elders, friends and family, and above all
everyone whose life experiences have been a constant
source for observation and learning.

Oṃ thath sath brahmārpaṇam astu

May our life and all that we do, be dedicated to
total self-control and unattached active engagement.

Acknowledgments

It is hard to write an acknowledgement for a work than has spanned over decades, even though the formal part might have been for only ten years or more. First, my sincere thanks to all those who read my blog posts and have contributed their inputs through comments online, in person or through mail. Internet and YouTube are relentless sources for information and education, when used wisely. How do you thank the many who contribute to these tools so generously their wealth of knowledge? I have also received suggestions or reading materials from many that have expanded the scope of my reach and learning. While mentioning some I am sure to leave out many others. Accepting this risk, I would like to mention the following with profound gratitude for their inputs and support: My wife Durga, our son Ganesh, his wife Jessica, Dr. S. Ramaswamy, Mrs. Chitra Murali, Mr. John Cain, Mr. Dilip Mathur, Mr. L. Raghavan, Dr. J. Tagat, Dr. A. Mohan, Mr. S. V. Ganesan, Prof. Babu, Mr. N.K. Dhand, Dr. TGK Murty, Swami Vireshananda and many more. Authors of the Foreword are also my close friends. Discussions with them along with Dr. K.K. Sankaran, Dr. N. Balasubramanian, Mr. Vijay Raghavan, and Mr. R. Gopalan have helped me to shape this book immensely. The Jnana Yoga discussion group has provided a forum to discuss and refine many of the models in this book. I am very much indebted to Mr. Logachander and Mrs. Abirami for their relentless support in these discussions for well over a decade along with Mrs. Komala, Mrs. Janaki, and Dr. Santharam.

My sincere thanks to Josh, Jordyn, Natalia and others in the editing and publication of this book.

Finally, a word of thanks to all the readers, especially those from the younger generation. You are the reason for whom this book is written. Even if a few among you learn to look at life in its larger context, an integral part of the universe at large, rather than being shackled by the limitations and constraints as isolated individuals or belonging to a small family, narrow social, religious, or political groups, my gratitude to you for that transformation and the joy it will bring forth for all around you.

Author Biography

Dr. Krishnamoorthy (Subbu) Subramanian, born and raised in Nannimangalam, a rural village in Southern India, graduated from Board High School, Lalgudi, Tamil Nadu, India. He received his undergraduate degree from Osmania University, Hyderabad, India and his Ph. D from MIT, Cambridge, MA. USA in 1977. He has over 45 years of experience working in the global manufacturing sector. His work has focused on research, new business development, innovation, and mentoring. He has worked with people at all professional levels from many nations and continents, from hundreds of companies and scores of universities. He is a distinguished fellow of two professional societies: ASME and SME. He has received the coveted Eugene Merchant Medal for Manufacturing. His professional work has been published extensively. He has authored the book: *The System Approach – A Strategy to survive and succeed in the Global Economy* and co-authored another book: *Thriving in the 21st Century Economy - Transformational Skills for Technical Professionals.* Now he serves as the President of STIMS Institute (www.STIMSInstitute.com), an advisory, consulting, and mentoring services organization that partners with businesses and universities around the world.

Dr. Subramanian is deeply versed in Hindu traditions, culture, and way of life in rural India. His upbringing by his grandparents and growing up in rural Southern India was a formative experience. He has witnessed poverty and affluence and experienced the way of life at all layers of economics in society. His interactions with professionals and their families from many nationalities and cultures have enriched his global view. This personal experience and exposure have impelled his study of Vedic Philosophy and its universal appeal.

He was introduced to studies in Philosophy through a few lectures at MIT by Swami Chinmayananda in the early 1970s. He has pursued self-study since the early 90s, which continues today and hopefully forever. He teaches classes for youth and adults on the theme of Spirituality in Practice (SiP). He explores the nuances of SiP in daily life through mentoring and volunteer work. He is the President of AASAI (American Association for Social Advancement of India http://www.aasai.org/), a non-profit charitable organization. He is married to Dr. Durga Subramanian. Their immediate family includes their son, daughter-in-law, and two lovely grandchildren Asha and Niraj. They live in Bay Area, CA. USA.

Foreword
1

For many 'spirituality' implies metaphysical. It tunes them off from further engagement. For them, 'spirituality' is something to do with abstractions unrelated to everyday concerns of our lives. Moreover, any thought of spirituality is to come well after retirement. That is also when they weigh the question of how to spend more of their time in their late years while also exploring the religion they are affiliated with and partaking in its practices. In other words, 'spirituality' is often perceived as a pursuit for old people!

Dr. K. (Subbu) Subramanian, the author of this book, takes a different view. For him, spirituality is about how to live our day-to-day life. He draws his ideas, arguments, and analysis from the ancient Hindu religious texts (Vedas and their derivatives) and the writings of Hindu seers. His ideas, however, are accessible as well as practicable for everyone, irrespective of their age, way of life or religious affiliation.

Subbu's ideas are applicable in any context. As an academic who teaches management, I see some especially valuable concepts for managers. I want to mention three of them: how to foster objective decision-making, importance of true knowledge, and the components of emotional intelligence. Let me briefly elaborate on these three.

Objective decision-making is at the heart of managerial life. Still, it is fraught with risks, especially since we all have biases. It is important to recognize that we need to work constantly and consciously to elevate ourselves above our biases. One essay in this book highlights three characteristics – desire, anger, and passion – that are the sources of bias that interfere with objective decision-making. A reflection on these sources of bias and a conscious effort to overcome them allow us to be more objective in decision-making. To foster such objective decision-making, we must acquire knowledge of the self and the environment. Another essay in this book on Vedic Philosophy and the Knowledge Economy describes that managers need to know how the environment operates and how they contribute to and are affected by it. Such knowledge allows one to develop objectivity in decision-making over time as it allows managers to rise above their biases. It is important in this Information Age to take the time to gather information, reflect on information, recognize how biases can affect both information choice and information processing, and move on to decision-making with a sense of impersonal detachment.

Finally, the above description of objective decision-making free from biases and the importance of knowledge for decision-making highlights the need for managers to master emotional intelligence to implement such decisions, Emotional intelligence calls for awareness (of the self and social) as well as management (of the self and relationships). In another essay using the parable of taking a horse to the water, Subbu shows how Vedic philosophy encourages us to maintain equilibrium among personal well-being (awareness and management of the self), social well-being (awareness of others and management of social relationships) and spiritual well-being (inner harmony that helps to see the self as an integral part of others).

In sum, the author has admirably succeeded in linking the ancient wisdom of Vedic philosophy to the needs of the modern world. His discursive yet logical writing style allows one to learn complex concepts, understand them in a contemporary context, and feel encouraged to apply them in their own life, adapting them to suit the occasion's needs. Thanks to the author's efforts, I hope that many readers will take advantage of the book to partake in the wisdom of our ancients located in the modern milieu.

Prof. U. Srinivasa Rangan

Luksic Chair Professor of Strategy and Global Studies

Babson College, Babson Park, MA 02457, USA

Foreword
2

Having benefited from attending the Spirituality in Practice classes under the banner of Jnana Yoga, we are excited to see this collection of essays, a distillation of the essence of our learning over the past decade.

Divided into three parts, Dr. Krishnamoorthy (Subbu) Subramanian introduces us to the basics of spirituality in the first section, exploring the gamut of its terminology, emphasizing for the readers the aspects of spirituality as a way of life in harmony with universal principles based in a foundation of rational and holistic thinking. Also included are very helpful discussions of steps of learning and other essential tools to help us embark on our quest to spiritual living. A lucid discussion helps the reader understand how spirituality extends beyond belief systems of religion, rituals, and theology to inform our life and living.

The second section discusses the basis of Vedic philosophy, the knowledge of self, as each one of us live and experience different planes of existence. The concepts of emotional and objective reasoning, as part of our interactions and connections with the world, are explored, especially as it relates to the individual journey from emotional beings through rational objectivity to that holy grail of Vedic philosophy - nonattachment and renunciation of the world while actively engaging within it. This, perhaps the most difficult concept of Vedic philosophy, is rendered without the complex language typically associated with it. This makes it accessible and engrossing to everyone not necessarily well-versed in the concepts of Vedanta or Vedic philosophy.

The third section is where the essence of teaching comes by relating our everyday experiences to spirituality in our inner selves, our interaction with each other, and nature itself. The ancient wisdom of *Bhagavadgītā,* which the author quotes extensively, has stood the test of time precisely as it applies to spiritual living in daily life. This is the section where the proverbial 'rubber meets the road'. With innumerable examples from his own life and observations, this section expertly incorporates the spiritual principles helping us learn in our quest to improve our experiences beyond physical emotions and reactions through rational objectivity to purposeful and impactful action. And finally, active engagement with the world combined with the detached worldview of a true yogi. The way we are all interconnected, and a part of the larger universe is the universal consciousness.

This book is an amazing accomplishment and culmination of outstanding efforts to bring forth an enriched guide to new aspirants interested in the spiritual path or existing seekers needing additional guidance to continue in their spiritual journey. Essays contained in this book provide a wonderful kaleidoscopic view into the world of spiritual knowledge and wisdom. It takes the reader on a journey based on sound principles of Vedic philosophy. As the reader dwells deeper into the essays, the understanding and transformation is intrinsic. The essays explore many concepts and assumptions with an analytical scientific view. Various aspects of human behavior, beliefs, practices, rituals, and ideas are explored and put to the mettle. The essays are thought-provoking, and the final product is a work of art that is fascinating and full of joy. A great collection that makes a relentless effort towards discovering one's own true self and eventually immerses us in the nectar of spiritual moorings.

The significant highlight of this work is the manner in which complex topics derived from Vedanta and mythology are illustrated. Several essays are interestingly formatted with titles as questions to arouse curiosity in any spiritual seeker. The core of these essays comprises the building blocks of the path of Jnana Yoga and include a rich blend of concepts referring to the *Bhagavadgītā,* Upanishad, and Eastern philosophies. This collection of essays greatly simplifies the

concepts, terms, and meanings of intricate notions and is very well organized to suit the levels of any reader and spark their interest. Readers who sincerely contemplate and comprehend the contents of these essays and adapt them in the daily and challenging times of their lives will benefit from the valuable concepts and thoughts.

Mr. Logachander Natarajan

Mr. Girish Sripathi

Dr. Shashidhar Harohalli

Members, Jnana Yoga Study Group, NH., USA.

Foreword
3

For millennia, scriptures, including the Vedas, the Upanishads, and the *Bhagavadgītā,* have offered important insights into the nature of the self, the workings of our mind, body, and the spirit, and our ways of living. *Bhagavadgītā,* or Song of the Lord, is a Hindu philosophical scripture in the form of a dialogue between the Pandava prince Arjuna and his charioteer Krishna in the epic *Mahabharata.* It is also a work of theology, spirituality, human psychology, and ethics. Through this dialogue, Krishna counsels Arjuna, teaching him the cyclical nature of birth and death, the permanent nature of the human soul within the transient human body, a duty to righteous action, control of the senses, and perils of attachment to materialism.

Over the centuries, several commentaries have been written on the Gita and the Vedic scriptures largely focused on the philosophical and spiritual insights. Relatively few have distilled these insights for practical application in day-to-day life. Spirituality in Practice by Dr. Krishnamoorthy (Subbu) Subramanian adds to this much-needed body of work, providing practice-oriented insights into Vedic Philosophy. It is a must-read book for anyone interested in eastern philosophy, applied to living a balanced life with happiness and contentment. This work comprises a collection of essays that condense insights from the eastern spiritual scriptures in a highly engaging, down-to-earth manner. The book clarifies the distinction between religion and spirituality and conveys the complex models of the nature of the mind, body, and spirit for the reader in a simple yet elegant manner without jargon. What makes the reading compelling is Dr. Subramanian's use of many real-life anecdotes, some from his own life, to illustrate key insights. The book is also replete with diagrams, tables, metaphors, and mnemonics, many of which are original.

Anyone who wishes to improve one's approach to ever-changing life situations and individuals seeking to understand optimum ways to engage in leadership will find this book valuable. As a practicing psychiatrist, I find several aspects of this book applicable to individuals struggling daily with existential challenges. Such insights are relevant today as we are facing a pandemic of emotional distress on top of a viral pandemic impacting all aspects of our lives.

Matcheri S Keshavan MD

Stanley Cobb, Professor of Psychiatry

Harvard Medical School

Boston MA 02115, USA.

1. Introduction

This is a collection of essays on life in general. In our rush to do better, feel better and be happy, we tend to miss a large part of who we are, what we already have, and the happiness which is natural and within us all the time. When we stop, look around and "smell the roses" on hand, then it becomes easier to do better in whatever we are doing. Good feelings and genuine happiness also come forth as naturally as the water flows downstream or the rain soaks the dry earth, or plants grow on their own nourished by rainwater! This is *Spirituality in Practice* (SiP)!

I was born and raised in a village in India. I moved to larger cities for higher studies and work, then for graduate studies at MIT, Cambridge, MA., USA. My long professional career created opportunities to interact with many people and their families across the globe. My upbringing in the villages and small towns in rural India has been a source of reference for comparison and connectedness with many cultures and their way of life I witnessed across the globe while progressing through life. I have personally witnessed poverty and affluence in many continents. I have experienced the culture and way of life at all layers of society. My interactions with many professionals and their families from many nationalities and cultures have enriched my global view. This personal experience and exposure have impelled my study of Vedic Philosophy and its universal appeal.

SiP is always a work in progress. While perfection is the goal, we need to keep the "I" or ego in check to gain the most of it, for peace and harmony within as well as collaboration and cohesiveness with all that surrounds us! So, we have named our blog site: Spirituality in Practice — SiP! This compilation of essays started as a series of blog posts over ten years ago at www.Sipractce.com. There are over 200 essays on this blog site. They have been edited and condensed into 76 essays presented in this book.

This book starts with an overview of spirituality and to address many questions about this topic. This overview also lays the foundation to understand and treat spirituality as a tangible and real aspect of everyone's daily life. We recognize spirituality as a non-denominational process exhibited through our thought and actions. We recognize that spirituality is one of the three legs of a stool required for a stable life, along with material/physical and emotional/social aspects as the other two legs. When we focus primarily on the material aspects of life or seek comfort through family and social groups, our life suffers from instability since we ignore spirituality as something that belongs to religious people with a monastic or secluded way of life. We hope to shatter this paradigm and false notion and present spirituality in practice as an essential for everyone's life.

A collection of five essays is found in the introductory section. Through these essays, we glide into an analytical approach, the basis for any philosophical study. Then we enter the realm of Vedic Philosophy and its relevance for daily life. We address the basics of Vedic Philosophy through a series of twenty-two essays. Spirituality in practice is far more engaging and applicable in various contexts in daily life. We explore this application-oriented discussion of Vedic Philosophy in the next chapter containing forty-nine essays.

In the end, we hope the reader leaves with a few takeaways: Vedic Philosophy is not abstract and metaphysical. The concepts proposed in Vedic Philosophy provide a simple yet comprehensive framework to describe and understand anything we wish to study or learn about. Life is not an aimless journey but full of potentials enriched by the soul within and the universe at large. We are alone if we choose to be, but we are also seamlessly part of everything since that is the way it is. True knowledge is not feeling isolated as individuals. True knowledge is to see us as part of the eternal and ever-present universe. The goal is to feel good through self-compassion but also work towards the peace and harmony of all, limitlessly. We are subjective when we see ourselves as a droplet of water. We become objective when we see ourselves as part of the whole, a larger body of water. We become increasingly objective when we are under self-control (in our physical perceptions), with non-attachment (in our emotions), and liberated in our thoughts from all that bind and isolate us as "I" or individuals (like drops of water). We gain true knowledge when we realize that all that is cognitive and all their enablers (laws of nature) are like two sides of a coin, like the waves on the surface and the deep ocean below coexisting, inseparable, and enabling the other.

To keep the discussion simple and easy to follow, the book is written as a collection of essays. Each essay could be read as an individual item or as part of a stream, depending on the reader's time, motivation, and personal needs of the moment. However you choose to read, we hope you gain some nugget of value each time that uplifts your spirits and a positive outlook on life.

We use simple schematics or illustrations to bring out the "model" behind the thoughts codified in Vedic Philosophy. We do not follow a single text or set of references, but it should be clear that all the materials contained in this book are from a large body of scripture collectively known as Vedic literature. Some interpretations and all the figures are original. The principles and framework outlined in the essays to convey the Vedic Philosophy are adapted from Vedic literature and many books written in English and Tamil to translate and convey their meaning by scores of authors.

The origins of Vedic Philosophy are not well known. They are treated as self-evident truths. The authors of Vedic literature are many. Our salutations to all these visionaries. We present this collection of essays with great regard and reverence to all of them. Our gratitude and reverence are also for many Saints like Adi Sankara and modern-day teachers such as Bhagavan Ramana Maharishi, Ramakrishna Paramahamsa, Swami Vivekananda, and many others. This author was introduced to formal studies in Vedanta by Swami Chinmayananda through his lectures. "Studies in Vedic Philosophy should not be an abstract intellectual exercise" was his repeated guidance through his lectures. Instead, all such studies should lead to their understanding

and application in our daily life. The theme of this book –
Spirituality in Practice – originated from this guidance!

2. Spirituality in Practice: Overview

Spirituality – What is it?

Life is a constant balance between our physical, emotional, and intellectual conditions. In the Sanskrit language, "condition" is described as *Upadhi*. It is a holistic understanding of what it is. Physical condition for each of us could imply our body and all its parts as material objects of nature, no different from all other objects or matter. As an example, our bone is a structured composite. It can be compliant up to a point and can be brittle and fracture at the extreme! A collection of such bones in different forms and shapes held together by muscles, tendons, and ligaments creates our body. Our bones are no different from the structural elements like the beams or pillars in a house! In this condition, the body of everyone and animals or other objects of nature are all the same!

Our physical body is sustained by the life processes (breathing, blood circulation, neural processes, sensory perceptions, vision, hearing...) that make us living people. Emotions are our ever-present perceptions and responses to our physical conditions. We are impulsive and reactive when we are subjective. We are reflective and considerate when we are objective. We shall discuss more on subjective vs. objective in future essays. Beyond our physical and emotional conditions, we are also endowed with the ability to think and reason. This analytical skill or condition is co-existent with our body and emotions from birth and as we age with time. Hence life at any time requires managing all three conditions – physical, emotional, and intellectual.

These conditions of who we are and how we live are like the ever-present waves on the surface of the ocean. The waves do not exist on their own. They are part and parcel of the deep ocean, supporting and enabling all the waves. There is no separation between the waves and the ocean beneath. All our physical, emotional, and intellectual conditions exist and remain inseparable from the vast nature (and its laws). Collectively they are called *Brahman* in Vedic Philosophy. Living with peace and in harmony must include acknowledgment of this reality.

Life from a spiritual perspective includes (a) Comprehensive look and management of our body and its functions, Emotions, and Intellectual needs, (b) Constant awareness of our inseparable union with nature and its laws (*Brahman), and* (c) Such awareness leading to an outlook of universality that "I" and the universe at large are one and the same, indivisible, eternal and omnipresent! Perhaps such graceful living is reflected in the Vedic pronouncements: I am Brahman (*Aham Brahma Asmi),* and May everyone, and indeed everything exist in peace and harmony (*Sarve' Jhana Sukino Bhavanthu)?*

How do I think, and for what purpose?

How do I reflect? Analyze? Ponder?

Why do I feel the emotions, and where do they come from?

Why do I choose to do all my activities?

Am I alone and unique? Or am I merely part and parcel of everyone and everything around me? Am I part of the Universe at large?

Finding answers to the above questions is the beginning of "spirituality". Answers to these questions set the path, direction, and way we engage our body, mind, and intellect in all their functions. Such engagement, in turn, determines the harmony one experiences within and with the world outside.

Spirituality may be described as:

An outlook, a way of living that promotes peace and harmony within as well as harmony with everything external limitlessly as part of the universe.

Spirituality is described through the pronouncement in the Upanishad:

Tat Thwam Asi (You and the Universe are integral in each other).

The evidence of spirituality in practice is best described by the following examples from *Bhagavadgītā*:

The enlightened living of a spiritually evolved person is like a breeze, which by its mere presence spreads the fragrance from the flowers for all to enjoy, in the process also leading to pollination and growth of the plants. The breeze itself neither recognizes the fragrance, pollination, or even its own impact on such effects.

Spiritually enlightened persons live like a lotus plant, which, while living all the time in the pool of water, does not get attached to it, as seen by the droplet of water dancing in its expansive leaf.

A spiritually evolved person, through their self-control, lives as his own friend in harmony with everyone and everything around him. Through the absence of self-control, one becomes one's own worst enemy!

Lao Tsu, the Chinese Philosopher of the 6th century BC, said: *The best of leaders are those who help others accomplish their objectives; when finished, others say that they did it by themselves.*

Do we need "Spirituality"?

Spirituality is an innate quality in all of us. Philosophers would say that the universe exists in spiritual harmony. Our individual perspective inhibits us from this inner harmony and hence the need for its constant discovery. Our choices and preferences in our thoughts limit our ability to see beyond such choices. Much of our experience – acquired through the body, mind, and intellect – are a measure of our spirituality. Our inner agony, and hence a lack of true inner contentment, arises out of our unwillingness to explore the subject at hand in resonance with our spirituality. True inner peace experienced within and harmonious existence with outside are evidence of spirituality in practice.

Why should anyone bother to take precious time off from other things to reflect on "spirituality"?

The above is a fair and legitimate question. Certainly, no one needs to reflect on "spirituality" for its own sake. We should not do anything in life without clarity of purpose. How do we choose what we want to do? How can we make this a natural habit in our daily life: at home, at work, in bringing up our children, in taking care of our elders, in taking care of ourselves, in our friendships? Often, we engage in life without even thinking of this basic question "Why am I doing this? How did I make a choice to do this instead of something else?" No one can provide specific answers to these questions. These questions are personal, self-initiated, and answered by one's own self. However, spirituality can:

Focus our attention on these basic questions.

Provide a way or method to steer our analysis.

Create confidence and courage to pose such questions to oneself.

Create a comfort to find answers, accept and live in comfort with such answers.

Ultimately engage in whatever we do with a sense of inner peace and harmony with the outside world.

To facilitate such self–inquiry is the beginning of the spiritual journey in life.

Can we not live well without spirituality?

Life presupposes an object of the universe capable of "breathing" or surviving in some fashion for its mere existence. Spirituality is much like that. As humans, we exist, distinct from other objects of nature, by our mere ability to make choices. Spirituality would seem to be the means through which we can understand the process we use to make these choices.

One could ask, "Can I live without breathing?" The answer is clearly "No." But we do not know anyone with perfect health or "breathing". There is always a shade of something missing or something that can be better. It seems to be the same with spirituality. One can always seek a better spiritual condition. But no one should forget that we are all spiritual in some way or fashion, to begin with.

Is it the same as religion?

The answer depends on your understanding of "What is religion"? Generally, any religion favors reflection and introspection, in turn leading to spiritual evolution. Such practices of self-reflection or introspection may be facilitated through certain faiths and beliefs. Each religion differs from the other based on the faiths and beliefs promoted by that religion.

To the extent that religion promotes reflection and introspection, there is a similarity with the beginnings of spirituality. But spirituality requires no allegiance to any religion, faith, or belief.

Ask yourself the following questions:

"Am I okay?"

"I am okay. Are you okay?"

"We are okay?"

"Are we all okay?"

Spiritual evolution progressively promotes a frame of mind that responds with the single answer "Yes" to each of these questions. It may be tentative at first but finally with resolve to all the above four questions simultaneously and without hesitation, limitations, or exception.

How clear and instinctive is your answer "Yes" to the above questions vs. how much do you rely on guidelines, beliefs, and faiths prescribed by a religion of your choice? – The distinction between spirituality and religion begins to emerge. The more instinctive the answer "Yes", the more your evolution in spirituality in practice. More hesitant and nuanced your answer based on references to teaching from any source; you may rely on religion or theology as your source of support.

It is important to note that in daily communications spirituality, practices of religion, being reflective, and introspective are all used interchangeably. As a result, being spiritual and religious is considered one and the same. Also, being spiritual is assumed to imply merely intellectual and, to some extent, to become reclusive. All these would appear to be arbitrary limitations imposed on spirituality.

Being religious helps to look at the world we live in a larger context yet bound by principles and moral codes of conduct. Being religious also promotes reflection and introspection. Hence being religious is a pathway for the two essential aspects of spirituality (i.e.): integration and harmony with the outside world as well as reflection and introspection and harmony within. But religion as a pathway is not identical to the end point of being spiritual.

The focus of spirituality is to recognize the unity of oneself with the universe at large. Such unity within and with the external brings forth an inner vitality, a calm yet determined purposefulness in life and in all its activities. As a result, spirituality is the springboard to engage in the dynamic world of activities while maintaining composure, stability, and consistency, which others might often perceive as being intellectual and reclusive.

Bhagavadgītā describes spiritual evolution as enlightenment. The enlightened person is described as:

One who appears to be asleep when others are awake and is awake when others are asleep!

Through self-control, one remains one's own best friend.

One who is steady and equal in response to the dualities of pleasure/pain, like/dislike, friend/foe, etc.

A judge in the legal system is not disposed to either party. They are equal in disposition to like/dislike, friend/foe, defendant/prosecutor, etc. The judge is objective, non-attached, and considers all evidence without favor or preference. This objective un-attached outlook is also at the core of spirituality. They are also the fundamentals for any professional – lawyer, teacher, doctor, engineer, politician, etc. – in any field. They are also essential for anyone in a leadership role in a team, family, project, work, business, etc. We can clearly see that spirituality leads to a higher plane in any activity, profession, or walk of life.

Does spirituality depend on your religion?

Religion usually is a tool – a steppingstone – to give you a few answers to get started. If you accept the answers as inalienable truths and if you live limited by such a world of faith and belief, then you live in the realm of religion. If you accept the guidelines from the religion as a starting point and eventually develop your own personal clarity on their basis through analysis and reflection, then you are well on your way to your spiritual journey.

Religion paves the way for spiritual evolution in all of us. Like the many mountain paths to the summit, every religion helps us ascend to the same summit. The summit is evidence of spiritual evolution. If the entire mountain range represents spirituality, what are the roles of religions, which merely lie on the surface of the mountain?

Referring to our four questions mentioned earlier, if you are "okay", why is it so? If you are not okay, why is that? The clarity in our answers is evidence of progression in the spiritual journey.

In the question "I am okay?" we can address three components: "I", "Am", and "Okay". Religions give us some starting definitions for each of these three words. Usually, these are in the form of dogma or moral codes, with which we can relate to one another. Reflection and further study lead us to answers which are universal and devoid of religion.

Then we can look at the other questions, "We are okay?", "Are we all okay?" and their components in the same fashion. Again, religions give us some starting definitions. Society and mode of living in harmony with each other within the society evolve through answers to these questions. How far and limitless is your understanding of the term "all"? Religious outlook accepts everyone within the religion as the same. Clear distinctions are identified across religions through real or perceived differences in faiths and beliefs. Spirituality sees no such distinctions of any kind. Spiritually evolved outlook sees the single entity – the *Brahman* or the universe of nature – as the substratum of all that appears distinct and different.

Is "spirituality" non-denominational? How?

Yes. The exploration of questions such as "Who am I? How do I make choices? How do I relate to the world around me? How can I find an inner harmony that permeates as harmony with the universe?" is spirituality. These questions apply to young and old, rich or poor, man or woman, and people of any nationality, religion, race, color, or creed. Indeed, the same questions could be asked to include all objects of nature, conceivable and beyond our cognition. As one begins to see this expansive nature of our existence and finds the same answer in every case (i.e.) the universe and I are integral and inseparable from each other (*Tat Thwam Asi*); I am Brahman (*Aham Brahma*), one would clearly say that spirituality knows no distinctions of any kind.

Is spirituality something for this life or for afterlife?

This is a difficult question to answer. Before answering this question, one must address the question: "Do you believe in the life after?" Spirituality and true inner contentment through it are real. We can relate to this in this life. If such contentment also satisfies your belief in life after, that is good. It will be a pity if one lives a life of discontent today, hoping for contentment in the afterlife. This would be like someone who does not care for physical fitness today and abuses his body, hoping to be in better shape in their old age. It will also be like seeking a fruit – real or imagined – while letting the one in hand slip away and fall into the dirt.

What are the steps to experience spirituality in our daily life?

All our experiences are the outcome of the connection of the inner person, the spirit or consciousness with everything external. Such connection is made through three co-existing connectors like strands of the rope. These three strands are knowledge, bias, and ignorance. All three strands co-exist all the time. The dominance of one over the other two determines the equilibrium which we identify as our experience for that moment in that connection.

Objectivity leads to our comprehension of all our experiences, their interplay, and how they come into existence as a reflection of the three connectors. Objectivity permits us to observe life as a spectator while also being the actor, director, and producer of life, as a stage play.

Reflection, meditation, and contemplation lead us toward recognition of the abstract themes or concepts that connect and unify all perceived differences and variations. Such spiritual evolution brings increasingly larger meaning and purpose for intangibles such as "love", "friendship", "generosity", "compassion", "absence of ego", etc.

Can we see evidence of spirituality in practice in day-to-day life? How?

There are many attributes or behavioral outcomes through which we can observe spirituality in our daily life. Examples are:

An attitude or connection to all objects and living beings, without differences: friendly, considerate; compassionate.

Without a sense of the possession or "ego": absence of singular ownership; without the feeling that the self is the only one responsible or the singular source of any event or outcome.

Even minded with respect to happiness and sorrow.

Forgiving in nature.

Practitioner of self-control: Ever steady in meditation, contemplation, and contented to be in union with the self.

Of firm conviction, with mind and intellect dedicated to a larger common cause.

One who is not agitated by others, nor cause agitation in others.

Free from the influences or anxiety due to joy, envy, and fear.

Pure; skillful; prompt (ever attentive, ready, and vigilant).

One who initiates all actions with a sense of renunciation of the self-intended purpose, Free of unrelenting wants.

Does not rejoice (endlessly); does not hate (endlessly); neither grieves (endlessly) nor desires (wants) endlessly;

renouncing the impact of good/pleasant and bad/unpleasant with faith based on understanding.

Even minded. Dualities are held in equal regards, such as friend or foe; in honor and dishonor; in heat and cold; in happiness and sorrow; criticism and praise.

Free from attachment or association (through clarity or understanding that all experiences result from the interplay of the three connectors (mentioned earlier).

Silent (because of calm contemplation); Contended in all matters.

At home, anywhere, and everywhere: Not rooted in any place or thing solely through emotional attachments.

Of stable mind, firmly rooted in the constant practice of self-control (Yoga).

Note: Above are listed as qualities of an enlightened person - *Bhagavadgītā* Chapter 12

How can I engage in Spirituality in Practice?

First, understand what spirituality is.

We are all okay. We are always in harmony with nature - within and without. We exist as an integral part of the universe.

The universe exists as a witness to the role and play of the Laws of Nature (*Brahman*)

The laws of nature (*Brahman*) are our nature itself.

Spiritual acts nurture the mind; the spiritual mind nurtures the intellect; spiritually oriented intellect promotes spiritual acts...

We can nurture spirituality by engaging in selfless acts. This can be through charity or helping others in need. This can also be done by caring for each other as fellow human beings in the common journey of life. Spirituality is also self-compassion! Engaging the mind to be consciously aware of the emotions and feelings of the self and others is also part of nurturing spirituality. Intellectually we nurture spirituality through noble thoughts.

Essays in this book explore aspects of Spirituality in Practice. Enjoy the reading and reflection. It is our small contribution to your journey of life.

3. Introductory Essays

Education: The Teacher, Student, and the Transformation

Emphasis on the "Process" of learning:

Education is a transformative process. Education happens when someone who wants to learn – the student – and someone to teach are both present. There is a famous verse from Upanishad. The students and the teacher chant this verse at the beginning of each class:

sahanāvavatu saha nau bhunaktu saha vīryaṃ karavāva hai
tejasvi nāvadhītamastu mā vidviṣāva hai
oṃ śāntiḥ śāntiḥ śāntiḥ

May the Lord (the Omnipresent) protect us as we rejoice by sharing what we consume, acquire greater abilities through education, and may such learning lead to greater glory. Let there not be deep-seated divisions among us.

Peace! Peace! Peace!

The question may arise:

Why do we see reference to "avoid deep-seated divisions" in the invocation? Relentless focus on one point of view, without accommodation of other ideas and thoughts, leads to deep-seated divisions. Life is not always Black and White. It is mostly grey. Often it becomes a matter of opinions and debates on the divisions or shades of grey! Education also requires a constant emphasis on the process of learning, enabled by proper tools that contribute to greater clarity and why the shades are that way. For one who is truly objective and scientific, the emphasis will be on the process of inquiry.

Through objective learning, the different points of view will be seen as outcome of the depth and breadth of our understanding of the subject matter on hand and our methods of reasoning, measurement, and analysis. While there could be differences in the data and its interpretation, for a truly scientific community (of students and teachers), there should be no differences in the tools used for analysis and the process of measurement or the analysis methods!

Indeed, true education is not a precise transmission of data and its pre-ordained interpretation (or opinions). Hence it would appear that through the above invocation, both the students and the teacher are urged to focus on the "process" of learning and not get distracted by mere evidence and their interpretation and the divisions they invariably bring about.

Learning about the basics of Vedic Philosophy and its application to daily life is our goal. We pray for this common goal between the author and the reader!

Steps of learning: Education is described in the Scriptures as a four-step process analogous to crossing a river.

First step: The teacher points the student toward the direction of the river. Both have an expressed interest in crossing the river (desired education).

Second Step: Next, the teacher helps the student wet his feet by entering the river. In the beginning, the depth of water may be shallow and just enough to wet the toes, then progressively deeper. It is the duty of the teacher to be sure that the student is stable and can withstand the river currents. It is also the duty of the teacher to ensure that the student does not get too deep into the water, or into the turbulent swirl, without adequate preparation to swim well.

This initiation to the field of study reminds one of the freshman seminars in US universities:

Freshman Honors Seminars program offers freshmen the opportunity to study in small, intellectually stimulating courses taught by distinguished faculty members from throughout the entire University. Seminars introduce freshmen to challenging standards of analysis and argumentation, oral as well as written. They accomplish this through intensive discussion, focused papers, and readings emphasizing critical interpretation. – NYU website.

Third Step: Now, the teacher points to the various features of the river, like the depths and shallows. At some point, because of the ability to deal with the various aspects, the student may feel at home with the expanse of the subject matter and can move about freely – offering beautiful explanations, annotation, summaries, new evidence, etc.

Fourth Step: For the student, well versed in the subject like the fish in the river, there will be a tendency to stay in the river too long or forever. Such students may offer brilliant explanations on the subject matter, at times extremely nuanced and difficult for others to follow or benefit from! At this stage, the teacher is required to help the student to cross the river and continue their journey of life. Education is not an end but a transformation to put the education for better use in society at large.

Note: Above story is part of a discourse in Tamil Language by Velukkudi Krishnan Swamigal.

Our studies in Spirituality in Practice follow the above steps as well. We get an introduction to the subject in chapters 2 and 3 (like recognizing the river and getting the feet wet). Through these essays the reader is exposed to subject of Spirituality and its context. Chapter 4 covers in-depth the knowledge and intricacies of Vedic Philosophy. In chapter 5, the reader is presented with essays covering various situations and topics where this fundamental knowledge can be applied under the umbrella of spirituality in practice. Enjoy the reading, learning, and transformation!

A Philosophic Reflection on Oil Lamp

In an oil lamp, the earthen cup or the brass container holds the oil. The wick soaked in oil provides the channel through which the oil is drawn to one end, where it burns to create the flame. While much of the oil is consumed through burning, there is also a small and gradual burning of the wick into carbon or ash as well. This transformation leads to the flame, its glow that illuminates the surroundings. As a result, we see the lamp as well as all the space that is illuminated. The glow from the oil lamp is not much different from the light from a candle.

Figure 3.1. Oil Lamp is made up of the stable or inertial lamp, unstable and volatile oil as well as transformative wick leading to the glow of the flame. They truly reflect every one of us as human – inertial, turbulent, and tranquil - with an inner glow of the Soul that enables and illumines everything!

The components of the oil lamp are the cup, the oil, and the wick. That nature of the world or the universe, which does not change on its own accord, we recognize as inertia or *Thamasam*. The earthen cup is stable. Unless broken into pieces or cracks have developed, the cup can be used forever. There are temples in India where the lamps are many centuries old. They are used even today. Churches use candle holders that are centuries old. This stability of material objects is amazing in a world where change is assumed to be normal and even expected.

"*Rajasam*" or turbulence is another property of nature. Just like inertia, there is nothing good or bad about turbulence. It is the variable aspect of our surroundings that enables life as we know it. The oil in the lamp is volatile. Under very low temperatures, it freezes into a solid. The oil vaporizes at higher temperatures. Hence ambient conditions – the surroundings – have a great influence on the behavior of the oil. Almost all aspect of our physical world relies on changes influenced by physical processes. We recognize these as chemical reactions, response functions, energy fields, etc. Without flow and volatile nature of oil, we will not have a flame, which implies no illumination. A lamp, as a source of light, acquires all its merits only because of the stable or inertial container and the turbulent or volatile fluid contained in it! Without these two – stability as well volatility (change) – there is no flame and hence no light and thus nothing for us to recognize as the lamp!

The property which enables us to become aware of the unknown hitherto, is called *Sathvikam or* Tranquility. The flame creates a glow leading to illumination. Thanks to this illumination, we see objects in and around the lamp. We become aware of their presence or existence. Like its cousin's inertia and turbulence, this property is neither good nor bad. It merely exists! Tranquility is always associated with turbulence and inertia, just as the glow of the lamp (illumination) is enabled by the stable cup and the volatile oil. In fact, all three properties co-exist. None of the three can exist in the absence of the other two!

The container is stable, and hence it can be measured in terms of its dimensions, weight, volume, etc. Such measures remain constant over time. There is a certainty associated with inertia*!*

The fluid – oil – is measured using the container in which it is held – such as the volume occupied or the weight added to the container! A liquid object is always quantified relative to something that is unrelentingly stable! Our emotions are known based on our actions, words, expressions through body functions, etc., and how they change with time, place, or circumstances! We are happy or unhappy relative to what we wish to be or relative to the happiness or unhappiness of someone else! They are always understood in relative terms.

Without a body, there are no emotions and hence no turbulence on its own accord! Next time you feel agitated, take a moment to reflect: Are you providing the container for the volatility to grow and thrive? Or are you using others as the containers to reinforce your turbulence or volatile nature? Just as the oil, which assumes the shape of the container it fills, our emotions also adapt to the nature of their container (our body functions).

The wick is a relatively insignificant part of the lamp in terms of its weight, size, volume, etc. It is very easy to ignore or dismiss the existence of a wick. It plays its transformative role – of transporting the oil, creating a space of controlled combustion. The same can be said of our intellect. Which part of our body is the home of our intellect? If you say "mind", then is it not the home for all our emotions and upheavals? In our daily stress and pressures, it is possible to relegate the mind and its role largely for our emotions (turbulence). It requires a concerted effort to assign a small but significant focus to the mind and its function to engage in thoughts and the transformation it can create for our emotions and body functions.

The flame of a lamp enables us to see all the objects in its glow. In a dark place, the glow of the lamp enables us to see the lamp itself. The same is true of our thoughts and ideas and their transformation into knowledge. Through our knowledge and understanding – the glow – we comprehend everything around us and the very enablers of such knowledge (i.e.) our body, mind, and intellect.

Darkness and illumination are complements of each other. The same goes for knowledge and ignorance on any subject. When the illumination is not adequate, our vision diminishes, and we rely on guesswork or judgment. This uncertain nature, with respect to our knowledge, is the source of our bias or turbulence!

One can extend such analysis and apply the analogy of the lamp to understand the role of the three connectors – inertia, turbulence, and tranquility – to progressively greater depth. We also learn that our knowledge, bias, and ignorance are all interconnected, laying the foundation for all our experiences. Perhaps such reflection, analysis, and understanding are suggested by the following verses. They are chanted at the end of almost all Vedic worship services, along with the offering of the lighted lamp to the idol at the altar (*Deepa Aradhana*):

The sun does not shine, nor the moon and the stars, nor the flashes of lightning, nor this flame of the lamp. All these shine through His luster

Katha Upanishad 2.2.15

Neither the sun nor the moon nor the fire shine there; having reached that place, no one returns; that is My abode BG 15.6.

All that we know is the result of our understanding through our knowledge of nature and the laws that govern nature. This knowledge – that accepts everything as parts of nature, and everything is enabled by the laws of nature – is the only true knowledge. On comprehending this knowledge, one acquires a stable frame of mind from which one does not return to the life of perturbations caused by our limited knowledge, bias, and ignorance.

Philosophy provides the reasoning behind the ideals we seek to live by in our daily life. It is an analytical pathway to understand the visible and invisible better. Idols we worship are the visible symbols of the invisible ideals. The un-flickering glow of the lamp – deep inside the sanctum – is our visible symbol of the idol. When we see the oil lamp and its flame, we implicitly understand Divinity and the God it represents!

"The un-wavering smile of a Yogi (one of self-control and constant internal reflection) is like the glow of a steady, un-flickering flame of the lamp" BG 6. 19.

Religion – The Door To The House That Exists Or Not?

"I think different religions are like different doors to the same house. Sometimes I think the house exists and sometimes, I don't" – Isaacson's biography of Steve Jobs, founder, and successful inventor/entrepreneur at Apple Inc.

Religion can be divided into three parts: One that promotes certain faith and belief system; the second, which provides certain rituals and guidelines to abide by; the third, a pathway for philosophical inquiry. Most religions are an amalgam of all three pathways.

Each religion is recognized frequently based on the belief system specific to that religion. Invoking the concept of God or some superhuman entity is common to all religions, even though the descriptions of God may vary from one religion to another. This aspect of "faith" uniquely relates to a religion's identity. Hinduism is seen as a religion with hundreds of Gods, the laws of Karma, and reincarnation.

Hope, stability, and permanence can be experienced through the door of faith. This door helps me to cope with situations and circumstances that I cannot handle when I am at the limits of my rational analysis. It is only through faith in some entity larger than my comprehension that I can come to terms with certain events in my life and in the life of others that otherwise seem miraculous on the positive side or beyond the limits of misery and suffering on the negative side. Yet, most of the time, after some reflection and after regaining my analytical process for inquiry, I can understand the cause and effect. I become more certain of the laws of nature are at play. At that point, the gateway of faith appears like a needless entrance to a non-existent house. Hence the house behind the gates of faith, the house of heaven and hell, and the pre-ordination through Karma and the reincarnation of life appear illusive.

Over a period, rituals get established to bring everyone into a common fold and create a sense of continuity. We show our affection, respect, and connection to each other in myriad ways through rituals established over the years. We shake hands, hug each other, etc. Yet, we don't think much about them if we live in a community where these rituals are seen as part of the norm. But, when we are not accustomed to them, then rituals appear strange and uncomfortable. The rituals in the baseball game would appear strange and unwarranted for soccer fans! Often, the rituals are questioned when individuals force them to exercise authority in areas where they do not have such a role or power! These individuals use religion and their rituals to open the doors to a house that does not exist.

The philosophical aspect of any religion is much needed. This is a door to the house full of promise. Yet very few seek to open this door of substantial value. Rituals evolve to codify the guidelines, which are the outcome of philosophical reasoning. The belief systems of each religion serve as the steps to ascend to the gates of philosophy. For example: How is it possible to relate to objectivity when we live in a world of subjectivity? Our experiences, the judgment they create, and our responses, as a result, are all subjective! But we can measure or calibrate our objectivity through a pointer, marker, or reference. One who is the most objective among us is identified as the "*Mahatma*". In this respect, God, the ideal for objectivity on all occasions and in all situations, is referred to as "*Paramathma*", or the Supreme Being. The path of analytical reasoning provides a logical framework for objectivity. Then the descriptions of God provide the necessary markers for calibrating my level of objectivity. More objective I am, the more the Divinity that shines through in my way of thinking and living! When one enters life through the door of philosophy, the role and purpose of all other doors in any religion may become mere passageways in the journey of life.

Words and Their Meaning

Proficiency in understanding the word, its meaning and their connection enhances the knowledge and skill of anyone and in any language. Such understanding also enhances proficiency in our use of words and what they stand for. In an invocation poem, the famous Sanskrit poet Kalidasa (from 4th Century India) describes Lord Siva and his wife, Goddess Parvathi, as inseparable just like the word and its meaning.

Despite their many possibilities, only specific meaning gets attached to some words, as a matter of use and convenience. Then through frequent repetition, that meaning alone becomes commonly accepted. While this may be OK in general, there are also pitfalls. There could be a greater benefit to exploring the in-depth meaning of several words and the context in which such meaning should be used. Here are a few examples:

Philosophy: Webster's Dictionary describes Philosophy as: pursuit of wisdom; a search for a general understanding; an analysis of the grounds of and concepts expressing fundamentals

Philosophy is an analytical and logical – cause and effect – approach to understanding any subject matter in depth.

This meaning is consistent with the fact that the highest academic degree in any field is Doctor of Philosophy, such as in chemistry, physics, mechanical engineering, music, languages, etc. Yet we commonly use this word – Philosophy – to represent an in-depth study of "What is life and how it should be lived?" Also, the expression "he is a philosopher" is generally used to refer to someone who is theoretical, reflective, and a recluse. Philosophy also generally stands for an in-depth study of sacred writings of any religion (scriptures) and a summation of knowledge derived from it.

We shall look at Philosophy in the essays in this book as an in-depth study of life, why it is that way, and how it can be lived with peace and harmony for oneself and also for all those around. Our studies and analysis will tend to rely on Vedic literature and the principle derived from them. They are not focused on any rituals or religious beliefs. These essays are intended to be non-denominational, applicable to anyone, in any aspect of life, and in any walk of life.

Yoga: Union with the self. It is a conscious and deliberate exploration of the "self" – the driving force within - with anything external perceived through our body, mind, and intellect.

Exploring the union or connection with the body and its functions through a series of postures and breathing exercises – *Hatha Yoga* – has now come to be generalized and regarded as "Yoga"- much like any machine that copies documents is now called Xerox machine

Exploring all our experiences as the union or connection with mind and its functions — *Thri Guna Vibhaga Yoga* – is the study and observation of the three Gunas (Connectors). It leads to "Objectivity" and hence a separation from all our preferences (duality) like love/hate, friend/foe, happiness/sorrow, etc. Chapter 14 of *Bhagavadgītā* provides a very good framework for this Yoga – conscious and regulated union with the mind and its three connectors. Each chapter of BG illustrates specific approaches for the use of objectivity and analytical reasoning.

I will teach you this secret knowledge (on how to explore our experiences objectively). On learning, these, the wise have reached a higher plane (a life of enlightened living with minimum perturbations caused by daily events and their experiences). BG 14.1.

Exploring the union or connection with the mind (the center for our intellect or thoughts) and its functions – *Jnana Yoga* – has now come to be generalized and regarded as "*Vedanta*" or Philosophy. *Jnana Yoga* leads us to a place where experiences are seen as an unavoidable part of living enabled by the Laws of Nature (*Brahman*). All exists as evidence of nature and its laws (*Brahman*)! Through *Jnana Yoga*, life becomes a process of exploring the laws of nature at work in all activities (from the beginning of life till the end).

Karma: Activity

Google search for Karma gives the following meaning: *"the sum of a person's actions in this and previous states of existence, viewed as deciding their fate in future existences; destiny or fate, following as effect from cause."*

The correct word or phrase for this Google meaning would be *Sanchita Karma* (accumulated effect of actions) or *Prarabdha Karma* (Effect of actions accumulated over many lifetimes)! Other phrases associated with *Karma* are *Nitya Karma* (daily activities; daily rituals), *Naimitya Karma* (activities leading to a desired end goal – like studying for an exam), *Kamya Karma* (activity to meet one's desires), *Nishkama Karma* (Selfless act), etc.

Karma may be understood as any activity in a broad sense. *Karma* may also be the appropriate activity for the moment leading to *Dharma* - the approach to carry out any activity for the right reasons by the right person and at the right time! Such activity is implied in the famous BG quote, *"KarmaniYeva Adhikaraste'* – you have an obligation to carry out your duty (*Karma*)".

Bhakthi: Loyalty, surrender, faithfulness, attachment, and devotion.

Above adjectives being the generalized meaning, *Bhakthi* is a combination of all the above. Over time *Bhakthi* has been assumed to stand for devotion or fully absorbed in the contemplation and surrender to the almighty or the Lord.

It is our awe to the greatest feat of others that inspires us to greater heights. Our awe of the laws of nature inspires us to explore further. When service for elders and the needy is not seen as a burden but as a calling, it is an expression of *Bhakthi*. Our loving relationship with a friend, children, and youngsters, not as a preference or ordained commitment but a pure expression of devotion to a larger cause, it is devotion or *Bhakthi*. Love and affection between the husband and wife is not a mere relationship of need and convenience; instead, an expression of loyalty, surrender, faithfulness, attachment, and devotion, best described as *Bhakthi*.

In all our essays, we shall use the above in-depth reflection to seek the meaning applicable to many terms we come across in Vedic Philosophy.

A Parable

Parables are effective means to communicate certain principles. There are many parables in all cultures with ancient histories. Here is a parable from Indian culture.

A mother in her old age was being cared for by her son, a man of extreme noble character. He did everything to be helpful to the needy. He was very compassionate to his mother as well as to others. His compassion extended beyond human beings and included caring for animals as well.

One hot day, a cow was standing in front of his house. It appeared very thirsty. The young man rushed to bring a pail of water to feed the cow. The old mother stopped her son and said, "Please do not waste the water. It is summertime, and there is not enough water to go around." The son being respectful for his mother, put the water away, even though he felt hurt in his heart for not being able to feed the thirsty cow.

The king was aware of this noble son and his kindhearted actions. The king ordered his soldiers to take large amounts of house hold goods, such as groceries, and deliver them to the young man's house. Concerned that his offer would be turned down, the king also ordered his soldiers to deliver the items quietly and without any knowledge to the young man. The soldiers carried out the king's orders and delivered the materials when the young man was not at home. They informed the mother that the goods were being delivered as per the king's orders. They also mentioned that the king sent two boatloads, but one of the boats capsized in the river due to heavy winds.

On his return home, the son was surprised to see a large lot of groceries. Recognizing that they were too much for his needs, he shared most of the goods with the neighbors. Then his mother informed him that the king had sent them. She also informed him that it would have been two boatloads, except that one of the boats capsized in the river and lost all its goods.

"Mother, do you know why only one of the boats capsized?" asked the son.

"Maybe there were heavy winds?" replied the mother.

"If there were heavy winds, would we have not lost both the boats, mother?" replied the son.

"Then what do you think happened, son?" asked the mother.

"I think we lost one of the two boats, maybe because you stopped me in the hallway from my feeding water to a thirsty cow yesterday?" replied the noble son.

Life is full of events. It includes a thirsty cow denied of water to drink; an old woman concerned about her needs more than the need for the cow; a generous son helping as many as he can; a noble king caring for his subjects; the ships that carry good; the ship that is capsized with the loss of the shipment it carries; interpretation of this loss by the mother and the son from their respective points of view, etc. – what is the common theme that connects across all these events? They are all "experiences" in the life of the mother, her son, neighbors, soldiers, king, and the cow! We start the next chapter with a few essays that address this simple question: What is an "Experience?"

4. Basics of Vedic Philosophy

Anatomy of Our Experience – The Source

The Sanskrit word "*Vasana*" has several equivalents in the English language. They could be a habit, nature, tendency, preference, experience, etc. Yet, all these words do not adequately describe "*Vasana*". It is the sum of the behavior of anyone at a given time because of evolution, hereditary, exposure to events and activities, and choices throughout life leading up to this moment. It is the result of all experiences. This is the description of "Who am I?" for anyone. Each of us is a product of our *Vasana.*

Then there are specific aspects to "Who am I?" at any moment. Two individuals exposed to the same set of circumstances react or respond differently. The experience of these two individuals is different. What contributes to such differences in experiences among each of us, making us stand out as "individuals"?

The methodology for anatomy of our experience(s) is very clearly laid out in the various chapters of *Bhagavadgītā*. We adapt extensively from this source for much of what is written in this essay and in the subsequent essays.

We start with the premise that consciousness exists, and it is everywhere. Our existence is enabled by our consciousness. As an analogy, we recognize fire by its evidence – heat, light, spark, smoke, etc. "Fire", which is intangible, becomes tangible, and we can describe it based on perceivable evidences. What is the enabler of fire? One could say that fire is an outcome of an "Exothermic" reaction. Then what enables such reactions? At some point in this analysis, we settle down with the answer, "It just happens." It is natural! It exists!

The consciousness is that which exists after everything else has been negated as "this is not it"! Another example: imagine yourself seated in a large room with many other people. You hear your name called out. You turn in the direction where the sound came from. There is no one to be seen. It was just a mere sound. But who is that inside of you who responded to the call? That "I" in you is enabled by consciousness! There could have been many in the large gathering with the same name, all of whom might have responded to the call! Then you hear the message describing a moment in your life that is known only to yourself! You are startled. You wonder how is it that anyone other than me knows this information? That "I" in you, who is aware of this secret and who is now wondering, is enabled by consciousness! Consciousness has no properties of its own. It is eternal, permanent, and ever-present. Consciousness enables us to perceive, connect with, and relate to anything other than consciousness.

Thus, we have two avenues to answer the question: "Who am I?"

- I am consciousness!

- I am a product of my experience (*Vasana*).

Our evolution in spirituality depends on the clarity and understanding of these two pathways and their interconnection. Anatomy of our experience helps us greatly in such understanding and clarity.

The word anatomy has the following synonyms: structure, composition, make up, framework, analysis, examination, and investigation. Anatomy of experience at each moment gives us a comprehensive look at who I have been, how I am evolving, and who I am likely to evolve into! This internal reflection can be merely for a better understanding of the situation at hand. It can also be for mid-course correction or part of a well-laid-out "internal fitness" program. This is the very first step in the process of Self-Realization. This fitness program – *Yoga* – is a parallel path to our physical fitness. This fitness program based on reasoning – *Jnana Yoga* - facilitates emotional and intellectual well-being just as the exercises in the Gym promote physical fitness.

Birth or origin of "Experience":

When consciousness gets connected with anything external to it, an experience is born. My eyes are closed. I open my eyes for a fraction of the moment. I set my eyes on an object. Now, I see something. An experience is born! The object existed all along. My eyes and my power to see existed all along. When I opened my eye, I could have ignored that object and might have set my sight on something else. Enabled by consciousness, the moment "I" got connected through my eyes and vision to this specific object, the specific experience – awareness of this object is born.

We acquire "experience" through our organs of the body. We see through our eyes, hear through the ears, smell through the nose, feel through the skin, etc. Even when we keep all our organs isolated, like being quarantined, our mind is active with all its emotions, feelings, likes, dislikes, preferences, desires, etc. In every case, a connection is made between the consciousness and something external to it. Then there are all those ideas, thoughts, and concepts. These are abstract, just like our emotions and feelings. But ultimately, all these intangibles are expressed and become evident through our body functions. Thus, the body, mind, and intellect are our portals. Through these portals, connections are made. Consciousness gets connected to the "external". This is the process for the origin of all our experiences!

We could describe our experience as a momentary event, a collection of events, or an accumulation of such events over a period. For example, I touch a hot object, and I feel the heat. This is a momentary experience. I talk to my friend. My conversation is a minute long. I have an "experience" as the outcome of this conversation. I have a childhood experience that spans over a decade, professional experience that spans several decades, married life or a lifetime experience, etc. Experiences are like the scenes in a movie, both long and short. Life is a collection of experiences.

I touch a hot pot, feel the heat, get burned, and get mad! Many who often cook, despite their best attention, occasionally get burned by contact with hot pot, but brush it aside as "just part of the job"! I hear something from someone. It does not seem to really matter to me. Someone else hears the same thing, gets excited, loves it, hates it, gets emotional, gets upset, etc. All of these are our "experiences".

If consciousness in all of us is the same, and if the hot pot or message or any external stimuli is the same, then why does each of us respond differently to the same apparent signal? This has to do with the nature of the connection between me ("I") and the external. This connectivity or nature of the connection is called *Guna*! We shall investigate it in detail in our next few essays.

Consciousness is omnipresent, functioning as if with eyes, heads, ears, mouths, and feet everywhere. Consciousness exists in all aspects of all activities, and hence it envelops all aspects of the world.   BG 13.14

Consciousness exists actively supporting all activities and functions through all sense organs, yet remains unattached, thereby devoid of the influence of senses or the experiences (of cause and effect) arising out of them. BG 13.15

Consciousness is inside and outside of all beings and things, which are movable (animate) and immovable (inanimate). Because of this subtle nature, consciousness is perceived to be both far and near.   BG 13.16

Consciousness is undivided and universal and yet may be perceived as being divided or manifested through individual acts, people, or things. This universal manifestation is the cause of creation, sustenance, and destruction of all things and beings (i.e.) all our experiences BG 13.17

Anatomy of Our Experiences – Understanding the Source

A large body of philosophic writings focus on describing the axiom "I am consciousness". The person who is clearly and totally aware of the consciousness is described as an enlightened person. As an ideal, consciousness is also referred to as God. Hence the mission in life is to acquire God-like or divine qualities as the natural aspect of our living. It is said that such a person lives like a lotus leaf that thrives in a body of water yet remains untainted by water. It is living like a breeze, which by its mere presence spreads the fragrance for all to enjoy, without itself being aware of the fragrance, spreading of such fragrance, or the joy it creates to all those who enjoy the sweet smell of fragrance.

Every one of us may not have the aptitude to work through the nuances and subtleties to understand what consciousness is and how it serves as the substratum of all our experiences. Very few, if any, can live permanently in this state of mind. It is sufficient as a starting point to accept that everything is enabled by "something". That something is consciousness.

Here are a few more examples: Each of us can relate to the laws of nature. Water flows from a higher elevation to a lower level. Apple falls from the tree. Planets rotate and stay in orbit governed by the laws of gravity. Chemicals react leading to new compounds. When atoms collide, we get a large release of energy. We may not know in-depth the true nature of all these laws of nature. But we know they exist. We also learn constantly and thus discover new laws which have been there forever! We also know that all these laws act the same way, independent of time, place, or circumstances. Such laws do not have any preference of their own. They merely exist! They are understood by their effects and evidence that are cognitive to us. The more scientific you are in each field, the better you become aware of the laws of nature pertaining to that field. Indeed, the laws of nature enable the lotus leaf to remain dry while soaked in water or the breeze to exist the way it does, as described above. We have myriads of laws of nature for all aspects of the universe. It is then conceivable to envision an enabler – the consciousness – as the sum of all these laws of nature that enable us to be who we are as living persons. We may never fully understand all the laws of nature and hence the consciousness they represent. Indeed, it has been said that one who truly comprehends consciousness is also aware of their limitations of such knowledge!

Now let us look at the alternative axiom: "I am a product of my experiences (Vasana)". This is the thesis of many books written on self-development, behavioral studies, guidebooks for better living, etc. These books are more like recipes, a means to an end. They are very helpful. But they cannot be the end by themselves. These books on self-development and better living tell us to avoid negative tendencies such as hate, anger, passion, jealousy, etc. Don't be driven to get whatever you want; we are advised. But you see the one next to you may be your friend, your colleague at work, your neighbor, or your relative who gets away with actions and effects totally unacceptable under normal circumstances. Should you not get angry or at least feel upset?

"Enjoy only what you have truly earned" and "Share all that you have with the needy" are two guidelines for better living. One rule discourages anyone from getting help as it might not reflect true effort for self-reliance, while the other implores us towards self-negation and to be on the constant lookout to help others! Aren't they in contradiction to each other?

We are advised, "Always Be objective." What does that really mean? Should I be cautious and frugal in praise or favor to my child as I am for my neighbor's child? If not, am

I being objective? How can I be harsh to my child and be objective when my neighbor is generous with favors and readily forgives her child under similar situations and circumstances? My mind is on an endless treadmill but going nowhere! I am unsure of my experiences and the contradictions between right and wrong that I must always arbitrate.

Let us take a closer look at the definition (i.e.) "When consciousness gets connected with anything external to it, an experience is born". The key to understanding any "experience" may not be a thorough comprehension of the consciousness or a total understanding of our behavior in the cognitive universe. Both these avenues are open for lifelong exploration. Instead, we need a clear and comprehensive understanding of the "connectors" and the nature of such connections with any event, which can be as brief as a moment or for any duration longer than that.

These connectors are the ropes or the screws, the rivets or the glue that hold the pieces together. These connectors are the same, independent of the specifics or the pieces they hold together. The pieces may be people (like my child vs. my neighbor's child), places, circumstances, means, situations, time frame, etc. Focusing on the connectors makes us less focused on the specifics of the pieces held together and their details. This, in turn, leads us to be less subjective (not driven by specifics). Instead, our reflection is based on a common framework, an essential requirement for objectivity.

Focusing on the connectors, we are also deliberately keeping in mind the two essentials – the consciousness and everything external to it – as the two ends of the connectors and the separation between the two. In due course, this separation between the two creates a non-attachment, much like the breeze and its mere existence. Hence, what appeared abstract, and intangible earlier becomes tangible and a way of life. To be objective is no longer the end. Instead, it is part and parcel of our thought process, observation, reflection, and analysis. This is an aspect of evolution in self–realization. We are constantly aware that our life is always a representation of the laws of nature – consciousness – in some form or other. We see ourselves only as a product of experiences when our focus shifts away from the connectors (*Guna*) and their role. This evolution of knowledge occurs without us even realizing the same! These are the end effects of the anatomy of our experiences.

We shall explore the connectors and how to recognize them at play in the next few essays.

As the wind blows, the flowers' scent or fragrance is spread around for all to enjoy. The wind itself neither recognizes the fragrance, the spreading of the fragrance, or the effect of the fragrance all around. An enlightened person participates in the activities of life and contributes to results perceived by others without them recognizing either the activity or its results. B.G. 15.8.

Any person who perceives the "connectors" – Guna – stands apart from the long-term traits and the short-term effects or reactions to events. Through such separation and analytical view of "experiences", enlightened living brings the joys associated with it. The rest struggle through the events of life as a burden and the emotional pain associated with them. In this manner of living, they miss the opportunity to realize the potential for a larger purpose in life and the wonder, awe or joy associated with it.   B.G. 15.10

Anatomy of Our Experience – The Connectors (*Guna*)

Connectors:

"*Guna*", a Sanskrit word literally means rope or the connector. The word "Attribute" is also used to represent Guna. The synonyms for attribute are quality, characteristic, trait, feature, aspect, and element. Each of these words equally well apply for the word *Guna*.

It is said that there are three connectors associated with every experience. They are like the three strands of a rope. Don't blame yourself or credit yourself for your experience. Instead, look for the connectors associated with your experiences!

The three connectors:

When I set my eyes on an object, I could become instantly aware of the object because I have very good prior knowledge about it. As a result, I am very clear on exactly what it is and what my next action should be.

I could have some knowledge of the object apriori, but I am not sure. This partial knowledge triggers some actions, which may or may not be adequate.

I could be unaware or ignorant of the object, so I am totally unclear on what I am seeing or what I should do next.

These are the three connectors – Knowledge, Partial Knowledge, and Ignorance or absence of any knowledge – associated with any event.

My experience associated with this event of my setting eyes on this object is a combined effect of all these three connectors.

For every person, the connection between the consciousness (the enabler, the driving force inside the person – Soul, *Dehinam)* and the external is established through their body, mind, and intellect as the probes. The signals received through the three ever-present connectors or links (*Guna*), are: Knowledge, Bias, and Ignorance.

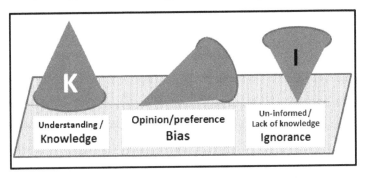

Figure 4.1. Three Connectors (*Guna*)

The three connectors co-exist all the time!

The co-existence of the three connectors is an important axiom. It should not be dismissed or set aside lightly. In fact, this axiom alone may be sufficient in many cases to find peace and harmony, even under complex situations and circumstances. Let us use a lighthearted example here: Consider someone calls you an "idiot". You might say, "That is very offensive," and get angry, upset, disgusted, etc. Ok, let us say someone calls me an idiot! If I do believe in the axiom above, I could think, "For certain, I could be ignorant of some things or some views; very likely, I am biased or partial to certain other things or views; but maybe there is also some element of knowledge in me as well, that can affirm or deny the accusation! If I think like that, I am not easily swept off my feet and enraged when I hear such a derogatory statement about me! The fact that knowledge and ignorance can co-exist drives me to reflect and think deeply. I am in control of my own self. I am not left to be swayed only by the opinion and judgment of others!

Co-existence of knowledge, bias, and ignorance is indeed the reality. One who understands the true meaning of this axiom and its implications is never swept away by the tides of praise or criticism. Instead, one resorts to internal reflection instinctively. Such reflection leads to the analysis and identification of the three strands or connectors and their relative proportions.

One among the three co-existing connectors is always dominant.

While all three connectors co-exist, one is always dominant over the other. It is the influence, or response to the dominant connector, modulated by the other two that we call our "experience". The dominance of one connector over the other two leads to an equilibrium that we identify as our "experience".

Tranquility (Sathvikam), turbulence or agitated activity (Rajasam), and stagnation or inactivity (Thamasam) are the three natural tendencies (equilibrium states) of any person. These tendencies incessantly bind a person (Dehinam) to his/her body (Deham). BG 14.5.

When knowledge prevails over bias and ignorance, we experience "Tranquility". When Bias is dominant, we are "Turbulent". We become stagnant or inertial when ignorance dominates over knowledge and bias! BG 14.10

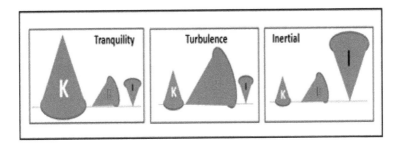

Figure 4.2. Three equilibrium states *(Gunathvam)* leading to our "experience" (*Vasana)*

64

Examples of using a balance to illustrate the three equilibrium states (i.e.) our experience:

Every merchant uses the weighing scale or balance to establish the equilibrium (measured weight of items sold Vs. money received).

Figure 4.3. Tranquility (Balanced state of mind)

Tranquility (*Sathvikam*)

No matter what the merchant sells, the item sold for a given weight (verified against set standards) is always the same! This implies that the balance, weights used, method of weighing – all follow the same standards and procedures. Everyone in this store (who uses the same balance, weights, and process) get the same result. People trust this merchant, each other, his balance as a measuring instrument, weights, and procedures. In fact, over time this shop sets the standard for honesty and integrity. Everyone respects this store and prefer to interact (shop) with this merchant. The prevailing experience for the customer, merchant and his workers and everyone involved may be identified as tranquil.

Figure 4.4. Turbulence (Biased state of mind)

Turbulence (*Rajasam*):

Consider the situation with another merchant. Whenever he sells, the expensive items come out below the promised weight, but it is not a problem for inexpensive items. When people complain and on weighing again somehow the expensive items needed few more pieces to reach the correct weight. But such re-weighing is not always done. Usually, it follows a quarrel from angry customers and their complaint. Sometimes the problem goes away when there are other workers at the weighing station. Each day the merchant went home upset and unhappy, but the situation was no better or different next day! One careful observer found that the merchant was putting his thumb in the scale (bias) to make more money off the expensive items, affecting the results based on his personal desire, greed, wanting to do favor for one customer over the other, etc. The prevailing experience all around could be easily recognized as "Turbulent" (driven by bias, attachment and preferences).

Figure 4.5. Inertial (Ignorant state of mind)
Note: a small weight attached to one of the pans, not readily visible!

Inertial (*Thamasam*):

For this merchant, there was never a case of getting the correct weight. No matter who tried to weigh, it was never correct. Even others could not help. Sometimes even the customers themselves were asked to weigh. They could not get items at the correct weight with consistency. Suspicion and uncertainty were growing. It became a habit for most people to feel that the merchant is not trustworthy. No one could figure out what was going on. The ignorance shrouding the overall experience may be characterized as stagnation or inertial. One day an innocent by stander tipped the balance over. The merchant found a piece of metal stuck to the bottom of one of the pans! The merchant and all his clients and workers ignorant of this have been growing upset all along, feeling relentless grief as long as they were clueless.

While the above examples may appear elementary, the truth is that all our experiences always fall into one of the above three equilibrium states. This assertion from Vedic Philosophy is noted in *Bhagavadgītā* as follows:

There is no being on earth, heaven or among the Gods who is free from these three connectors (Guna) or their equilibrium states (Gunathvam) arising out of nature.

B.G. 18.40.

Consider a rope with three strands. Consider the grip or feel of a rope with strands of different materials or of different gage, strength, and such properties. (e.g.): rope, where the three strands are made of three different materials (cotton/nylon/wool or copper /steel/aluminum). Clearly, the strength, endurance, flexibility, feel, use, etc., of such a rope, depends on each strand its role and properties. You begin to see why two people could connect with the same event differently – depending on the nature of the "rope (and its strands)" they use as the connectors!

We can use the above axioms to look deeper into our analytical view of our "experience". This requires a further in-depth understanding of the three connectors and how to recognize their properties, role, and effect. It also requires pointers to identify the dominance of one over the other two.

Such an analytical look at life and experiences develops a natural separation. We can view our experiences as the scenes in our movie (the life) and "I" the audience in the movie! We can always resort to a common methodology or framework to use – to identify the three connectors and the dominant strand –irrespective of the event, time, situation, circumstances, etc. The consistency in using such methodology in all situations facilitates objectivity in our outlook on its own accord! Such an analytical and dispassionate look at our experience with a consistent methodology as the backbone is another elementary step towards self-realization (*Yoga*). May be we can call this as the **Connector- science** or language of the Conscience! We shall pursue these details in our next essay.

Connectors and their identifiers:

Knowledge brings clarity to the situation. The cause and effect are clear. The objective or the purpose is well identified. The role and responsibilities of the people involved are all clear. There is clarity on the means or tools available as well as the circumstances. There is a sincere effort to understand the laws of nature at play. Reflection, analysis, and contemplation always precede any activity where there is abundant knowledge!

Bias occurs when our knowledge is partial or incomplete. We do not acknowledge our incomplete knowledge. Instead, we have the urge to act. We make choices driven by our impulses. (e.g.): It is a quiet evening, a little bit after the sunset. It is a bit dark. I hear the sound. I have a thick wallet with some cash in it. I am attached to my money. I dislike the thought of losing it. The sound I hear is the creaking noise of the door being slowly opened. I can imagine an intruder, ready to snatch my wallet. I wait a bit longer. I am sweating. Then nothing happens for a while. I gather my courage and move closer to the door. I learn that the door had swung open. I was ignorant of the blowing wind. There is no one in sight, but I am convinced that someone is lurking unseen. I grab my wallet and run as fast as I can, but I am not sure where to go. In the process, I trip and fall. I am mad at the stone that tripped me! It goes on ...

Ignorance shrouds our capacity to think and reason. Even our passion and desire, and attachments are subdued by an envelope of lethargy and depression, and a total lack of purpose. The irrationality from ignorance is distinct from the irrational behavior of someone with partial knowledge and a biased point of view. We shall see more details on this in our future essays.

Knowledge in its pure form adds illumination *(and knows of no ill effects). Dominance of knowledge may be perceived through tranquility, contentment, and pure happiness.* B.G. 14. 6.

Bias is *evidenced through turbulence or agitated activity. It is rooted in desire or passion. It is seen as an outcome of our unbridled attachment. Turbulence leads to endless chain of activities, each unable to satisfy or full fill the need or the desire* B.G. 14. 7.

Ignorance leads to stagnation or inactivity. It leads to irrationality or blind attraction. Ignorance may be perceived through despair, gloom, and hopelessness B.G. 14. 8.

Knowledge is affiliated with happiness and contentment; Bias leads to endless chain of activities; Ignorance shrouds the knowledge and leads to lack of direction. B.G. 14.9.

Anatomy of Our Experience – Using the Connectors as the Guide

Our "experience" is governed by three connectors (*Guna*) – Knowledge, bias, and ignorance. Their relative proportions create equilibriums states (*Gunathvam*) through which we comprehend the effects of the laws of nature at play.

Everything happens governed by and because of the Laws of Nature. We breathe, and as a result we enjoy the sweet smell of flowers! Whether we understand the laws of nature pertinent to each event or not, we remain under the influence of their invisible hands. If we comprehend the laws of nature at work, then the observations, effects, and consequences are all clear. With such knowledge, we can choose to become "observers" of our "experience". When we do so, we see that our experiences are not a continuum, but discrete events, like the scenes in the hands of the movie editor.

Our ability to stay focused and remain composed and contented – whether we comprehend the laws of nature or not – is enhanced by our faith in the laws of nature at work and the singular source representing all of them, which may be identified with as the Universal soul, the consciousness.

With such faith and understanding, we remain in harmony and as part and parcel with the universe at large (*Thath Thwam Asi*).

The following verses are useful guides to better understand the three equilibrium states (*Gunathvam*):

When tranquility and contentment are perceived in every avenue of the body and its functions, one can recognize that knowledge has prevailed. B.G. 14. 11.

When bias or partial knowledge prevails, we see turbulence or agitated activity. Greed or desires of endless nature are their sources. They set in motion an endless chain of activities, each unable to meet the need, unease, and longing. B.G. 14. 12.

When ignorance prevails, we see stagnation or procrastination. The result is gloom or darkness, ineptness, lack of direction, or lack of a sense of purpose. Their origins are attraction born out of illusion. B.G. 14. 13

It will require a sustained and in-depth study of these verses to gain their full import. For example, consider from the above (B.G. 14.11) the phrase "contentment is perceived in every avenue of the body". When total and complete knowledge prevails, we are not only contented emotionally and intellectually, but we see the evidence of the same in the words we speak, in the expression in our eyes, the sound we hear, etc.

We can also learn about the dominant connector based on how one proceeds forward in a time of crisis. Crisis need not be only a calamitous event. Crisis can be simply a moment of decision-making. We are making decisions all the time. The more intense and calamitous the situation, the decision-making takes a "crisis" proportion. How we make our decisions or how we make our choices is greatly determined by the connectors. Here are a few more guidelines on the role of connectors at any moment of decision-making:

At a time of crisis, higher levels of knowledge and hence tranquility transform a person to a higher plane (of reflection and consideration of the situation as a whole). B.G. 14.14.

When knowledge is the dominant connector, the decision-making process is focused on the laws of nature at play and their understanding. The emphasis is on the "process" of inquiry. This brings a consistent approach to all times, situations, and circumstances. The details and specifics surrounding the decision-making process are merely used as evidence. We call a person with such a state of mind as "professional". This may be a lawyer, doctor, musician, teacher, etc. This is like an impartial judge or jury, for whom the process – upholding the law – is the only goal, no matter who is on either side of the case! Objectivity is second nature to a person or group of people or in a situation where "Knowledge" has a dominant role over the other two connectors.

In fact, most of the time, we are at peace and in harmony within, thanks to the laws of nature at play. But like a good meal, while we enjoy it, but tend to forget that soon after! Make a list of all the things you do each day. If you include your breathing, digestion, assimilation, brain functions, etc., you are engaged in countless activities each day! Now make a list among them when you felt agitated, perturbed, or were at a total loss (lacking any direction whatsoever). Very likely, they are no more than a few, a handful at best! But it is our impulse or bias to action in most cases and the ignorance of that truth which overwhelm us to see our life as a constant chore and misery! The few saints who realized this have exclaimed, "I am Happiness"!

At a time of crisis, dominance of bias or partial knowledge (and attachment to it as the total truth) leads to turbulence or agitation, further resulting in an endless chain of activities (each unable to full fill the desires, needs, and wants). B.G. 14.15

We frequently find ourselves with a false belief that action is required here and now. Hence, we fail to step back and reflect. Most of the books on self-development focus on this aspect and provide scores of guidelines. One simple principle is enough: Simply take a deep breath, step back and ask yourself, "What am I doing? Why? What are the laws of nature at play here?" When you are unable to step back, call upon your faith – in God or some larger force – to give you the strength and courage to step back and reflect. It is this capacity to "rein in your horses" that is called *Yoga*. The reflection that follows is the beginning of Self-Realization.

At a time of crisis, dominance of ignorance leads to stagnation or procrastination, or inactivity B.G. 14.15.

Dominance of Ignorance is the most difficult for one to recognize on its own accord. If you are ignorant, you will know about it only if you permit someone else to point out that to you! But if you are also biased and unwilling to let anyone, give you that information, then you will never get out of your ignorance. In that situation, you are in a vicious cycle. You wish to decide or move forward, but like a frog in the well, you are stuck! On the other hand, if you are knowledgeable about the possibility of your being ignorant, you open the door for others (with knowledge) to inform you on what you need to know. This is possible if and only if you genuinely believe in our earlier axiom: Knowledge, Bias, and Ignorance – all three connectors – co-exist all the time!

It is said that knowledge and tranquility arise as the result of proper or virtuous acts, which in turn leads to clarity and absence of blemish (purity). The result of partial knowledge is agitated activity, in turn leading to sorrow. Absence of skills for analysis and discrimination (between right and wrong) is the fruit of ignorance. B.G. 14.16

In the following table we have summarized many details on the connectors (*Guna*) and their characteristics. This table is developed by adapting many verses found in *Bhagavadgītā* Chapter 14. This tabulation is intended as a simple guide to reflect upon and manage any activity that is part of anyone's life at any time.

Life is like a river with its constant stream of experiences. Their contours change constantly between the calm flow of water to a swirling white water and all alternatives between them. But viewed from this simple model of connectors and their role, each activity becomes merely a representation of the three connectors and their equilibrium!

Knowledge leads to understanding and analytical skills; Bias leads to agitated activity; lack of direction and illusion, is the result of ignorance. B.G. 14.17

Higher levels of knowledge through tranquility and its effect on contemplation, reflection, and analysis elevates one to the higher level of accomplishment of the intended goal; When Bias, is dominant, it leads to agitated activity of endless nature with no end in sight. Preponderance of Ignorance sinks a person to the lower levels, losing ground constantly. B.G.14.18.

Table. 4.1. Using the Connectors as a guide
Source: B.G. Chapter 14

Connectors	Knowledge	Bias	Ignorance
Features or characteristics of the three Connectors (*Guna*).	Knowledge adds illumination and clarity for the problem on hand	Bias arises out of personal needs and wants and our attachment to them.	Ignorance is driven by illusion, fantasy, or irrational expectations
	Knowledge binds a person through genuine sense of happiness	Bias binds a person to endless chain of activities	Ignorance binds one through lack of directions.
	Knowledge can be recognized through the happiness and contentment focused on the well-being for all.	Bias can be recognized through associated endless chain or recurrence of additional activities, without a sense of closure, satisfaction, or fulfillment.	Ignorance shrouds the knowledge and leads to gloom, malaise, lack of direction.
How can one perceive the dominance of each connector?	When knowledge, or illumination is perceived in every aspect of the subject matter one can recognize that as tranquility and its effects.	When Bias is dominant one is drawn into greed or desires of endless nature, driven by intense personal needs, initiation of endless activities due to a lack of satisfaction or	When stagnation or inactivity prevails, the result is ineptness, lack of direction or sense of purpose and illusion (attraction born out of ignorance).

		contentment, unease, and longing.	
At a time of crisis or when a decision needs to be made, the dominant connector leads to:	True knowledge transforms a person to a higher plane of existence (of total self-control and unattached active participation).	Bias leads a person to more activities, merely to satisfy growing personal wants and desires which continue to remain as unfulfilled.	Ignorance leads stalemate, procrastination or one being shrouded by delusion.
The result of dominance of each Connector:	Proper or virtuous acts and purity or clarity on the sense of purpose.	Duality such as Happiness / Sorrow.	Depression and despair
Each Connector Leads to:	Composure and understanding	Greed, anger, and sorrow	Lack of direction and delusion
Impact on the intended purpose under the influence of each connector:	Rise to the higher level (through engagement with self-control and the reasoning and logic that occurs as a result)	Ambivalent (due to reasoning being constantly overruled by desires and its insatiable needs and wants)	Sink to the lower level (since the reasoning and logic never surfaces, like the fire being shrouded by the ashes eventually gets quenched).

Anatomy Of Our Experiences: Objectivity

Objectivity – in action:

Our "education" at any level is intended to facilitate our skills to identify the three connectors: knowledge, bias and ignorance on the chosen field or subject of study. Their relative proportions and how to sort them out reflect proficiency in education! One who is good at this skill becomes "expert" in that field of study. As we have noted in our earlier essays, the elements of the philosophic approach are nearly identical. It is not a mere coincidence that the highest degree awarded in any field of study is called "Doctor of Philosophy". The best researcher in any field has the best knowledge of the laws of nature in that field, the limitations (ignorance) of such knowledge and possible wrong interpretations (bias) of the same! The same can be said of any professional: best doctor, surgeon, musician, carpenter, etc. Understanding the connectors, when it is explicit and analytical and quantitative, we call the process "scientific". The more intuitive, inferential the process, we call it creativity or "common sense"!

Leaders in any activity can see these three connectors at play distinctly and clearly. The leader will not always be the one with the highest level of knowledge or the scholar. In many situations, it may be the one who can see the evidence of "bias" distinctly. In some other situations, it may be the one who recognizes "ignorance" and is willing or daring to speak about it! Remember the story of the child calling out, "the emperor has no clothes"?

Consideration of all evidence and equal emphasis on all three connectors – knowledge, bias and ignorance – and their relative content (Equilibrium states) is called "Objectivity (*Sagunathvam)* ".

An objective person is not swayed by his knowledge nor tends to understate or diminish the evidence pertaining to bias and ignorance. An objective frame of mind treats all three connectors with equal weight or merit. The Sanskrit word for this is "*Sa- Gunathvam*" (i.e.) enabled by an equal regard for all connectors (*Guna)* and their equilibrium states (*Gunathvam).* A person of objective nature is regarded as an "enlightened person".

Objectivity is evident when a person – through intense reflection and analysis – ultimately relies on their own "self". They have a firm and balanced frame of mind, where opposites such as happiness and sorrow, dear and not so dear, praise and blame are equal in effect. They have a value system where a piece of clay, a stone and a piece of gold are of equal merit. B.G. 14. 24.

To be objective requires three considerations: detachment, non-attachment, and renunciation.

We shall look at these three features in this essay and the following two essays as well.

Objectivity is evident when a person (who has transformed or moved beyond the three connectors of Knowledge, Bias, and Ignorance) perceives honor and dishonor, friendship, and enmity as equal in merit. Such a person has a frame of mind that sees "self" as separate and distinct from everything external to it. Hence such a person does not initiate any actions based on personal or self-driven needs. B.G. 14. 25.

Such objectivity is easier stated and difficult to exercise. It will invariably require a frame of mind with a balanced outlook at all observations. It is akin to a judge's perspective, for whom in their constant search for truth every evidence presented in the case has equal merit. This objectivity is the foundation of our jury system, where a group of fellow citizens, totally unconnected with the case (detached), look at the evidence and render judgment with non-attachment (without any consideration of self-driven needs). It is the fundamental basis of the justice system that the truth – or the judgment as a result – as seen by these jurors would also be found to be the case, even when scores of other impartial observers analyze the same evidence. The objectivity described here is the basis of our modern civilized society!

The natural questions that would arise are: Should we not seek to be more knowledgeable all the time? Isn't bias bad? How can ignorance be of the same weight as knowledge?

Recognition of the existence of bias and ignorance is not the same as cultivating them! It is by avoidance of acknowledgement when it exist we foster more ignorance and greater bias! One inadvertently and unknowingly hurts oneself by ignoring this valid evidence! Hence, to be objective – with equal weight for knowledge, bias and ignorance – is not a punishment or error. Instead, it is the pathway to the reward we seek (i.e.) true knowledge of the subject matter.

Any suggestion that evidence of knowledge will be preferred apriori also results in a bias or attachment of some sort. The goal should be that the knowledge and tranquility, as a result, should evolve as a natural outcome of our objective analysis of all the evidence. It is stated that true and comprehensive knowledge is perceived on any subject matter only when we see evidence pertaining to that in every avenue! In such situations, the person becomes an embodiment of knowledge in every aspect of their life. The following may be a good example to illustrate the point.

"Non-violence" – *Ahimsa* – as seen by Mahatma Gandhi was not merely avoiding injury to animals or living with a vegetarian diet. Instead, non-violence implied no violence of any kind in thought, actions, desires, and intents. He describes the blind allegiance to limited forms of "non-violence" and the bias it creates as follows:

"The trouble with our votaries of Ahimsa is that they have made it a blind fetish and put the greatest obstacles in the way of the spread of true non-violence in our midst. The current and, in my opinion, mistaken view of non-violence has drugged our conscience and rendered us insensible to a host of other and more insidious forms of violence like harsh words, harsh judgments, ill will, anger, spite and lust or cruelty; it has made us forget that there may be far more violence in the slow torture of men and animals, the starvation and exploitation to which they are subjected to out of selfish greed, the wanton oppression and humiliation of the weak and the killing of their self-respect that we witness today than in mere taking of life".

Any individual with high objectivity on any subject matter becomes recognized as the anvil or frame of reference against which all others shape and mold their knowledge. All of us need not become "Mahatma Gandhi", nor is it our goal. But anyone can develop skills with respect to any subject matter to exercise true objectivity through equal regard for all evidence perceived through all three connectors. Such objectivity elevates the person to the highest levels of performance with respect to that subject matter.

Objectivity, as outlined above with the example pertaining to non-violence, can be extended to any personal or societal matter. When we say we love someone, what does it objectively mean: Acts of kindness, compassion, and intimacy when a situation is conducive, but a sense of despair and unwillingness as an undercurrent most of the time? Does the term "Quiet quitting" is nothing more than an elegant way of admitting ignorance and bias or a true reflection of non-attachment? How does objectivity shine through in our practices of religion, ethics, morality, politics, democracy, etc.? These are questions for exploration for anyone as individuals as well as members of society. These are also questions that can be addressed through Spirituality in Practice.

In summary, objectivity is an outcome or culmination of: Detachment: self-reflection, analysis, and reasoning; "externalizing" all our experience. (acquired through our perception, feeling, and thought) to treat them as evidence.

Non-attachment: through tempered desires that are focused on the larger common good.

Renunciation: through a true recognition that anything and anyone are all integral and enabled by invisible forces of nature, collectively known as Brahman.

Non – Attachment

Scriptures are the vast ocean of knowledge and wisdom. One can get immersed in them to the point they become academic documents for mere intellectual exercise. To prevent such pitfalls, we have codes of conduct or golden rules such as: "Do unto others as you would have them do unto you". One could summarize the lessons from *Bhagavadgītā* as "May all manner of living to be dedicated to total self-control and non-attached active engagement".

Many questions that follow are: What is life? Manner of living? Control? Self? Self-control? Total Self-control? Vs. Partial self-control? Dedication? Non-attachment? Engagement with non-attachment? Once? as much as possible? Lifelong quest? etc. Exploration of these and many such questions and their understanding is the essence of any study in Philosophy. Exploring such questions may indeed be the essence of all scriptures and in any religion.

At first sight, "non-attachment" may seem weird, unreal, or imaginary. Instead, non-attachment is the true nature of our existence! There are hundreds, if not thousands, of activities we engage in every day. Yet we don't remember all of them or dwell on each. Consider the following examples:

You have driven your car for 1000s of miles in your lifetime. You have certainly bicycled many miles. For certain, you have walked 1000s of steps each day and millions of steps over the years! Each moment is an event, an activity. You had to be fully engaged in the event at that moment. Your life in the next moment depends on being active and properly engaged in the moment before! Yet how many of these moments occupy our thought or memory? Hardly a tiny fraction. The rest of the time, we are in a true or natural state of non-attached active engagement.

Our heart beats every moment from birth to death. Yet we may recall only a few moments when it pulsates abnormally due to joy, sadness, or malfunction! The rest of the time, our heart is functioning in a state of non-attachment with respect to the person – the "I" in me!

These are a few of countless examples where we consider something relevant. They are far fewer than the moments that merely happen and we exist.

It is said that *Brahman* is that "*which enables the fire to burn, the wind to move*", etc. The fire burns anything in its path, and the wind moves the objects in its path as well. They represent the laws of nature. These laws merely exist. They have no preferences or choices of objects, people, duality (likes/dislikes), etc. We exist merely as the representation of the laws of nature. True comprehension of this basic reality is non-attachment.

The principle of non-attachment is capsulized in the axioms: You exist as an integral part of the universe (*Thath Thwam Asi)*; One who understands the *Brahman* (non-attachment), becomes one with *Brahman* (*BrahmaVith Brahma Eva Bhavathi*).

Non-attachment does not mean the pursuit of life in isolation or as a monastic. It is a state of mind, knowledge and understanding rather than merely a way of life.

Non-attachment is not a choice. It is the recognition of reality as it exists. The world is a sphere (and not flat) and it is not a choice. It is mere acceptance of reality as it exists. Everything else (attachment) is the choice which leads to the duality (I/you, mine/yours, love/hate, like/dislike, friend/foe, etc.)

The reflection of the moon and its wavy appearance on the surface of the water is a reality for one who sees the reflection alone. This is how we engage and amuse a child. But as one grows up, the knowledge of the moon, the waves on the surface of the water, and the reflection which leads one to see reality and not the wavy moon as it is perceived (through attachment to limited knowledge). That knowledge of the reality of nature and laws is non-attachment.

When we are in a car, on a bicycle or in our shoes, we move with these objects as if we are one and the same. Every one of us knows that we are distinct from our car, bicycle, or shoes. Can you observe such a distinction between the "I" in you and everything else? That understanding is non-attachment.

Every event in life (and in every moment) is a response to the laws of nature. An angry person disappears in our mind when we understand the sources of their anger. Then we see a person with issues that need to be resolved. Non-attachment leads to the constant pursuit of the laws of nature at play.

A dispute starts as a discussion and eventually an argument. Enlightened conversation begins when the participants become "non-attached". The subject and enunciation of different points of view come into focus. The duality of "I said this, he said this", "I agree – you disagree", etc., that occupy our mind disappears. Such emphasis on non-attachment may be pursued by one, many or all the participants. The opportunity to remain "non-attached" to gain the most value out of the discussion is equal and open to all, any time and all the time!

The practice of non-attachment – conscious awareness of the association of the self with anything specific other than the self (or consciousness) – is also called *yoga.*

A musician performs at best when they are in total unison with the music. They exist non-attached to everything else for those moments *(Gana Yoga).* The best performance in the concert is recognized in those moments when the musician and everyone in the audience exists in union with the music (in a state of non-attachment from everything else).

We engage in many activities without even being aware of them. As one becomes proficient in any activity, non-attachment becomes involuntary. Non-attachment reflects the level of perfection achieved with respect to that activity.

An enlightened person remains self-restrained, with a firm sense of purpose, with thoughts and reasoning centered on non-attachment. Such a person is friendly and compassionate to all and hates none. Free from self-driven needs and their effects, such enlightened person remains equal in composure in happiness and sorrow. B.G. 12. 13,14

The non-attached person is neither disturbed nor disturbs their environment or the world. They remain free from joy, anger, fear or worry B.G. 12.15

When there is abundance, we are ready to give up and share. Non-attachment is a measure of our mindset about the abundance of anything: Abundance of love, caring, generosity, truth, accommodation of others, etc. We are afraid to lose the little of what we have. The "little" may be a reality or a perception in our mind.

Non-attachment brings with it freedom from fear of any kind. Since we are not afraid, we are free to speak the truth, ask the most innocent questions and probe any subject to its ultimate details to unearth the laws of nature at work.

Attachment is a measure of intimacy with respect to any activity. Non-attachment evolves when intimacy is reduced. When I look at shoes as a means, my attachment to the shoes is minimal. I can get in and out of my shoes with the same ease as an ascetic can enter and leave any home, town, or country where he is invited as a guest! But I might have difficulty departing the company of loved ones since my attachment is far more intense than that of an ascetic!

Non-attachment evolves when our goal or purpose expands. Caring for one's needs or caring for the family by themselves does not suggest absence of non-attachment. But relentless emphasis on narrow objectives and personal or self-driven needs is a sure sign of attachment.

We understand from the above the shades and details of "non-attachment" largely through reflection and analysis. As a result, one can say, "I agree". In that frame of mind, non-attachment becomes or exists as a natural aspect of life. When we say, "I do not disagree", non-attachment remains a concept limited to an intellectual exercise. If it is only conceptual, there is anxiety: How does one realize the existence of non-attachment and relate to it in practice beyond mere intellectual exercise? That is the essence of Spirituality in Practice.

Many of us do not grow beyond our immediate self-driven needs and concerns. We use the rules and codes of conduct from the scriptures as the crutch. Rarely we explore the truths or the laws and why they are like that. Non-attachment remains merely a concept heard of, or literal words learned from scriptures.

Whenever non-attachment is not instinctive and implicit, we see a division between a person (individual) distinct from the universe of which the person is part of. Can this duality be eliminated? Can we see the indivisible and expansive nature of "I", as an integral part of the universe (*Thath Thwam Asi*)? We have a burning desire to answer these questions and experience this reality. Yet, non-attachment (our natural state) can remain like the amber glow in the burning coal covered under a layer of ash. The coal, the heat and the energy all exist.

Meditation, yoga, retreat, and rituals like prayer services are all means for learning the principle of "non-attachment" through practice. We see such a practice-oriented approach in religions to appreciate and embrace non-attachment. Practices of self-denial are common in Buddhist and Jain traditions. A strict pathway ordained in Hindu tradition is *"Na ithi bhavam (*An attitude that relinquishes connection with everything*)"*. It is explained as follows:

It is said that when one negates everything that creates attachment through the principle that it is "not something" or "not relevant" or "not connected" to me, one ultimately becomes in union with Brahman (state of non-attachment) – Brhadaranyaka Upanishad (700 BC)

When the pleasures of material objects leave us, our mind becomes stricken with grief. On the other hand, if they are voluntarily forsaken, it produces infinite peace and tranquility of mind – Vairagya Shatakam

"Non-attachment" is the reality. Every religion and scripture teach this fundamental truth in its own unique ways. Each of us is a living example of non-attachment at play – described as the hand of God, divinity, laws of nature, etc. – along with everyone and everything in the universe. I, as an individual, exist differently from others only in my mind, conditioned by my thoughts from the moment of birth. We evolve and grow in our comfort with non-attachment through faith, belief, sustained effort, and practice. We transcend from "not disagree" to "agree" through reflection and understanding. Volunteering and caring for the needy are examples of activities that promote our understanding of non-attachment. In business practices, professionals are called away from their daily place of work and the attachment they create to focus their attention on larger common goals. Through such practices, the outer layer of ash – the attachment to the duality that I am distinct from the rest – is removed.

The Yoga of Renunciation
(Sanyasa Yoga)

There is certainly a benefit to consciously and deliberately withdrawing from anything that distracts you the most. Examples: Quiet time for children, Time off from T.V. or cell phone, offsite business meetings in secluded places, quiet and lonely walks, etc. The more conscious and deliberate the withdrawal, the more conspicuous it seems to be. But what happens if withdrawal is a natural part of one's way of life? Will that be equivalent to the yoga of renunciation (*Sanyasa Yoga*)?

In the Hindu tradition, during one's lifetime, four stages are prescribed: Childhood leading to becoming an adult, life as a family member, gradual and sustained withdrawal and finally renunciation (*Brahmacharyam, Grahastham, Vanaprastham and Sanyasam*). This hierarchy suggests that renunciation is the fourth and ultimate stage, coinciding with the late period of one's life. The image of the persons with a minimum of clothing and possessions as the renunciates (*Sanyasi*) has been reinforced in Hindu culture. Renunciation associated with religious leaders and theologians is also noted in all religions and cultures. While these views and perceptions are valid and relevant from certain points of view, do these notions cloud our thinking and distance us from an important and valuable role of the "Yoga of renunciation" in our daily life?

The word "*Sanyasa*" in the Sanskrit language stands for "that which separates or dissociates from ...". To disassociate from or renounce something requires a pre-requisite of attachment. Hence renunciation is generally associated with giving up or abdicating desires. But renunciation need not be merely an exercise in negation. As you grow older, with a deep inner feeling of "been there, done that", renunciation may appear easier to practice. Is it more of a convenient excuse? Instead, the yoga of renunciation may apply to anyone at all ages.

Yoga refers to a conscious and voluntary exploration of the "self". This process of inner exploration can be associated with any activity. Thus, we have *Karma Yoga* (conscious and voluntary engagement in activities with mindfulness – a mind that is focused on the present), *Bhakthi Yoga* (Conscious and unrelenting faith in a larger order – the Lord), *Jnana Yoga* (relentless search for knowledge and understanding of all our thoughts and choices for action and faith), *Dhyana Yoga* (Yoga of meditation), etc. *Hatha Yoga* stands for conscious exploration of our physical body and its parts and their movements. But each of these Yoga Practices require the yoga of renunciation (*Sanyasa Yoga*) as a pre-requisite.

As a child, one has many interests and preferences. But as we grow up, we make choices. Often, they become confusing, difficult and, at times, painful. Could this be a place to practice the yoga of renunciation?

As we grow older, there are preferences that we exhibit or habits that we imbibe as a part of life. Then we come to a crossroads where these habits or choices are not conducive to healthy living. The most common example is the need to give up salt or sweet for various health reasons. Could these be situations to practice the yoga of renunciation?

There are times that a discussion drifts into derogation or mockery. You feel uncomfortable, but you cannot walk out as it will be obvious and uncomfortable for others. Perhaps this is a moment to practice the yoga of renunciation.

In the above situations, the yoga of renunciation, might make one appear quiet, recluse, aloof or not fully engaged. Yoga of renunciation is recognized in a Tamil proverb:

For one who appears to be recluse and aloof, pay twice the attention. His mind may be active and alert to matters that most others would be missing!

Silence as a form of renunciation can be seen in three avenues: (a) One can remain quiet as a matter of convenience

(b) There is a fear of the outcome – such as angering someone we like or letting down someone close to us – and hence we remain silent (c) Silent dis-association is seen as the best for the moment, but clear action and follow up is already planned in mind as the next steps with a commitment to follow through. There is no assurance that the desired outcome will happen, but there is an unrelenting commitment to the larger goal (which is not self-centered at its core) and the process. These three pathways for the practice of yoga of renunciation are described as follows:

Renouncing activities which a person is obliged to perform is not proper. Abandoning such activities in the name of renunciation arises out of a hidden desire and attachment. It is declared as ignorance in the practice of the yoga of renunciation B.G. 18.7.

The work or activity which is perceived as an obligation to be carried out, but it is not performed as a response to the influence of duality – love/hate, like/dislike, fear/bravery, etc. – is not renunciation. Instead, it is abandonment arising out of turbulence or an agitated state of mind. B.G.18. 8.

Activities which should be performed are appropriately carried out while abandoning unbridled attachments to the outcome are described as tranquil activities in the pursuit of the yoga of renunciation. B.G. 18. 9.

Enlightened Living: A seamless blend of three pathways for self-control.

In a literal sense, life is the process from birth to death, where birth implies the time when the heart starts pulsing, and death when the heart stops pulsing permanently. If that is your understanding and you are contended with such a clinical definition, you are likely to be one in a million! Most people would like to add more details to the above definition. For most people, it is not a life when your heart pulses and nothing else happens! Most people would converge on the definition of life as a collection of activities and the collective experience because of such activities.

Are these activities chosen at will, or do I let the activities determine and define who I am? In other words, do I choose to act based on reflection and analysis, or do I merely react? It is this unique ability to choose what we want to do at any moment that distinguishes the human from all other objects in the universe. It is always wise to think before you act; look before you leap! But what do you want to think about? What do you want to look for before you leap?

A committed effort towards reflection, analysis and finding answers which lead to the conscious choice of our activities, can be summarized as Enlightened Living. For such a choice, one needs an awareness of who am I, the entity who wants to think, who wants to look before the leap. What are my choices? What is my process for analysis and decision-making? Reflection inwards to find answers to these and many related questions are called self-control or *yoga*. The root of the Sanskrit word *Yoga* is *Yuj* (union with the self).

The many facets of enlightened living are detailed in various scriptures like *Bhagavadgītā*, Upanishads, etc. Aspects of such enlightened living are illustrated schematically in the figures below. Every element of our thought and action described in these figures is a subject for scores of books and insightful literature in many scriptures. Vedic Philosophy states that all of them are enabled by and witnessed through a large body of forces of nature collectively identified as *"Brahman"* and reflected by the symbol

We live only through three pathways: our body and its capability to act or engage in physical activities, our mind, and its ability to feel or experience emotions and the intellect through which we think, reflect, reason and analyze. The three pathways described in the Vedic scriptures are:

Karma Yoga (which emphasizes selfless action).

Bhakti Yoga (which emphasizes faith and worship, leading to a calm emotional state of mind without duality such as like/dislike, love/hate, etc.) and

Jnana Yoga (where the intellect is held in check with the single-minded thought that the Universe and I are integral in each other - *Thath Thwam Asi.*

All three pathways of enlightened living co-exist. There is no function of the body, devoid of mind (and emotions) or intellect (and thoughts). This continuity of the various facets of enlightened living is illustrated in figure 4.6.

The process of enlightened living leads to self – realization. What happens after that? This confusion arises when we think of the three pathways of self-realization as a linear sequence. But what happens when the three pathways are inseparably interconnected? The living human body consists of muscles, nerves, and blood veins. We can recognize each independently. We can treat or correct each on its own accord. Yet, the living person is an embodiment of all these aspects of human anatomy working in unison. The same can be said of the three pathways for Self-control (*Yoga*). Self–realization remains the center (the intent, heart, and soul) of such an enlightened person in every aspect of their living.

Figure 4. 6. Interconnected nature of Self-control through Action, Emotion and Reasoning

One who understands the concept of Self-Realization thinks they do not participate in any activity, even though engaging in all activities, such as seeing, touching, smelling, eating, working, and breathing. B.G. 5. 8.

In all activities such as speaking, relaxing, holding an object, even in the momentary acts such as winking, the enlightened person remembers that all these are responses of the sense organs abiding in their senses (as influenced by the Laws of Nature (i.e.) Brahman). B.G. 5. 9.

A person with deep roots in the concept of the highest enlightenment (Brahman) performs all activities abandoning all attachments to them. Such a person is not stained by the work (Karma), just as the lotus leaf is not wetted by the water in which it resides. B.G. 5. 10.

Those who perform their activities with body, mind and intellect or reasoning, even if it is only through body functions or sense organs, through self-control and hence without attachment to those activities are called enlightened persons. B.G. 5. 11.

Through the true knowledge of the self that the person residing within remains unattached, the ignorance of the living objects is destroyed; then, such a living being shines with tremendous knowledge, like the sun in the shining sea. B.G. 5. 16.

At that stage of awareness or enlightenment, the living beings soar with knowledge, self-control, and commitment. They aim for a larger cause from which there is no return. In this process, all the actions are cleansed by their knowledge and understanding. B.G. 5. 17.

The enlightened person conquers birth and death even in this world! They have reached the state of unattached existence (Brahman). Such a person has neither faults nor equals. Hence discrete events such as birth and death do not occupy his mind. B.G. 5. 19.

Such a person neither rejoices on obtaining their likes nor grieves when the dislikes are bestowed, remaining steadfast in the unperturbed knowledge, knowing that they as a person reside within the laws of nature (described as the Brahman residing within the Brahman). B.G. 5. 20.

Having disconnected themselves through the process of non-attachment, they find the happiness of eternal nature through the union with the Brahman – the concept of total self-control and unattached active participation. B.G. 5. 21.

Any person, with detachment from external objects, with eyes focused steadily and with control of all body functions, sense organs, mind, and intellect, focused on sustained contemplation on the laws of nature and their interactions, thereby totally freed from desire, fear or unrelenting anger, is a liberated person. B.G. 5. 27, 28.

Mind Over Matter

Why do people who can handle complex issues at work become extremely agitated about simple matters in their personal life? Why do we refuse to see the limitations or blemishes in one situation when we can accept the same or look over them as acceptable or inevitable in other situations? Why can one guide and counsel total strangers but find it difficult to provide the same support for their children or close ones? These are among the scores of situations, all of which are real. Are they all situations that require reflecting on the principle: When "mind "is intimately tied to the "matter", the mind goes through perturbations as the material objects change with time and circumstances? Instead, can we manage the "mind" as a purveyor of the "matter" – (i.e.) mind over matter?

Anything that exists, that which can be perceived, experienced, understood or reflected upon, are all parts of the Matter (*Prakriti*). That which resides in the matter, leading to actions (of the body), emotions (or feelings) and thoughts (intellect), is the Mind (*Purusha,* Self or Consciousness). The self or the mind (I) cannot be perceived devoid of the matter (the universe). Yet, the mind (I – the self or consciousness) is the means to perceive all aspects of the "Universe".

This mind/matter interconnectedness is illustrated through many analogies: The flame that illumines (the mind) does not exist without the torch (matter). The flame connected to the fire appears to be unique (just as the mind, connected with each of us, gives us a sense of identity as individuals). Illumination (property of the self) is inherent in every object that functions as a torch (matter enlightened by the mind).

Here are a few quotes from Uddhava Gita:

Just as fire manifests differently in pieces of wood of different sizes and qualities, the self or consciousness, having entered the bodies in all forms, appears to assume the identity of each. U.G. 7. 47.

The various phases of one's material life, beginning with birth and culminating in death, are all properties of the body and do not affect the soul or consciousness, just as the apparent waxing and waning of the moon do not affect the moon itself. Such changes are enforced by the imperceptible movements of the time, a property of nature. U.G. 7. 48.

The flame appears and disappears at every moment, and yet this creation and destruction are not noticed by the ordinary observer. Similarly, the mighty waves of time constantly flow, like the powerful currents of a river, and imperceptibly cause the birth, growth, and death of innumerable material bodies. And yet the soul, which appears to be constantly forced to change with time, does not perceive the actions of time. U.G. 7. 49.

When the mind perceives nothing, then nothing exists! In this state – when the mind exists without any connection to the matter - all dualities (love/hate, life/death, joy/sorrow, respect/disrespect, friend/foe, praise/criticism, relative/not-related, ...) cease to exist. It is this state of calm contemplation that we seek when we meditate. This state of mind leads to the highest level of objectivity. This is the state of mind of a devotee when they worship the Lord in total surrender, without any thoughts or connections. This is the state of mind of a spiritually evolved person: One of calm contemplation, independent of the situation and circumstances.

The Sun evaporates large quantities of water by its potent rays; later water returns to the earth in the form of rain. Similarly, a spiritually evolved person accepts all material objects and at the appropriate time when the proper person has approached him to request them, he returns such material objects. Thus, in accepting and giving up the objects, he is neither entangled nor in-separably attached to all such objects.   U.G. 7. 50.

Even when reflected in various objects, the sun is never divided, nor does it merge into its reflection. Only those limited by their reasoning would consider the sun as divided and merged into its many reflections. Similarly, although the self is reflected through different material bodies, the self remains undivided and nonmaterial U.G. 7.51.

These scriptural writings should not become cursory reading materials or abstract statements adding to our confusion! They are powerful means to explore the perturbations in our mind and how to return the mind to a calm and tranquil state.

One will begin to see in the above their universal principles only when every aspect of life is understood as something external and does not belong to the individual "Self". In that awareness (state of mind), the field of activity (the matter) becomes irrelevant. With this frame of mind, the deep and subtle principles enunciated in the scriptures – of every religion or philosophy – come to the foreground. In that frame of mind, one becomes equipoised and not affected by the ebb and flow of life experiences. Perceived differences in race, religion, culture, ethnicity, personal connections, etc., all give way to a larger universal principle: *Thath Thwam Asi* (You and the universe are integral in each other). In this state of mind over matter, the writings in the scriptures become relevant and purposeful.

Few more verses on the concept of "Mind over matter":

Neither people, the presiding deities (God), my body, nor the planets, past actions or time are responsible for my joys or sorrows. The learned men proclaim that the mind alone is the cause which sets the wheel of worldly experiences (dualities) in motion. Bhikshu Gita Verse 43

The mind alone indeed creates the powerful sense of objects (matter or the universe as we know of it) and thereafter proceeds to create the connections through the three connectors (Guna) – knowledge, bias, and ignorance - which in turn result in all our perceptions or experiences. Bhikshu Gita Verse 44

The mind is mightier than the mighty! He, who brings the mind under control, is indeed the God of all Gods!! Bhikshu Gita Verse 48.

Those who have not conquered their mind, which is truly difficult to conquer, of irresistible speed and which inflicts pain where it truly hurts, creates false divisions of friend and foe amongst people. *Bhikshu Gita Verse 49*

Holding on to this body, which is only perceived through the mind, one becomes blinded by the notions of "I" and "my"; in this endless darkness, they roam around with the delusion of "this is me" and "this is the other". Bhikshu Gita Verse 50

The dualities (love/hate, life/death, joy/sorrow, respect/disrespect, friend/foe, praise/criticism, relative/ stranger, ..) are self-inflicted through the mind. If sometimes a man unwittingly bites his own tongue with his own teeth, then with whom can he get angry for that pain? Other than one's own self, no one can give us joy or sorrow. Bhikshu Gita Verse 51.

Oh, son, therefore restrain the mind with the right understanding. This is the essence of yoga. Bhikshu Gita Verse 61.

Mind Over Matter – Practical Aspects

It is said that "Success is getting what we want; Happiness is wanting what we get". In these definitions of success and happiness, the operating word is "want", which is determined by the mind and its connection to the world of matter.

Based on our discussion in the previous essays, our perception (experience) of want would be governed by the dominant role of one of these three connectors. When knowledge is dominant and hence tranquility prevails, there would be a clear sense of purpose for our want, with an intended good for a larger cause. (e.g.): I am happy when I see my actions create a smile in whomever I meet. When bias is dominant and turbulence (*Rajasam*) prevails, the want is more in the nature of desire with a self-fulling need. This want is never fully satisfied. (e.g.) I am happy when my actions bring smiles to my family member or someone close to me. No sooner this thought crosses my mind, I am off to the next step: Who is the one close to me? The purpose of engaging in positive actions that bring a smile is lost in my mind that is searching for the close one! Thus starts the series of a chain of events, waves of happiness and sorrow. When ignorance is dominant resulting in an inertial state

(*Thamasam*), my mind has no focus or sense of purpose. Even the smile in others brings a frown in me as it is seen as a mockery. Or it brings memories of fear and delusion totally disconnected and tears of sorrow!

The Self (I) behind all these experiences is one and the same. This constancy of self in the world of experiences (through the mind and its connection to the matter) is true knowledge.

The connection between the mind and matter is also one of our awareness of the sense organs and their role. They collect and transmit signals to the mind. They also act in response to the signal from the mind. There is no noise when the tree falls in the forest with no one to hear. Our ear does not send any signal to the brain, and the brain does not perceive the noise of the falling tree! To a large extent, the role of the sense organs and their senses (sight, sound, taste, touch, and smell) can be under the control of the mind only through voluntary separation from them.

Connections of the mind with the matter can also be actively managed through its direct control of the sense organs. This process of separation from the sense organs or their active control by the mind is what we call the initial steps of "Yoga". Even when the sense organs are held in check, the mind can wander through the realms of emotions and thoughts. Voluntary conditioning of the mind – to remain still and hence detached from the emotions (perceived through the body, mind, and intellect) – is achieved through meditation. This is the next step in *yoga*.

Mind over matter could take unexpected twists and turns in our daily life. As an example, what you see – through the eyes – and hence perceive as the real, may not be what it is! The classic example is the mistaken view of the rope as a snake and the fear that engulfs our emotions. The surprise of discovering the rope, where it was seen as a snake only moments earlier, brings a sense of relief and joy, and newfound safety. All these are aspects of the mind over matter. To be constantly aware of this interconnected nature of mind over matter is an aspect of Spirituality in Practice.

Every moment of life is an exercise in "Mind over matter". Our communication is always challenged by what we say vs. what was truly intended. Conversely, there are challenges to what is heard vs. what is understood. The greater the attachment and bias, the more anxiety, grief, and suffering. A major focus of Buddhist teachings are lessons to manage the mind over matter to be free of desire and attachments.

"Ignorance" as the primary connector between mind over matter leads to serious mental health issues. The field of Psychotherapy and counseling is rich in addressing these issues. In many situations in personal relations, innocuous observations result in misperceptions and totally irrational outcomes. How often do we observe something and perceive it to be something totally different? How often do we hear words incorrectly or comprehend them inaccurately, yet believe what we heard is the truth? All these are situations that require proper management of mind over matter.

Totally innocent events tend to become twisted and turn into heinous effects depending on the observer and their perceptions (the mind). Is it not useful and necessary to seek a set of observations and look at the pattern instead of jumping to a conclusion on a single piece of evidence? If the education on sample size and their statistical significance is used in our daily life, there may be far less noise and commotion in our daily life.

How often do you jump to conclusions? As a metaphor, how often do you fire first and aim later? How often do you facilitate gathering relevant information before decisions are made? Whether you jump to conclusions will be evidenced by your openness to new information. The greater your engagement in such a broader base of observations, reflection and analysis more is your effectiveness in managing the mind over the matter.

Our willingness to change our mind is not a weakness if the mind is consciously aware of the mind over matter. Constant effort to seek more information or observations and a complete willingness to change our minds when faced with new evidence is not a symptom of being indecisive. This open-minded nature should not be sacrificed for fear of being seen as weak or a flip-flop.

People tend to develop a preference for things merely because they are familiar with them. In social psychology, this effect is sometimes called the familiarity principle. Such effects are involuntary conditioning of the mind. They reflect an absence of control of the mind over the matter.

Observation and reflection is not a one-way street. One who has constant control of his mind over the matter is free to say or hear whatever he chooses at a given moment since his mind is open to the response and modify the action accordingly. If you are not totally attached to your thoughts or actions (the matter), your mind will exhibit that freedom. When the focus on mind over matter becomes natural, there is a liberation from the constraints that inhibit most of us and most of the time! This is best described as analogous to the lotus leaf, which lives in the water, sustained by the water, and yet remains untainted by the water!

Events and circumstances surrounding them are all aspects of "matter". Observation, inferences, conclusions, and decisions are all the various aspects of the "mind". The objectivity displayed by the mind will be noticed only through the next set of events which could be a decisive action or seeking more data or information, probing, experimentation, etc. All of these are, again, aspects of "matter". Thus, we see that mind and matter are inseparable and intertwined. When "mind" is intimately tied to the "matter", the mind goes through perturbations, just as material objects change with time and circumstances. When the mind is held in check and used as a tool and as an enabler, the objectivity of the observer increases.

Inability to treat the mind as distinct and separate from the matter is considered a fallacy (Maya – illusion). To understand the interconnected nature of the mind and the matter and the nature of the connectors is described as the first step towards acquiring true knowledge. Mind, the matter, and the connectors (*Guna*) are all means or agents. The Self (I) merely exists as a witness and participant in this play of mind, matter, and their interconnectedness. One who understands this independence of the Self (I) is considered truly liberated. In this unattached active engagement, one reaches a state of true liberation. This is considered true knowledge.

The true knowledge of the Self (I) merely as an observer brings untold joy and happiness, which cannot be described. It is truly the outcome of self-realization. In that state of knowledge or awareness, our common perceptions of joy and sorrow (and all other dualities) disappear. This is not a metaphysical state. Instead, it is merely the fine-tuning of our understanding of the mind over matter.

Upanishads are scriptures, part of the Vedas. They contain Vedic Philosophy in a summary fashion. Kathopanishad is one of the most well-known Upanishads. It contains a simple analogy to explain the subject of mind over matter:

Figure 4.7. Mind over matter: Consciousness, charioteer with reins, and the horses as sense organs.

Our body is like a chariot to which the sense organs and the senses are yoked like horses. Mind, like the reins, enable the charioteer (soul or consciousness) to hold the horses (i.e.) the senses in check. The soul rides on the chariot, and the road is the world of objects (perceptions, feelings, and thoughts) over which the senses move. If the reins are not held firmly and wisely, the senses and organs like vicious horses will get out of control, and the chariot will not reach the goal but will go round and round in cycles of births and re-births (life of constant tumult of duality - like/dislike, happiness/sorrow, joy of birth/fear of death, etc.). Anyone who controls his mind will find his senses like good horses driven by a good charioteer. Kathopanishad. 3. 4, 5 to 9

Simply put, when you want to manage your "mind over matter", one could say, "Rein in your horses!"

Spirituality in Practice – Contrast between the Two Pathways

The question "Who am I?" can be answered based on an analytical understanding of our experiences. This analysis starts with the axiom that "All our experiences are the outcome of the connection between the consciousness and anything other than that (perceived as the cognitive world) through our portals of body, mind, and intellect". All such cognitive effects end up in three connectors: Knowledge, bias, and ignorance. Our focus on these connectors and their nature and the details surrounding them is the means for better understanding our experiences. This analytical approach leads to a natural separation of "I" – the consciousness – and "I" – the individual or our cognitive existence. Separation between the two aspects of "I", when it becomes a natural aspect of life, it is described as enlightened living. This explicit awareness of the consciousness and everything other than that is also described as "self-realization".

Such enlightened living is reflected in the "Divine" or spiritual qualities we exhibit in our day-to-day life. The analysis of our experience could be flawed or insufficient on occasion. In those situations, we find ourselves limited by our responses and fail to exhibit the strength of divine qualities. This is "unenlightened living". In theological terms, such behavior may be termed as "demonic" in contrast to the "divine" or "angelic" qualities. Hence, life, in general, is a spectrum between the two extremes: Enlightened and Un-enlightened Living.

Bhagavadgītā Chapter 16 lays out clearly the contrast between the enlightened and unenlightened manner of living. We present the following extended excerpt from this chapter. The goal should not be to dwell on the extremes. Instead, the goal should be constant vigilance of these two pathways and an attempt to steer the ship of life, more towards the enlightened and more away from the unenlightened way of living.

The qualities of enlightened living (also described as "divine" qualities) are:

Fearlessness; tranquility; self-control through analysis or introspection; steadiness or consistency of purpose; self-less giving to those in need; Self-less nature evidenced through actions; study of scriptures, austerity or contemplation as a means of self-control; straight forwardness; nonviolence; truthfulness; freedom from anger or passion; renunciation of intensely self-focused needs; peacefulness; absence of deceit; sincere and kind consideration to the needs of others; steady mind unaffected by desires; gentle manners; modesty; vigorous; forgiving nature, tolerance or fortitude; purity as reflected by the absence of malice; absence of uncontrolled pride.

B.G.16.1 to 3.

We also find these qualities extolled and sought after as the blessings from the Lord as part of all prayers in any religion and the chanting during devotional services.

Qualities opposed to enlightened living are:

Lack of commitment to principles; hypocrisy or ostentation, arrogance; deceit of oneself through their own pride; anger arising out of desire; insensitivity, disrespectful; lack of knowledge or understanding.

B.G. 16.4.

The unenlightened are not aware of the distinctions between activities that require involvement, and that should be avoided. They also lack a clear mind which reflects sustained analysis, proper conduct befitting the occasion, and truthfulness. Such unenlightened persons say, "A person is nothing more than a physical being brought about by the union (between a couple) caused by passion. To them, in this world, there is no other purpose, reason, basis, truth or higher order (Laws of Nature, Brahman or God)". These unenlightened persons, due to their lack of reasoning, participate, indulge, or bring forth fierce activities, leading to the destruction of the world or space in which they exist, which they treat with enmity. Such (unenlightened) persons pursue their activities filled with insatiable desire, self-serving reasoning or hypocrisy, pride, delusion, or attachments to the world of activities and their effects. They pursue fulfillment of their desires as their only goal. The result of such pursuit is an obsession with endless anxieties which end only at the person's death. Such unenlightened persons driven by endless desires and tied down by passion and anger strive to attain or gather wealth (or material benefits) for their personal gratification, if necessary, even by improper or unlawful means. Such people speak out of ignorance, "This is my gain today. This desire of mine shall be met today. This is my wealth, which I shall acquire more or further again. This is my enemy, and I shall eliminate them. I shall identify more enemies for their destruction. I am the king, who is perfect, and my strength brings me happiness. I am wealthy and superior by birth, and no one else is equal to me. I shall conduct the rituals of sacrifice and give away wealth in the name of charity, as a means for my enjoyment". Such unenlightened persons bound by the web of desires and confused by limitless thoughts or notions and influenced by the joys of their desires fall into the trap of their own making (described as falling into a foul hell). In a self-conceited manner, such unenlightened persons of inflexible reasoning, driven by their pride in personal belongings, offer sacrifices only in name and not according to the principles or basic values – of total self-control and unattached active participation. These (unenlightened) persons of malicious nature driven by their self-centered pride (ego), power, desires, and anger show their contempt or anger towards nature and the larger order it represents (or the Lord) in their own bodies and in that of others. B.G. 16. 6 to 18.

"Divine" qualities lead a person to an enlightened life. The unenlightened person remains as such due to their bondage or attachments to the "pairs" such as pleasure/pain, happiness/sorrow, love/hatred, etc. They inhibit self-control and liberation from such attachments. Human beings: Be aware that you are born of "Divine" qualities.   B.G. 16.5

The evidence and the outcome of these two pathways – the enlightened and the unenlightened – are readily recognized at their extremes. But, for most of us, life is a constant spectrum of experiences between these two extremes.

The Essence of *Bhagavadgītā*

1. It is the law of nature that everyone and everything in the universe is constantly involved in activities of one kind or another.

2. Activities may be momentary in nature or may involve lifelong pursuits. "What is the proper or appropriate manner to participate in any and all activities?" – This is the question raised by any person seeking enlightened life.

3. Every activity occurs due to the confluence of five aspects: (a) The objective, reason, or purpose of the activity (b) the person(s) involved (c) means or circumstances (d) impact or consequences, and (e) the laws of nature or the Divine influence.

4. Without recognizing these five aspects, anyone who believes that he/she alone is responsible for any activity is lacking in wisdom. Such partial or self-centered view on anything is described as "ego"!

5. Consideration of all these five aspects is enabled through reflection, analysis, and contemplation within oneself. This process of internal reflection or assessment

regarding the activities of life is called "self-control". It is also described as the union with the "self" (*yoga*).

6. Through internal reflection or Self-Control, a person remains their own best friend. In the absence of Self-Control, a person becomes their own worst enemy.

7. Our participation in all activities involves one of three attributes or Equilibrium states (*Gunathvam*): (a) Tranquility: Analytical, reflective, and contemplative (b) Turbulence: Impulsive, emotional, based on wants and needs, (c) Passive submission: Lack of both analysis and emotional attachments and largely based on inertia, delusion, and ignorance.

8. It is the law of nature that our body, mind, and intellect is connected to everything external through three connectors like three wires or ropes (*Guna*). These three connectors are knowledge, partial knowledge (bias), and ignorance. While all three co-exist, one of these connectors dominates the other two, setting up three equilibrium states: tranquility (*Sathvikam*), turbulence (*Rajasam*), and inertia (*Thamasam*). There is no activity or experience which is free from one of these three equilibrium states arising out of nature.

9. Tranquility leads to wisdom, understanding, illumination, and clarity. Happiness derived from

contentment is associated with tranquility. It permits transition from one activity to another with ease and with a clear comprehension of why such transition is needed. Thus, a tranquil attribute at the time of crisis or transition transforms a person to a higher plane or higher level of performance.

10. Turbulence is rooted in excessive desires or passion arising out of the needs and wants of a person. Turbulence leads to unsatisfied needs and wants, which in turn leads to the initiation of countless other activities, unease, and lack of contentment and longing without satisfaction. At the time of crisis or transition from one activity to another, turbulence merely compounds and increases the level of activity, confusion, and chaos. The result of a turbulent approach to activity is sorrow.

11. Passive submission is due to the lack of a sense of purpose or direction. This inertia, indecision, and procrastination shroud knowledge and understanding. The dominance of ignorance leads to association with activities based on illusion, grief, delusion, and despair.

12. Tranquility leads to WISDOM, through which one can perceive the same and changeless presence of the laws of nature (Divine presence) in every aspect and beings of the world.

13. Turbulence or agitated approach to activities, through self-driven desire and attachment, leads to separation or division of various kinds. This results in the wisdom that perceives many divisions – I/others, race, religion, politics, rich/poor, etc. – even though the same laws of nature are at work and with the same effect!

14. The wisdom that leads to unalterable attachments to one or few activities, objects, or effects, as if it were the whole of life, ignoring the true realities and narrow scope pursued is declared to be born of ignorance.

15. Tranquil mind leads to REASONING that helps to discriminate between appropriate and inappropriate activities and between bondage and liberation. An agitated mind leads to discrimination between right and wrong with flawed logic or reasoning influenced by one's wants, needs, or attachments. Through lack of understanding whatsoever, the reasoning which leads one to conclude inappropriate activities as appropriate and everything else in reverse is due to ignorance (like being blindfolded).

16. Tranquil nature leads to CONSISTENCY or stability in the control of the mind, life processes, and in the enlightened pursuit of the activities of life. Turbulence leads to stability that constantly relies upon one's wants

and needs as the sole purpose of any activity. The foolish dependency through which one constantly falls back to sleep, fear, grief, dejection, and passion is described as the consistency associated with inertia or an ignorant approach to activities.

17. The experience, which appears like poison in the beginning but transforms into nectar in the end, that pleasure of transformation is associated with the HAPPINESS of the tranquil approach. Such happiness is derived from the purity or clarity of the mind and its power of reasoning within oneself. The happiness which begins as nectar but slowly transforms into poison (due to the inability to satisfy one's increasing desires or needs and wants) is associated with a turbulent approach. The happiness at the beginning, as well as in its continuation, is deceitful to one's own self and leads to a lack of direction; such happiness is associated with ignorance or passive submission.

18. Through the process of self-control, an individual can dissect every activity into segments until each segment of activity can be identified with its associated attribute or equilibrium state (*Gunathvam*).

19. To identify the dominant attribute, it is necessary for a person to develop a frame of mind that evaluates all three

connectors and their equilibrium states as equal in merit. This requires objectivity and non-attachment.

20. Constant internal reflection with a frame of mind that treats all three attributes or connectors with equal value is called "Total Self Control" (*Sagunathvam*).

21. Such "Total Self Control" brings with it a clarity or understanding of the cause and effect associated with activities. The enlightened understanding leads one to see all activities as the ebb and flow or tides on the surface, resting on the deep ocean, which is invisible, calm, and merely exists! The ebb and flow of life and its activities are caused by laws of nature, which are universal and omnipresent (*Brahman*), like the deep ocean supporting all the tidal waves on the surface!

22. "Total Self Control" also brings with it an objective frame of mind that treats all opposites as equals. For example, one does not see the difference between one wave and another in the ocean; one also does not see the difference between the crest and the bottom of the wave, as all parts of the wave are composed of the same water. Such frame of the mind treats opposites such as love/hate, happiness/sorrow, like/dislike, pleasure/pain, rich/poor, etc., with equal regard. It is the same frame of mind that sees commonality in all perceived differences

such as race, religion, gender, color, creed, nationality, etc.

23. Such a person with "total self-control" remains steady and unaffected by all aspects of life and its activities. Such steadiness and stability permit one to comprehend the enabling laws of nature (*Brahman*) and everything else as the enabled! The enabler – laws of nature – merely exist and are indescribable (*Nirgunathvam*). They are objective and unattached. The enabler in all of us is the soul or consciousness. It is analogous to a person within who cannot be harmed by weapons, burned by fire, wet by water, or swayed by the wind.

24. A person with "total self-control" participates in all activities of life and yet remains unaffected by them. This is analogous to the gentle breeze, which spreads the fragrance all around, and yet neither recognizes the fragrance, the act of spreading the fragrance, or its effects. Such steadiness brings with it a value system that treats a piece of gold and a piece of clay with equal regard, another example of objectivity and non-attachment.

25. Such enlightened participation in the activities of life (duty) is required of every individual. Withdrawal from appropriate activities or withdrawal due to fear or

apprehension of results are both undesirable. The purpose of "total self-control" is not to become a recluse or to withdraw from life and its activities.

26. "Total self-control" and the objectivity associated with it are best achieved when all activities are initiated with an externally focused objective and not self-centered. This is described as Unattached Active Participation.

27. Such unattached participation brings with it a joy and purpose in life which has no equals. Those who recognize this unique mode of participation in life and its activities fully enjoy life.

28. When an individual conducts their life with "Total self-control and unattached active participation", for those moments, the person is in union with the highest form of enlightened existence or the conceptual state of "*Brahman*".

May all manner of existence in life be dedicated to Total Self Control and Unattached Active Engagement.

Athma Bodha (Knowledge of the Self) – Who am I?

Following is a summary based on *Athma Bodha* (Knowledge of the Self) authored by Saint Adi Sankara (700 – 750 CE).

Who am I?

There are two aspects to "Who am I?" or the "knowledge of the self".

One is cognitive, which we can relate to readily.

The other is the in-cognitive forces of nature (*Brahman*), the enabler or substratum of everything cognitive.

I am a cognitive person:

Each of us can identify ourselves by our name, appearance, age, family, connections, education, job, accomplishments, etc. In this knowledge of the self, our life in general is a "product of our experiences". These experiences are the outcome of connectors (*Guna*), i.e., our knowledge, bias, and ignorance through which we are connected to the experience. Depending on their proportion, these connectors create a sense of duality, such as like/dislike, love/hate, etc. The goal in life for inner peace and harmony within and around is to maintain an awareness of all these connectors *(Sagunathvam)* which leads to objectivity. In this process, the dualities are held in check, and the emotional upheavals gradually vanish. We are equally at ease irrespective of our situation or circumstances or the people around us.

Our thoughts are the seeds for all our experiences. By reducing the number of thoughts, we are left with a smaller number of experiences to manage, as described above. "I think, therefore I am," states the French Philosopher René Descartes. It is our mind and its thoughts that lead to our emotions and hence our feelings and actions. "Control your mind, you are in control of yourself" is the guiding principle for life by Lord Buddha. The role of thought and its impact on our actions and the way we live in the cognitive world has been addressed earlier. See essays on Mind Over Matter.

In the Cognitive Universe everything is a tradeoff between Subjective Vs, Objective. Let us elaborate on this further here. Each thought can be directed into a circle focused on "I" and "mine", as shown in figure 4.8. Alternatively, the thoughts can be directed externally to "We" and "ours". Each excursion through the cycle is an experience. Many cycles of life and death can be metaphoric to a multitude of cycles corresponding to the many experiences. The fewer our thoughts through a calm and quiet mind, the less is the number of cycles experienced. We live in a state of calm tranquility. In other words, minimize the journey through the two sets of circles and closer you are to liberation from the tumultuous nature of life and its journey.

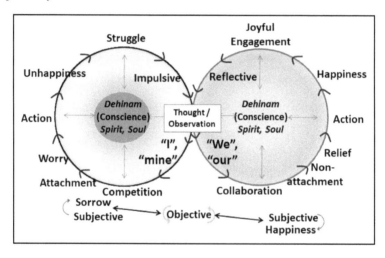

Figure 4.8. Managing our thoughts in the cognitive "I": Subjectivity Vs. Objectivity

These two circles are also analogous to the wheels of a bicycle. For the bicycle to move forward smoothly, we need two actions happening simultaneously: (a) Apply the effort through the pedal to the rear wheel invisible to us (i.e.) focus the effort for the success of others through non-attachment; such effort also ends up useful in the progress of oneself analogous to the bicycle movement and the journey. (b) focus farther away beyond "me" and mine", with a longer-term goal and vision. It is analogous to our attention away from the handlebar we are holding on to and the wheel immediately in front of us. The more we are fixated on the handlebar and the front wheel at every moment, the greater the risk of losing balance and the bicycle tipping over! For the journey of life to continue with inner peace and harmony – there must be a balance (objectivity) and not sway to one extreme or another (through the duality of like/dislike due to subjectivity governed by opinions, bias, and judgments). In bicycling, we maintain balance and do not sway to either side, with progress in the journey as the goal. In real life, the goal is also to progress with a balanced frame of mind (seek objectivity) as best as one can in whatever we do.

Figure 4.9. Managing our actions in the cognitive "I": Subjectivity Vs. Objectivity; Attachment Vs. non-attachment.

The above might appear too analytical and conceptual. After a brief period of learning, everyone bicycles with ease and comfort. Similarly after a little bit of reflection and practice, Non-attachment, reducing the number of thoughts, steering them towards others – rather than "me" and "mine" – and focus on the larger common good (looking ahead instead of fixated on handlebar and front wheel) can become parts of our routine life. When we seek them out and use them as a routine, as a way of life, we ride through the pangs of life and its dualities such as happiness/sorrow, love/hate, anger, jealousy, vanity, etc. with ease. Life as a journey becomes easy to manage like spinning the wheels or riding a bicycle!

I am the in-cognitive or subtle person:

On sustained reflection, we also come to realize that anything cognitive and all the connectors are enabled by laws of nature. I am enabled by and exist as evidence of nature and the laws that enable nature. This enabler is defined as *Brahman. It* is devoid of anything tangible, cognitive, or connective (*Nirgunathvam*). This comprehension leads us to also acknowledge the transient nature (like reflections in a mirror) of all the Cognitive aspects and the connectors (*Guna*) that we call life.

The cognitive (*Gunathvam*) and in-cognitive or subtle (*Nirgunathvam*) are the two inseparable aspects of anyone or anything. This is the answer to "Who am I?" or knowledge of the self.

Below are two additional illustrations to capture the essence of the knowledge of the self.

Imagine anyone or a group of people on a boat. Think of the boat itself. All that are the cognitive aspects of the "self". People on the boat cannot sway or lean excessively to one side of the boat or the other. Otherwise, the boat will capsize, and everyone will fall into the water. Anyone who is

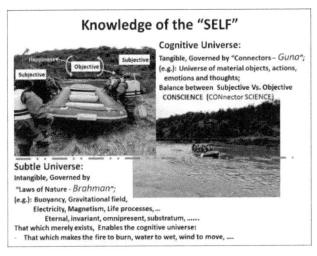

Figure 4.10. All that floats Vs. Buoyancy.
Cognitive Vs. In-Cognitive - Enabled and the Enabler

aggressive and wants their own way and hence leans beyond the limit to either side will also tumble into the water. These are examples of subjective nature, yielding to personal bias or selfish motivated choices. To float well and remain steady, everyone and the entire group in the boat must maintain a balance between the two sides. This is analogous to maintaining the balance between duality, such as like/dislike, happiness/sorrow, etc. Striking this balance is objectivity (*Sagunathvam*).

The connectors and their judicious balance (*Sagunathvam)* are all part of the mind and its function. Attempts are being made to explain the inner working of the mind through neural science. But what is this "science"? All forms of science are our attempts to observe and explain nature's subtle and in-cognitive laws or forces. It is defined as "*Brahman*".

While maintaining the balance, people in the boat should also be mindful that the boat and everyone and everything on it are all afloat thanks to the body of water! This ability for anything to float is enabled by "buoyancy", which is in-cognitive. The invisible buoyancy is necessary for everything cognitive (all that is floating) to exist that way! This is *Brahman* (that which enables the fire to burn, wind to blow, water to wet, objects to float in the water, etc.); the sum of all laws of nature that enable who we are and what we do. *Brahman* includes nature (forces that enable the planet and the universe to exist). *Brahman* represents the universe, and all that enables the universe to exist.

In the above illustration, we recognize two co-existing states: the cognitive (everything including the water) and the in-cognitive or subtle buoyancy and its role (the enabling force that makes all that is cognitive to float and enable the water its ability to sustain the floating). True knowledge of the self, comprises of both these co-existing states.

In many respects, the answer to "Who am I?" is also analogous to two sides of a coin. On one side of the coin is cognitive – our identification as individuals with our name, personal details, preferences, like/dislike, etc. This is the world of opinions and judgment – subjectivity. Through analytical reasoning, we strive to be objective, with a balanced frame of mind. The other side of the coin is the forces of nature (Brahman) that enable everything, all aspects of our being.

There is no such thing as a one-sided coin. We tend to remain focused on one side of the coin or the cognitive side, as if it is the whole coin. This is our illusion, or *Maya*. Being aware that there are two sides, and they are inseparable, is true knowledge and wisdom. Being tied to one side of the coin, we often identify ourselves as individuals. We remain "materialistic". When our perspective shifts to the other side of the coin, we see ourselves as limitless, as an integral part of the universe at large (*Thath Thwam Asi; Aham*

BrahmaAsmi). On this side, we remain "spiritual" –
connected to the enabler, the laws of nature, spirit, soul,
consciousness, or *Brahman*!

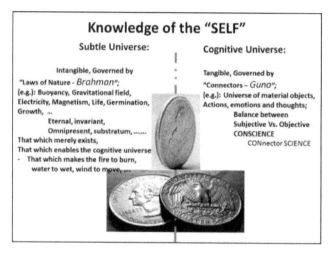

Figure 4.11. Cognitive and the Subtle (Enabled and the Enabler)
are ever present together like the two sides of a coin!

Summary:

The floating boat cannot exist without buoyancy. A coin
cannot exist without its two sides. We as individuals or
anything we can relate to have a cognitive state and an in-
cognitive or subtle body of laws of nature (*Brahman*) which
enable the cognitive to exist. Spirituality in Practice is the
recognition of the two sides and staying focused on both
simultaneously as best as we can. Recognition of this truth
is "Mind Over Matter" discussed in earlier essays!

Symbolism of "AUM"

In Vedic Philosophy, the Sanskrit word or symbol AUM has profound meaning. Is it a syllable or word, or is it a sound composed of many components? Extended discussions can be found in the Vedas and their annotations through Upanishads and the many scholarly writings that have followed over the past two millennia. In this essay, we look for the symbolism of AUM that is useful for our daily life in the context of Spirituality in Practice.

ॐ has both theological as well as philosophical implications. Here are a few excerpts.

The Prashna Upanishad:

"Those who have become established in AUM, what happens to them after death?"

The sage replied:

"AUM is both internal or intrinsic and transcendent or beyond limits. Through AUM, one can attain the personal and the impersonal".

"The three sounds of AUM when they are separated cannot lead one beyond mortality; But when the whole of AUM is realized as indivisible and inter-dependent and when that understanding goes on vibrating in mind, one is freed from fear, being awake or asleep".

Thaitriya Upanishad:

"AUM is the supreme symbol of the Lord. AUM is the whole, AUM Affirms; AUM signals the chanting of the hymns from the Vedas. The priest begins with AUM; Spiritual teachers and their students commence with AUM; The student who is established in AUM becomes united with the Lord".

The Mandukya Upanishad:

AUM stands for the supreme reality. It is changeless. It is a symbol of what it was, what it is, and what it shall be. AUM also represents what lies beyond the past, present, and future.

Source: The Upanishads – Introduced and Translated by Eknath Eswaran.

With the above description of ॐ and with reference to the description of *Brahman* in our earlier essays, we can see that ॐ is a symbolic representation of the term *Brahman* which itself is a collective noun for all laws of nature.

The above, as articulated in Vedic Philosophy, is noted in great detail in *Bhagavadgītā*, which has been the basis of many of our essays earlier. There we learned the following:

All that is cognitive are recognized through the three connectors (knowledge, ignorance, and bias) and their relative magnitude, which determines tranquility, turbulence, and inertia. To truly comprehend the reality and role of the connectors, one needs to step away from the three connectors and their immediate influence. This is the process

139

of self-control. Such inquiry through reflection and meditation leads to a state where the connectors are merely sources to gather evidence. The observer through the process of self-control evolves to become unconnected with the world of objects, the playing field of the connectors. At this stage, non-duality (absence of love/hate, like/dislike, friend/foe, etc.) becomes the very nature of an evolved person. Self or consciousness itself becomes the embodiment of enlightenment. Such enlightened existence enables a way of living, being in union with unattached consciousness while remaining alive in the cognitive world. Each person evolves into their own personal understanding and absorption of the above concepts.

The Sanskrit letter ॐ appears to codify the philosophy consistent with the above description. Let us look at such symbolism in the following. We do not intend this as an authentic reproduction from the scriptures. Instead, we offer this merely as a suggestion, a tool for better understanding the Vedic philosophy and its application to daily life.

The Sanskrit letter ॐ has a symbol "**3**", which we could use as a reminder of the three connectors. We perceive all our experiences through these three connectors. This "**3**" can also represent the three-fold aspects of the cognitive world (i.e.)

Body, mind, intellect.
Physical objects, emotions /feelings, thoughts /concepts.
Being awake, deep sleep, dreaming
Knowledge, Bias, Ignorance
Tranquility, Turbulence, Inertial.

Self-control implies that while being part of the cognitive world and being under the role of the three spheres listed above, one can pull away from the influences of these. The "arc", representing the extension away from the "**3**" in the ॐ, would seem to suggest such an extension away from the self, the process of self-control and introspection, while still being connected (living) in the cognitive world. The "**o**"– in the ॐ merely exists. It is not connected with the other parts (representing the cognitive aspects) of AUM. By its mere presence, the "**o**" completes the AUM. Without the "**o**"– the entire symbol of AUM – and by inference, all that it represents – is not complete or ceases to exist! These are the same descriptions ascribed to *Brahman* in the Vedic literature: *Brahman* merely exists; *Brahman* is wholesome; *Brahman* has no properties; by Its mere presence, everything becomes real (cognitive) and acquire their properties - enables the fire to burn, the wind to blow, etc.; One who understands the *Brahman* remains as *Brahman*; I – the self or consciousness – am the *Brahman*.

With the above symbolism in mind, we can see that represents the entire Vedic philosophy. For example,

"The three sounds of AUM when they are separated cannot lead one beyond mortality; But when the whole of AUM is realized as indivisible and inter-dependent and when that understanding vibrates in mind, one is freed from fear, being awake or asleep".

When AUM is seen as the symbolism of the entire Vedic philosophy, and when such philosophy is understood and appreciated by an individual, for them, all events of life are causal, governed by the connectors, and the entire life (or every moment) as viewed by being centered on Consciousness or laws of nature or *Brahman* is changeless since every moment is a mere repeat of the moment before or after. The consciousness within is merely that which is engaged in the process of observation and analysis of the connectors and their inter-play!

Astu: So be it!

During the Vedic chants, there are passages conveying the blessings of the Lord to all those present. When the chief priest recites these verses, the others in the retinue of priests would say *ThaTha Astu* (we concur with that). In its shortened form, it is stated as *Astu* (so be it). *Astu* also stands for a philosophical outlook in life, where life is lived every moment as it happens.

There are times in life when acceptance of reality as it is – *Astu* - may be the best option. Consider the situation of a family with an Alzheimer's patient. One of the neuropsychiatrists described it as "Heaven for the patient, hell for everyone around". In a poem titled *Bhaja Govindam* (verse 22), the poet states that the *enlightened person wanders around like an innocent child and like a mentally disabled (crazy) person*. This statement is very appropriately illustrated in a movie in which a young girl and an old professor afflicted with Alzheimer's disease play with each other blissfully. Their limitless union with nature is illustrated in a scene where they are both blissfully asleep on the lap of an elephant also in restful sleep!

Some of the Vedic sayings quoted in this movie are:

Thath Thwam Asi: Let us forget our names, relationships, memories, being, past, and present. When we live our lives shackled by these limitations, we fail to see the larger grandeur of nature or the universe, of which we are an integral part of.

One should be aware that truth always stems from awareness; where there is no awareness, there is no truth. Awareness is the limitless exploration of who we are and how we exist in a limitless union with the universe. Everything is part of cosmic consciousness (*Thath Thwam Asi* – You and the universe are integral in each other). Does such a mind exist? – Yes, if we accept: *Aham Brahma* – I am *Brahman*.

Does it mean the concept of "*Astu*" – so be it, or live in the moment, only for those who willingly or unwittingly live a life of isolation from the realities of life? What is the role of *Jnani* (the learned or wise one with true understanding) in the real world? These are real and serious questions any practitioner of Spirituality in Practice must confront.

Thath Thwam Asi (You and the universe are integral in each other) is a fundamental truth. Is there any other way you can think of yourself? Each of us is made up of material objects. Our body functions, emotions, and thought processes are governed by the laws of nature. This fundamental truth is not an injunction but a mere acknowledgment of the reality as it is! *Astu* – so be it.

If one can dwell in the above thought all the time, as a parallel stream to all the ebb and flow of daily life, then there is an unattached but active engagement. Perhaps this is the wakefulness or awareness declared in the Vedas? This parallel existence is like the lotus leaf that lives, grows and thrives in a body of water and remains dry (not wetted). While we engage in all activities of life, our mind (that is awake, alert, and aware) tells us in the background *Astu* (so be it) for everything good/bad, happiness/sorrow, strength/weakness, love/hate, comfort/discomfit, etc. My grandmother practiced this equanimity by constantly reminding herself, *Ishwaro Rakshatu* (Everything is God's will)!

Figure 4.12. Lotus leaf in water:
Analogy for Non-attachment

There may be only very few who truly comprehend the above simple truths. Only one in those millions may practice the above all the time and consciously live true to the dictum *Aham BrahmaAsmi* (I exist as Brahman). *Astu* – so be it.!

Among the thousands of persons, one perchance strives for perfection (to live with an awareness that "I am Brahman"); among those rare few who strive successfully, only one perchance knows Me (the Lord, the Brahman, the Supreme, the omnipresent substratum of the universe). B.G. 7.3.

Then what happens to the rest of us?

Everyone knows the difference between the "ideal" and the "achievable". While the Vedic scriptures teach us the ideal simple principles, the rest of us can easily learn to recognize reality as it is by distancing ourselves – mentally and intellectually – from any event at any moment. This practice of self-governance is called *yoga* (union with the self). This can also be thought of as "mindfulness". This practice of yoga can be momentary, frequent, active, or lifelong. Whatever the duration of this unattached active engagement, there is bliss, tranquility, and genuine happiness for that duration. Let that be our focus! So be it – *Astu*!

Thath Thwam Asi: You And The Universe Are Integral In Each Other

Thath Thwam Asi is considered as one of the grand pronouncements (*Maha Vaakyas*) of Vedanta (Knowledge derived from Vedas) or the essence of Vedas), In the most direct and simplest translation, it means: You are that. Here, the words "you" and "that" are two entities. "You" represents the "Self" or the person making the inquiry, and "that" represents everything the person can relate to or anything other than the Self. There is an extensive body of literature and scriptures that dwell into each aspect of this three-word phrase" "You", "That" and "are".

You or the Self is the person (*Thwam*). What you can comprehend external to you or deep inside of you is the Universe (*Thath*). You – the person – exist as part of everything that you can comprehend or relate to, or aware of. This remarkable axiom may be understood through the video: https://www.youtube.com/watch?v=0fKBhvDjuy0

The video shows a man enjoying a picnic in the lakefront park in the center of Chicago. Then the viewing area expands ten times each ten seconds. The view expands to one-meter square in size, ten square meters, etc. The view goes past the earth's orbit, the solar system, our galaxy, and beyond. In about 24 increments and at X 10^{24} square meters, the view covers the panorama of what might be seen from the edges of the universe, as far as we know of it. In every one of these views, the man in the park is exists, albeit increasingly smaller and ultimately minuscular part of the view. The narrator aptly states, "Our Galaxy looks like dust in the vast emptiness of the universe; the richness we see around us is an exception". Yet, we are all undeniably part and parcel of this universe: *Thath Thwam Asi.*

Then the video dwells deeper inside the person, covering one-tenth of the area every ten seconds. The view diminishes to expose the skin, the veins, the cell, the genetic double helix, the molecules, the atom, and the field of electrons. At $X10^{-16}$ square mm, we arrive at the smallest unit of material or energy field in each one of us, the nucleus of the carbon atom!

Whether we go far away or deep inside of us, we are nothing but part and parcel of the universe. This video provides us with a visual image of this reality. So, what? Why is this important to know or realize this basic truth? If "I" am indeed so integrally connected and in union with the universe, then why do I not see this connection as a matter of course? We pursue some of the answers in our essays.

Who Is A Spiritual Person?

Who is a spiritual person? Google search came up with images of mostly people meditating, sitting in silence in some remote place. Persons identified in this search as "spiritual" were the Pope, Dalai Lama, and Mahatma Gandhi.

Figure 4.13. Images of a spiritual person.

Mahatma Gandhi is considered a spiritual leader for his explorations of truth at all costs, caring for the poor and eliminating the caste system, and his work on other social issues. Martin Luther King, a close follower of Gandhi and a pastor, is not readily recognized as a spiritual leader. It requires a research article titled: "Dr. Martin Luther King, Jr. as Spiritual Leader" to affirm that. His Spiritual leadership is one of vision for equality for all, hope, faith, and altruistic love – all considered essential qualities of a spiritual person. "Spiritual" is also associated with "religious" unless the separation is made explicit. Sonia Sotomayor, U.S. Supreme Court Justice, states, "I am a very spiritual person. Maybe not traditionally religious in terms of Sunday mass every week, that sort of thing".

Dr. Margaret Paul, in her blog, writes:

A spiritual person cares about people, animals, and the planet. A spiritual person knows that we are all One and consciously attempts to honor this Oneness. A spiritual person is a kind person. You can go to church or temple or other places of worship regularly and say your prayers every day without caring about loving yourself, others, and the planet. You can practice yoga and meditate every day without being conscious of what is loving and what is not loving in your thoughts and actions. You can belong to a spiritual group and devotedly follow the teachings yet still be judgmental toward yourself and others in your daily life.

Spirituality may not be an end state. One may be spiritual for a moment or for periods of time. Spirituality is like our health. We are in good health under most metrics and most of the time! No one is ideal and hence 100% spiritual all the time, just as there is no one who is 100% healthy all the time.

Spirituality is reflected in our actions and way of life with a clear emphasis on our spirit, inner person, or consciousness (Analogs: reality = rooted in what is real; totality = in total or as a summation, etc.).

Spiritual person is objective (based on reflection and reasoning) and not subjective (rush to judgment). A spiritual person is decisive but open to changing their mind based on further observations or evidence. Spiritual person reflects, acts, and does not shoot from the hip (judgmental).

Self-control and a calm state of mind – hence yoga and meditation – are the building blocks of a spiritual person. But they are merely tools and not the end by themselves. The reflective nature of a spiritual person should not be mistaken for a recluse. The objective nature of a spiritual person makes them speak the truth or express views that may not be crowd-pleasing. A spiritual person sees truth/lie as an outcome of evidence and not based on any preconceived notions. Objectivity enables the spiritual person to be at ease with a wide circle of people, situations, and activities. A spiritual person seeks out situations where a real need exists. This makes them service oriented and caring. Addressing a real need is the motive and not a false sense of "savior of the world" mindset.

Spirituality, by its nature, dispels deep and unbridled desire or passion for anything or anyone. This is non-attachment and not detachment. A spiritual person is fully engaged in any activity due to their mindfulness on the forces of nature Brahman. Their the mind is not distracted by momentary perturbations, likes, unbridled desires, wants, needs, built-up emotions, etc.

A spiritual person is aware that ignorance is inherent in oneself. This awareness of self-ignorance permits the spiritual person to be kind to the self. Awareness of the potential for ignorance allows the spiritual person to be kind to others and understand their preferences and biases. To the extent any religion teaches methods to promote this tolerance, spiritual person can also be seen as religious.

Spirituality is like the sunshine, wind, or space that exists all around. While these ideals are expressed, each of us must find ways to reduce them to practice them in our own ways.

A spiritual person recognizes that the subjective world around them are the result of the three connectors: Ignorance, bias, and knowledge/understanding. Thus they can focus on the consciousness within oneself and remain steady or unshaken.

A spiritual person relies on their own self. They have an objective and balanced frame of mind, where opposites such as happiness and sorrow, dear and not so dear, praise and blame are equal in effect. They have a value system where a piece of clay, a stone, and a piece of gold are of equal significance.

A spiritual person perceives honor and dishonor, friendship and enmity as equal. Such a person does not initiate any actions based solely on personal or self-driven needs.

A spiritual person (of Self-control through internal reflection) reflects divinity through his thoughts, words, and action.   B.G. 14. – 23 to 27.

Shades of Karma

Karma is a Sanskrit word. It is very frequently used in Vedic Scriptures. The same word takes on several meanings depending on the context in which it is used. *Karma* is used to refer to the rituals to be performed in honor of the elders who have passed away. It also refers to religious practices in daily activities. "It is my *Karma*" implies that which is pre-ordained. *Karma* could also imply duty or the right thing one is required to do. There are many prefixes that create phrases such as daily work, for certain purpose or steps in a project, accumulated effect of actions, and impact of actions over generations - *Nitya Karma, Naimithya Karma, Sanchitha Karma, Prabodha Karma,-* respectively.

Kri is the root of the word *Karma;* it means to do or to act. Hence *Karma,* in any of its uses, refers to an action. The guiding principle for *Karma* from *Bhagavadgītā* states:

Your responsibility resides in performing your duty (Karmani Eva AdhikaaraAsthe'). B.G. 4.27.

What is this duty? Does it change with time and circumstances? Are my duties different from your duty? Are there many duties? What are the shades of duty? Shades of Karma?

Following is an illustrative story:

Once upon a time, a king sought ways to find happiness. His prayers were answered by a wise man and his advice: "Find the poor man in the far-off village, tending to the field. He will explain to you the source of happiness"!

The king traveled to the village and found the poor man in his tattered clothes and with a bare minimum of resources. But he was happily tilling the field, getting ready to sow seeds and grow crops. His happiness seemed to know no bounds. The king asked, "What is your source of happiness?" The poor man replied, "My King. I am certainly very limited in my means and resources. But I have figured out how to divide my resources for proper use. I share a quarter of my resources to feed my parents. That is my obligation, as I am nothing but a shade of the past. I share the second quarter with my wife. She is an integral part of who I am, and we care for each other. I share my third quarter with my siblings and neighbors who are in need for reasons and circumstances beyond their control. This is my righteous behavior to society, to be the keeper of my brothers and sisters. Finally, I share the fourth quarter of my resources with my children, who are the future. It is for these four quarters that I am also tilling the land now. So, my King, I grow whatever I can in the field, just as a means for taking care of these four quarters. Since my entire life has a meaning and purpose, I have little time to worry about anything else. I am happily engaged in all my life activities merely to carry out this duty – my Karma". The story is illustrative. It gives a broad framework for the advice, "Do your duty".

Each of us has three dimensions of time to contend with – the past, present, and future – and the obligations that pertain to these time periods: Preserve and protect our legacy - what made us who we are today; Strengthen the present as a core; Plan and ensure the future is well paved for. These three dimensions of duty apply to every one of us. While the past and the future are always external, the present has two components: intimate and personal (represented by the care for the wife in the above story); the second is external to oneself, represented by the siblings and the neighbors. Thus, we have four shades of duty: Pertaining to the past, present (internal and external), and the future. The above story can give us a universal framework to focus our efforts, carry out our duty and find genuine happiness in the process.

When one sees one's duty only through the narrow prism of "I" and what pertains to me, then duty becomes narrow and self-centered. When we do not grow out of these narrow confines, the prescription for boundless joy through one's duty becomes self-limiting. Instead, desire becomes the driver with the attachments that come with it. There begins the slippery slope. Any well-intended objective devolves into a self-driven process. Lack of satisfaction and hence, unhappiness are the end results.

Thath Thwam Asi (You and the universe are integral in each other). This principle helps to broaden our perspective of our duty. We can think of our duty in every aspect of life: our land, air, water, space, nature, workplace, our thoughts, ideas, emotions, and people we know... We are connected and part of this larger universe and in four dimensions: past, present (intimate and external), and the future. Our duty broadens to all these aspects. Viewed from this perspective, the duty is boundless and never self-limiting. They are the limitless shades of Karma?

Renouncing activities, a person is obliged to perform (Karma) is improper. Such abandonment arises out of our desires and ignorance B.G. 18.7. *The activity which is perceived as an obligation to be carried out (Karma), but it is not performed for reasons of fear, sorrow, or physical pain. Such withdrawal from duty arises out of an emotional or agitated state of mind. In this case, the person does not gain the fruits of such action. Such abandonment is a response to attachments to the "pairs" such as pleasure/pain, fear/bravery, love/hatred, etc.*

B. G. 18.8

All activities which should be performed and carried out appropriately, while abandoning influences caused by desires and the expectation of results of such actions are described as tranquil activities. B. G. 18.9

The ACTIVITY (Karma), which is appropriate to be performed are carried out without blind emphasis solely on the results and which is carried out without attachments to "pairs" such as love/hate, happiness/sorrow, etc., is a tranquil activity (Sathvikam Karma). B. G. 18.23 All activities carried out to meet one's desires and with a need to fulfill personal or self-driven needs and attachments, even though carried out with great passion, is agitated or turbulent activity (Rajasam Karma). B. G. 18.24 All activities undertaken for reasons of uncontrolled desires without any consideration of the effects or consequences, loss or negative impact, injury or harm, and beyond one's capability are acts of ignorance (Thamasic Karma). B. G. 18.25

Every person at any moment in life has activities to be performed (Karma) that are appropriate for the moment However limited in significance they may appear, it is better to perform such activities of obligation belonging to oneself (SvaDharma) rather than attempting to perform the roles or activities belonging to others (ParaDharma). B. G. 18.47.

The last verse is highly instructional. Duty (*Karma*) is a highly self-governing process. Too often we are ready to point out what "others should have done" instead of focusing on "What is my duty? Have I done it well, to the best of my ability?"

Every House Is Different; All Residents Are The Same!

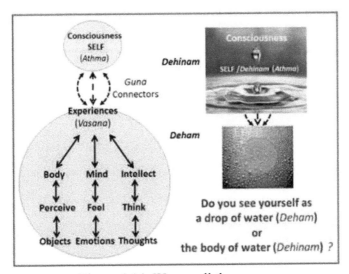

Figure 4.14. We are all the same -
like the droplets of water in a body of water!

In a crowded place, someone yells out your name. Among the hundreds of people in the crowd, you respond instinctively. There are two or more people in the crowd with the same name – not a common occurrence, but it happens. Each of them responds instinctively. Are we defined by our names?

I went in search of the house where I was brought up in a village in rural India. Not many large-scale changes in these places. Yet there were some changes. Families had moved on. People now living there were mostly new to the community. As I started slowly explaining my background – my parents and grandparents and the many things that occurred at that place nearly fifty years ago – a crowd gathered. I was nobody moments ago, became somebody recognizable to a few. Are we defined by our parents, past generations, and family?

There is an alumni association that connects us with the school or college where we studied. There is a driving license, ID card, or Bank Account that distinguishes us from the rest. Then there is the Visa and a Passport that defines if we belong to a given nation or not. For a group of people in a nation, those from outside are "aliens" like the species from outer space! Even our pets know the difference between their owners and visitors.

There is a deliberate and willful separation of each of us from the moment of conception to the moment of death. Everybody is different. We are like a house or container – a product identified by others through our body and its features and how it evolved; Our "house" is filled with our emotional experiences and the impact they create every moment to separate "me" from the rest of us; Our "house" is full of thoughts we think of or express. There are a million ways we can see each of us as different from the other. "I" am differentiated from others through tangible evidence –

the house or the container – collectively identified as "*Deham*", which literally means the body or our mortal existence.

Why do the scriptures proclaim that "I" and the Universe are one and the same (*Thath Thwam Asi*)? How can each of us, the "many" can be "one and the same"? Let us go back to the moment when your name was yelled out in the crowd. You responded. Who was that "you" – the resident in your house or container – that responded? Think for a moment. If that was not your name, you would not have responded. Someone else with that name would have responded. Who is that "someone else"? Perhaps I would have responded if I had that name. Then who is that "I"?

Let us continue this thought experiment a bit further: If I had an identical background in all aspects (name, family, school, nationality, body, emotions, and thoughts …), I would be thinking, talking, reacting, and doing everything exactly like you. But neither of us would respond if we were not alive and conscious!

Consciousness – the inner person, one who resides inside of "me" (*Dehinam*) – may be the same inside of you and everyone else. In each of us, that consciousness conditioned by its identification through the body, mind and intellect – *Deham* – acquires the perceived separation. It is like a person inside a house or a car. If I, you, or someone is inside a house or in the car, the person gets identified with that container. Imagine a bucket of water. Separate it into droplets. Each droplet takes the shape of the container in which it is placed, can be tainted with different colors, etc. We see each droplet as different from the rest and different from the water in the bucket. We live a life of different droplets, even though the origin and properties of each of us is like the droplets in a bucket of water. *Thath Thwam Asi?*

Let us do another thought experiment. As scientific knowledge progresses, we learn that we are all part of the same gene, modified ever so slightly. Everything we perceive through body functions can be increasingly described through laws of nature. Our emotions and thought processes – cognitive skills – are all being laid bare as evidence of our Knowledge, Bias and Ignorance. The planets, solar system and all that exists in the universe are being explained through the laws of nature. After over one hundred years, the laws predicted by Einstein – Gravitational waves – are now being confirmed. There may be laws that we don't understand forever. But one cannot imagine anything that exists which are not governed by the laws of nature.

Let us call the sum of all these laws (known and yet to be discovered) – which are intangible and perceived only through their effects – as *Brahman*. Each of us exists, enabled by the laws of nature. We exist as mere witnesses to the laws known and unknown. This simple and self-evident truth is proclaimed in the scriptures as "I" am Brahman (*Aham Brahma*).

Viewed as isolated drops of water, everybody is different. As a drop in the bucket of water and as a witness to or evidence of the laws of nature, everybody is the same. Swami Chinmayananda has described this as follows: Electrical bulbs in a circuit may be of different sizes, shapes, color and in different locations – like the different "body" we see. But they all come alive – as sources of light – enabled by the same electricity (Consciousness). We witness the same intangible electricity through the tangible and different bulbs.

What are the laws that help us see each of us as the water in the bucket rather than as the water isolated into droplets? We have attempted to explain these laws in the essays on "anatomy of our experiences". The differences we perceive as individual houses while not realizing the common resident in all of us are enabled by the "connectors" – *Guna*

– between the inner self or consciousness and everything external to it.

All our perceived differences come from our experiences. They are the result of the connectors (Knowledge, Bias and Ignorance) and their equilibrium states (Tranquility, Turbulence and Inertial). Whenever this connection is understood, the knot created by the "experience" vanishes; we become unhooked from our Subjective outlook and frame of mind. We become objective: (i.e.) We see ourselves as an integral part of the lifegiving force, forces of nature, the enabler, soul, Consciousness, *Dehinam*, inner person, Aum or *Brahman*. We see ourselves not merely as a droplet of water but as an integral part of a body of water!

Three connectors – Knowledge (Sathvam), Bias or attachment to partial knowledge as the whole truth (Rajas) and Ignorance (Thamas) – bind the inner SELF (Dehinam) to everything else (the tangible, physical world – Deham) relentlessly and without fail. B. G. 14.5.

All aspects of our existence as individuals and separated from each other – everybody is different – *is nothing more than the effect of these three connectors (Guna).* B. G. 14.19
Such wisdom leads to divinity, where we see everybody is the same *(this is described as the wise who acquire the qualities of God).* B. G. 14.19

Enlightened Living:

Progression from Self-Control to Total Self-Control to Un-attached active Engagement.

Following is a letter from a publication under the "Dear Friend" column, which provides advice to the readers:

"Dear friend: I am 77 years old, my husband 84 years old. We have been married for 53 years. Ours is a "Love marriage" as opposed to the traditional arranged marriage. It was rough in the early days as his parents did not approve of our marriage. He married me despite such resistance from his family. "Opposites attract" is true in our case, as we are both different in our habits and preferences. I am an extrovert, and he prefers to remain contained within the family. He will adjust and go along with me, even if that was not his choice. I have also adjusted myself by giving up my work life and career. He had lots of work-related travels. While at home, we used to quarrel and argue a lot. But in the end, he would give up when I shed my tears. This is how my life continued for more than four decades.

Now that he is retired and mostly at home, he is demanding attention all the time. I prefer to go out and do some social service, while he wants me to stay home and take care of his aging health. While he seems to have a sense of insecurity, I am getting old and easily tired. The future looks bleak. Our two sons are settled and far away. My husband appears to be depressed but refuses medical attention. We are both

constantly at edge and angry at each other. There is no
peace of mind.

Can you please help?"

In a Japanese movie:

Husband (Isao Hashizume) and wife (Kazuko Yoshiyuki) have been married for 50 years. For her birthday, the husband asks the wife what she wants for her birthday present. She replies that she wants a divorce! The wife's request for divorce sends the entire family into chaos.

The details narrated by the 77-year-old Indian housewife are almost identical to the circumstances outlined in the Japanese movie! Life is the same no matter where you live in the world or what cultural background one comes from!

The advice would be the same in both these examples:

Long married life is largely based on mutual trust between family members. When trust and mutual respect is restored in thoughts and in mind, a life of peace and happiness returns.

Trust is an abstract feeling, a conditioning of the mind that overcomes anxiety and despair. Living does not have to leave each of us helpless and miserable, reliant only on others to remove our anxiety and despair. Introspection and self-reflection can be the best starting point for any situation of anxiety and despair. Self-reflection is also the beginning of self-control. See essays on Mind over Matter.

Through self-control, one remains one's own best friend; through lack of self-control, one becomes one's own worst enemy. B.G. 6.6.

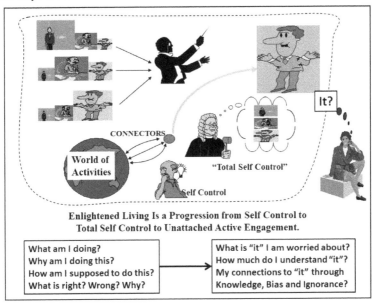

Figure 4.15. Enlightened living.

Self-control begins with an internal reflection: Who am I? What am I doing? Why? How am I supposed to this? What is right, wrong, and why? Raising these questions and to find answers requires a calm and contemplative mind. Yoga and meditation are means for such calming the mind as the step towards self-reflection.

Self-control also implies disconnecting oneself from the personal nature of any activity. It creates a separation between "I", the inner person – who is reflecting and analyzing – and "I", the person who feels happiness or suffering, misery and let down. Instead of having two individuals – the husband and the wife in our examples above – we now have two different persons inside of each: The reflecting "self" Vs. suffering and seeking help "self". While the acceptance and resolution between two individuals – the husband and the wife – may or may not happen, the resolution between the inner "I" and the external "I" is well within reach of each of us! This discipline for internal dialogue and finding answers on one's own accord is described as "*Jnana Yoga*", or intellectual union with the self.

Through such internal dialogue, we create separation or distance from the questions posed earlier. In the beginning we find we find the common word "I" and its connection to the subject matter. What happens when we separate all these questions and "externalize" them (i.e.) make them separated from "I" or "me"? The readers are referred to the earlier essays on "anatomy of our experiences", "Subjective Vs. Objective", "Each house is different, and all residents are same", etc.

Through the separation from the world of activities, we start with a clear focus on what is "it" the activity I wish to study or reflect upon. This is the initial step for Self-control. Now we can reformat all our questions as illustrated in Figure 4.15. We begin to see that all our experiences are subjective and personal. These experiences lead to our emotions through our connectors of Knowledge, Bias, and Ignorance. As three strands in a rope, they create the "knot", through Tranquility, Turbulence or inertial which we call as our experience, emotions, happiness, sorrow, etc. Untangling the knots requires an objective outlook on all evidence. This total self-control is like the work of any judge. With this objective outlook we use the world of activities like a symphony, like a conductor of music in an orchestra! It is the Intellectual Union with the Self (Jnana Yoga). This progression from Self control to total self-control to unattached active engagement is described as enlightened living.

Knots in a rope exist only if the rope is tangled in that way. When we untangle the rope, the "knot" mysteriously disappears! It is equally true for all our experiences. When we untangle the knot called "experience" by decomposing it into the prevailing knowledge, bias and ignorance and the role of the predominant connector, we understand the situation reasonably well. The pre-existing experience and its emotional nature disappear!

This Jnana Yoga helps to clarify the prevailing knowledge, bias and ignorance and their equilibrium states of tranquility, turbulence, and inertia. We become less subjective and more objective. This is the progression from self-control to total self-control.

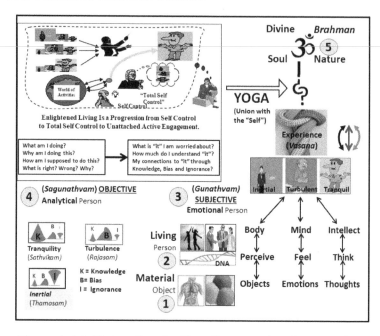

Figure 4. 16. Untangling the "knot" or emotional connections from our experiences through Self-control.

Through total self-control, we begin to perceive the reality that no matter how you look – as a material body, living person, emotional individual, or a reflective and objective saintly person – all of these are facets of nature. They are all enabled by infinite, invisible laws of nature. These are the enablers! The "I" that was the subject of every question posed earlier is merely an enabled, as much all-other facets of my body, living or emotions and feelings. "I" as an entity no longer exists except as part of the universe and enabled by the laws of nature. This collection of all the enablers is identified by a single word *Brahman* or a single symbol ॐ

The progression has brought us to a point where we can see that "I" and all my experiences is none other than the effects of the prevailing laws of nature, *Brahman* or ॐ.

The apple falling from the tree is not independent of the gravity that pulls it down. The boat that floats is not independent of the buoyancy that supports it. We begin to see that "I" and all my experience are none other than the manifestations of the laws of nature, *Brahman* or ॐ. The invisible hook, connection or attachment that was binding me through my perceptions, feeling or thoughts to everything other than the force of nature gets removed. "I" exist and operate, having progressed from Self-control to total self-control to un-attached active engagement! This manner of living is recognized as "Enlightened" in the scriptures! Swami Chinmayananda describes this as follows:

We acquire all "Experiences" through our Body, Mind, and Intellect. When all experiences are exhausted, we become in union with AUM or Consciousness"

The challenge faced by any one of us: How can we use such an analytical framework for an enlightened living when one is in the middle of a crisis? It is neither useful nor compassionate to suggest this analytical technique to someone in crisis or for one who has never practiced internal or self-reflection. They need a safety net to be pulled away from their turbulent waters. That is the role of religion, the family and society at large. At the same time, those who are on safe ground and are unwilling to learn and practice such analytical framework to manage their daily life may find themselves at some point or other in their life, in the swift currents of life and its flow without any help or recourse.

Self-reflection and analytical reasoning require a properly functioning mind. See essays on mind over matter. Wisdom is also required to separate anxiety and despair caused by mental health vs. issues driven by lack of analytical reasoning. Such education, knowledge and wisdom may be needed in society at large. It is especially the need as we grow older and as we focus on caring for the elders in the family!

Maya – That Which It Is Not.

The Sanskrit word *Maya* (that which it is not) is derived from its roots *Ma* (not) and *Ya* (that). *Maya* is often described as the illusion or perceiving something other than what it is. It has simple practical implications in our daily life. It also has profound philosophic implications in our role and purpose in life. A brief description of the illusion (Maya) in our daily life is noted as follows:

Reflecting or dwelling on the sense objects (body and its organs) as being real, a person gets attached to them. From this attachment or affinity arise all desires; from these desires is born anger or envy; from envy is born confusion, and from confusion, the loss of memory, clear vision or purpose in life. This results in a decline in reasoning, which further leads to the "death" of the person. B.G. 2. 62 and 63. Every person in the entire world exists in three states of connection (Knowledge, Bias, and Ignorance) with the world external to him/her. Without this understanding, they see the world as shifting and ever-changing (Illusion). Hence, they do not comprehend the eternal, constant or unchangeable reality of their existence. B.G. 7. 13

The view that any one of us is defined by our body and mind and trapped by our experiences is *Maya* or illusion. Steeped in this view, we see a divided world of self-driven needs, preferences, attachments, "I", my family, circle of friends, etc. Limited in this perception, we find it difficult to go beyond to see the larger forces of nature, which are eternal and universal (common to all).

The totality of our existence has been described as constituted by five layers, illustrated in figure 4.17.

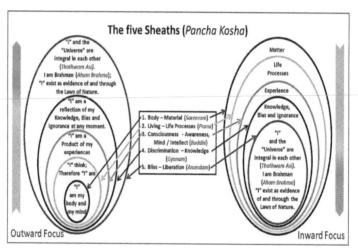

Figure 4. 17. Five layers of existence (*Pancha Kosha*)

Source: *Vivekachudamani* (Crown Jewel of Knowledge and Understanding) - Swami Sankaracharya–Verse:154 to 212.

The five layers consist of:

Our body which one can touch and feel (Defined by our name, height, weight, etc.). It is nourished and sustained by the food we consume.

All our body functions and life processes, such as breathing, digestion, perception, voluntary and involuntary responses, and mental faculty ("I think therefore I am")

Our experiences resulting from the body and its functions connected to anything external. ("I am a product of my experiences").

Our understanding of the experiences based on the connectors *(Guna)* – knowledge, bias and ignorance and the dominance of one over the other two ("I exist as a witness to my emotions, feelings and duality (like/dislike) and their ebb and flow").

Our existence as a result of the forces of nature which create and sustain our body, life processes, experiences and the understanding of the evolution of our experiences. "I am *Brahman* — I exist enabled by and as a witness to the Laws of Nature; *Thath Thwam Asi* – the universe and I exist as an integral part of each other".

The above five layers of our existence are interconnected. These five layers of our existence is the reality, the truth, which merely exists. They are inviolable. They are self-evident. It is the larger order. These layers can be visualized looking outward, starting from our physical body. The layers can also be seen as an assemblage starting from the universe at large and looking inwards, also illustrated in Figure 4.17.

Everything we see or comprehend are an interpretation of the above truth. Such interpretation or perception varies depending on the time, context, and circumstances. They are like the millions of reflections of the single sun. Relying on these reflections or interpretations as the truth is described as an illusion (*Maya*).

Let us explore a few of the impacts of this illusion in our daily life:

In the material world, we believe that we live on solid ground when we also know that the earth's core is nothing but molten magma at constant flux. Our planet itself is on a unique journey in its planetary motion while we build all things that we believe are fixed – like bridges, dams and skyscrapers. We mine or drill deep for minerals, fuel and water. We are torn apart by our feelings and emotions as if they are the governing forces, while we are balanced delicately between a few universal forces (Gravitation, magnetic and nuclear forces, life sciences, etc.).

Recognition of this illusion helps us to find a perspective between what is significant and insignificant in our daily lie. Recognition of this illusion helps us to focus on larger issues, such as protecting our planet (since we exist in a delicate balance on this planet on many dimensions – earth, water, ocean, air and space). We think we are individuals and hence unique and special when we also know that every one of us – indeed every living object we know – are enabled by biological processes governed by the same laws of nature! Recognition of this illusion eliminates the fear of death and helps us to cope with grief. Attention to better living habits become tools to manage the biological processes as part of daily living (rather than means to meet self-centered needs for beauty as an expression of vanity, longer life, etc.).

We think we are unique since our experiences are specific to us, ignoring the reality that everyone's experiences are rooted in the same three connectors – knowledge, bias and ignorance – and the dominant connector for the given moment. Mindfulness of this illusion (or reality) helps us cope with any event in life with even minded approach. It also helps us to be respectful of others and their needs; Exploring the connectors at work becomes the way of life instead of impulsive reaction to events and circumstances. Tolerance and forgiveness evolve on their own accord. We also find the courage to challenge and stand up against discrimination, racism, and bigotry, because it is the right thing to do (and not as a personal mission to meet one's needs). Non-duality (between happiness/sorrow, love/hate, like/dislike, etc.) becomes second nature to a person who is constantly aware of this illusion.

Even in trivial matters like a conversation, what I said and my intent behind that may be totally misconstrued. This misunderstanding can happen – and frequently it does – even among people intimately known to each other. Debating and arguing about what was said and perceived is illusion! Focusing on the nature of the communication and the reason for the miscommunication arising out of the three connectors at play is the wisdom required in that instance (and in many other situations in our daily life).

These five layers (sheaths) can be understood inside out – starting from the understanding of myself as a material object, expanding outwards until it is realized that "I" and the "Universe" exist as integral in each other. Every atom is part of the Cosmos; the cosmos cannot exist, rejecting any atom as outside of it! Conversely, the "I" can be understood starting from the universal view (I exist as the representation and witness to the laws of nature at play (I am Brahman) working downwards to "I am made up of material objects one can touch and feel". Not recognizing this interchangeable nature of the five layers of our existence is also an illusion (*Maya*).

Another aspect of our illusion (*Maya*) is the notion that these five layers we described above are independent of each other. It is generally believed that when you are young, you need to worry only about your health and personal wellbeing and as you grow older, you can focus on understanding your experiences, role and your purpose in the larger order.

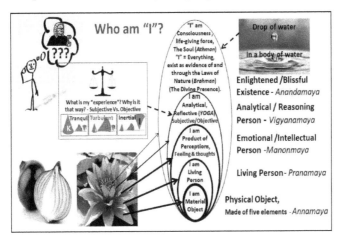

Figure 4.18. All five layers of "I" co-exist.

The reality is that all five sheaths (layers) co-exist. None of the layers exist without the others. A lotus flower is made up of layers or petals. An onion is made up of layers. The lotus or onion does not exist without its layers. For a given moment, one can discard certain petals of the flower or the layers of the onion. But our removing or discarding them does not deny their existence (or co-existence). They merely exist. They are all parts of nature.

"We exist as part of nature. Our existence becomes evident through five layers: Material object (Sareeram); life processes (Prana); consciousness or awareness (Budhi); Knowledge and understanding of the discrimination between the three connectors (Jnanam) and "I" as an

integral and inseparable aspect of the larger order or laws of Nature (Thath Thwam Asi; Aham Brahma).

Liberation (from the notion of birth and death; from the constantly changing and momentary influences of our experiences) is gained through an understanding of the above inseparable and interconnected layers of our existence.

This is the simple truth. By this knowledge and its practice, one lives a life of eternal peace." ——— *Viveka Chudamani* (Swami Shankaracharya).

The four layers – Material, Living, Emotional and Reflective/reasoning centered – of our existence is readily obvious to everyone. This is the "Material" world. We see ourselves as "individuals" when viewed through these layers. The fifth layer is known as the laws of nature, enabler, soul. Spirit, Consciousness or *Brahman*. This fifth layer co-exists and enables all the other four layers to exist. It is permanent, changeless, eternal, in-cognitive, and objective (without identifiable differences between person, place, time, situation, context, etc.). This common, undivided nature of everything is schematically illustrated in Figure 4. 19. Our divided and partial view of anything based only on the material or cognitive aspects is illusion (*Maya*). This is pointed out in the prayer song of the poem Knowledge of the Self (*Athma Bodha*) by Saint Adi Sankara as follows:

I meditate on the Self, residing in the deep wells of our hearts. It is Real Knowledge, Eternal Happiness, the state reached by those who have transcended to the fourth state of consciousness, which enables/illumines all our experiences during the waking, dream, and the state of deep sleep. I am that perfect Brahman, not the identity associated merely with my physical and identifiable material body.

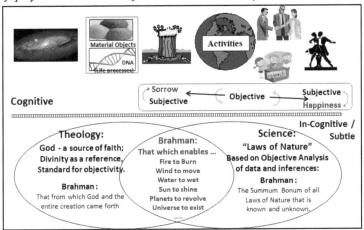

Figure 4. 19. Universe as Cognitive (Enabled) and In-Cognitive (Enabler)

We desire to be special through our needs and wants as an emotional being. We become special by objectively managing our needs and wants (in the fourth layer) as reflective and analytical people! Everything I know and everything I don't know is part of nature. *Sarvam Brahma Mayam.* I am part of nature (*Aham Brahma*). This knowledge or awareness is the fifth condition or layer of human beings - the state of bliss (*Ananda Maya*).

Vedic Philosophy - Summary

Vedic Philosophy provides a simple framework to study, analyze, observe, and practice any aspect of whatever we do in life. In summary, Vedic Philosophy states that: Everything in the Universe exists in five realms or conditions:

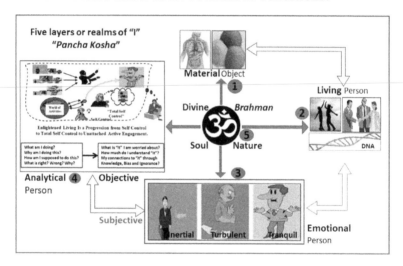

Figure 4.20. Basics of Vedic Philosophy – Summary

Material Object: All that is perceived; Anything one can study and manage through the many field of Sciences.

Living Person: All that can grow, be born, live and die. Anything one can study, learn, and manage through Life Sciences.

Emotional Person (individual, family, society, nation, ...): Life – experience, governed by the duality of like/dislike, happiness/sorrow, friend/enemy, good/bad, evil/noble, etc.

This is the subjective universe – of impulsive action and reaction. This is also the world that comprises all fields of human endeavors: arts, music, education, sports, religion, politics, career, economics, culture, society, and family...

Analytical Person: One (rooted in contemplation, analysis, and reasoning) who sees everything through three sets of connectors and their effects.

This is the sphere fostered through self-control leading to unattached active engagement. It permits our awareness of the universe like two sides of a coin – Cognitive (enabled) and in-cognitive (enabler).

Blissful Entity: Person in a true state of realization that he and everything exist as the effects of laws of nature (Everything is *Brahman*). One for whom the grand Pronouncements from Vedas – *Thath Thwam Asi, Aham Brahma. Sarvam Brahma Mayam, Pragjnanam Brahma* (You and the Universe are one and the same; I am *Brahman;* Everything is *Brahman;* Consciousness is *Brahman)* are self-evident!

We are objective with a sincere effort to understand the cause and effect. When our effort fails, we persevere while also accepting the reality as it is, as part of nature (*Brahman*) ॐ (Eternal, objective, omnipresent, intangible forces of nature). *Brahman* is in-cognitive. It is identifiable only through the above four realms. It is the cause, the forces of nature behind all the effects perceived or understood through all our perception, feeling, and thought.

As the all-pervading space remains unaffected or unchanged, the enlightened person – of total self-control and unattached active engagement – remains seated everywhere (in body, mind and intellect) and yet remains unaffected.
BG 13.33

As the single sun illumines the entire world, the single universal concept of Brahman – total self-control and unattached active engagement – has the potential to pervade and illumine all our activities and the entire Universe.
BG 13.34

Our physical, social, and intellectual aspects of life fall in one of the above five realms or conditions. They are interconnected. We live our life as a balancing act across all three spheres. We recognize these three aspects as material, emotional and spiritual world.

What is it that enables all the material objects? - nature.

What is it that enables all living things and beings? – nature.

Why are we subjective and hence attached to everything? – It is an aspect of our mind and thinking – aspect of nature.

Can one observe and understand the prevailing laws of nature in any of the above? - Yes, that is within human nature!

Personal	Family	Universal
Economic/ Material / Health	Social / Feelings / Emotional	Harmony / Thoughts / Intellectual
Physical wellbeing	Emotional wellbeing	Spiritual wellbeing.

Figure 4. 21. Wellbeing in life is a balancing act
across three legs of a stool: Material, Social and Spiritual.

What is this "nature"? - That which enables everything else!

Fire to burn, wind to move, eyes to wink, ears to hear...

Can I ever be free from being subjective?

One can be more subjective or less subjective. It reflects as increased objectivity.

What is the most objective? - Independent of time, space, objects, circumstances, etc. – (e.g.): nature and its laws.

Can I identify this immense collection of laws of nature and its effect with a singular term - *Brahman*!

Everything is Brahman: *Sarvam Brahma Mayam*

I am part of nature, and hence I am Brahman: *Aham BrahmaAsmi*

With the above knowledge and its connection to all four tangible layers, my knowledge is complete (to some extent)! I am happy, blissful.

This is the Blissful layer: *Ananda Maya.*

This layer is also known as the soul, consciousness, divine...

"I think, therefore I am" is a philosophical thought that recognizes the first four layers or conditions.

"I am, therefore, I think", states the Vedic Philosophy. It includes the fifth layer. This realm is also stated as "I am consciousness" – *Pragjnanam Brahma.*

All five layers co-exist like the visible relentless waves, the invisible deep ocean, and the wind currents, enabling the waves! We experience them through our Material, Social and Spiritual portals.

One can arrive at this knowledge or understanding as the end point of sustained study. One can also gain this knowledge instinctively as the starting point through reflection, meditation, and contemplation!

5. Spirituality In Practice: Application In Daily Life

Leadership Through Spirituality in Practice

Internal and external focus through Yoga and Meditation: Yoga and meditation are tools for exploring the "self" or the "inner person" in two dimensions: Internal and External focus.

Yoga or union with the self can be through reflection on any activity. Yoga lifts us from a subjective outlook to an objective frame of mind. Objectivity increases when we move from *Gunathvam* (Recognition of connectors and their roles) to *Sagunathvam* (Equal treatment for all three connectors and their roles) to *Nirgunathvam* (Connectors become irrelevant when every action is observed merely as a reflection of laws of nature at work – I am *Brahman*).

Meditation is calming the mind to focus or concentrate. Such calming of the mind is necessary to engage in yoga as described above. Meditation has three stages:

Focused Attention (limiting the thoughts on a specific activity like breathing, prayer, etc.)

Open mind: where the mind is calm on its own accord without relying on any object or event.

Love and Kindness: where the mind is open and expansive – inclusive of anyone and anything and excludes none.

The inner reflection (deep within) on the connectors and external focus (through a calm mind which is inclusive of anyone and anything and excludes none) can be seen as the two dimensions of evolution for any person. These are also the two dimensions of evolution for anyone as a leader as illustrated in Figure 5.1.

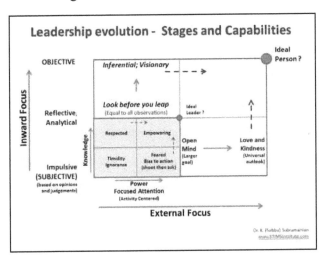

Figure 5.1. Leadership styles that reflect internal and external focus.

Knowledge and Power as two dimensions of leadership:

Lao Tsu, the 5th century B.C. philosopher, describes four kinds of leadership styles as related to Knowledge and Power. Knowledge pertains to the objectivity in our connection to the activity while power can be seen as the ability to influence others (external to the self). Leader without knowledge and power is timid and not respected. One with power but without knowledge intimidates others.

Fear prevails as the leadership style. Leader with knowledge but without power is merely respected for their scholarship. A true leader combines power with knowledge, enabling others to act independently. They feel empowered by the leader.

External focus can be activity-centered, goal centered or for common principles such as for the good of humanity at large. The three stages of meditation enhance skills for external focus in a harmonious way through focused attention on specific activity, open mind and loving kindness. These three stages are also the basis for all religions in their effort to spread harmony across society at large.

The more one explores the inner self one can progress from being impulsive to reflective. A reflective person can see a larger order and hence transforms into a visionary. Internal focus may be Subjective (opinion-driven) and hence personal or objective (non-attachment) and hence generally agreed upon by many (like the judgment in a jury system or the analysis and conclusions in scientific research). The goal of any form of education is to move away from subjective to objective treatment of the matter under study.

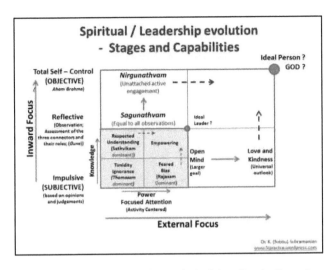

Figure 5.2. Leadership through Spirituality in Practice.

Activity-centered leadership seems to be the basis for most education on leadership. But one can see a larger space for leadership as a way of life. This realm for limitless exploration for leadership in life, beyond specific activity or professional work is Spirituality in Practice. It is the highest level of internal focus, together with limitless inclusion of everything and everyone. Those rare few who make it their way of life are described as the "enlightened" person. They set the ideal and serve as the beacon for others to emulate and follow. However, everyone can aspire to exhibit spiritual leadership in the way we think, feel and act (i.e.) in the way we live. Through those moments, we display evidence of divinity! This model for leadership evolution through spirituality in practice is illustrated in figure 5.2.

On Teaching the Basics of Spirituality to Children and Young Adults

"We don't think of self-reflection and philosophy until we grow old, after suffering through many aspects of life" — Is this the truth or just an opinion? Who wants to take the time when one is young to reflect on what is life and how it should be lived? In *Bhaja Govindam,* a poem written in the 8th century, we see the following verses:

When you are young, you are attached to playing; as a grown-up you are attached to your desires, passion, and sensual pleasures; when you are too old, anxieties rule over you. Anyone attached to the Supreme (Brahman) at any time? Verse 7

Who is your wife, son, family? This notion of family is indeed very strange. Who are you? Where do you come from? Oh, brother, think of that truth here and now. Verse 8

It is natural to think that we become "philosophical" as we grow old – and after we are beaten up in the school of hard knocks. Maybe that need not be the only way.

We teach children languages, culture, prayer songs, epics, moral values, etc., along with their secular education. Maybe we can teach them a little bit of secular philosophy in simple language for their understanding and practice from early ages?

"Objectivity" is taught at school through analytical methods and "Science" – governing laws/effect – in every subject we study. Subjectivity occurs due to limited data, bias, opinions and judgments and objectivity based on reflection, analysis, and reasoning. We are taught that subjective decisions can be partial; hence we have standards and protocols to arrive at impartial and objective decisions. When it comes to life and exploring the questions of what life is and how it should be lived, analytical tools and objective outlooks are not pursued seriously. Instead, we become "subjective" – governed by opinions and judgments – unknowingly in our daily life and in all our activities. This starts from childhood! In due course, life becomes a heap of "experiences", not an organized collection of events with a rationale for each experience and why it is that way. Is this the ash covering the amber glow of the objective self?

Spirituality starts with probing the following questions: Is life a clutter of experiences (like an untidy house)? Can life be fashioned into a well-laid-out and organized set of experiences (like a well-kept and welcoming home? Like a well-oiled and well-maintained machine that serves the purpose for a long time?)

We start the journey of spirituality by asking the questions of "Who am I? What is life?" and finding the answers in the following order:

In the beginning, life appears to be a random collection or aggregate of experiences like material objects filling a house. Knowledge, Bias and Ignorance and their roles identify the basis and nature of our experiences – like the contents in a house acquired based on identified needs. Standing back, through introspection and reflection (meditation, yoga: objective assessment) – we can find the experiences that need to be preserved and where they belong – like a house free of clutter. Life is a balancing act between subjective experiences, their perturbations, and objective experiences and the harmony they foster.

Vedanta teaches us that we are enabled by objective life-giving forces – *Brahman* – all the time throughout our life. Focus on the laws of nature behind all the experiences makes life a well-maintained and welcoming home with a common and unwritten purpose that permeates everywhere: Peace and harmony within and cohesion with everything that surrounds us.

There is no "Perfect" home, but a good home is easily recognized by all. Similarly, there is no "perfect life", but divinity in our actions and manner of living is easily recognized when present. It is radiated through our reflective mind seeking objectivity and the governing laws of nature as a way of life.

The above are not difficult concepts to discuss and teach. Of course, that requires an adult who understands the above – the teacher in the family. A 75 yearlong study at Harvard Medical School on longevity in life suggests the following conclusions: People who are isolated from others and feel lonely live shorter life. It is the quality of your close relationships that determines your longevity in life. People with good close relationships from their 50s lived well into their 80s. Good relationships protect our brains with better and sharper memory for a longer time. Good relationships include active engagement. They do not preclude arguments and emotional exchanges

In all of the above, consistency is the need and "perfection" is not the requirement.

Spirituality is noted when a person is reflective and analytical (and hence objective) at will and not driven by moods and circumstances (subjective). Through such self-reflection, one remains one's own best friend. Through lack of introspection, one becomes one's own worst enemy.

Having cleared the mind and emotions of its cobweb (by clearing out the emotional and biased view of life and its experiences), the spiritual person is at ease with anyone, at any time and under all circumstances. We witness this as divinity in their actions and way of living.

To be at ease with anyone, at any time and under all circumstances, maybe the ideal situation. But "perfection" is merely a yardstick to calibrate and measure progress.

Are you at ease with many at any moment? Are you at ease within and in harmony with others occasionally? Are you free of moment-to-moment mood swings and opinions, even for a short time? —- These are also evidence of divinity in daily life.

Spirituality promotes engagement and away from isolation. It promotes closer relationships with many. Since they are based on the active engagement of the mind all the time – living in the present, looking for the balance between subjective vs. objective outlook – they are also good for the body as much as they are good for the mind.

Are you the adult in the family? Are you ready to teach the above to your children and other youngsters?

Are you the child or the young one in the family? Are you ready to seek out such education on spirituality at a young age? – the earlier you start, the better off you will be!

The Steady (Un-Flickering) Flame At The Altar

The idol in a temple symbolizes the ideals we aspire to become part of our nature. The idol also symbolizes the ideals deep rooted in us. Our visit to the temple and the viewing of the idol is an effort to confront our bias and ignorance and overcome their limitations in due course!

Near the idol in any template is placed an oil lamp. The flame of the lamp illuminates the space. Through this illumination, we see the idol. The flame itself remains still (motionless) in the absence of any breeze or crosswind.

The devotee who stands in front of the idol offers his/her worship to the Lord. In this process, the devotee is in a state of deep contemplation and reflection (*Dhyanam*). While the body remains still, the contemplative mind of the devotee reflects on the connectors. In due course, all perturbations and wave-like oscillations of the mind subside into a calm stillness on their own accord since the cause and effect of all emotions are understood, and the roles of the connectors at play become clear. With a still mind, the intellect reflects on all thoughts, and they too cease to exist after some time since all thoughts are also the results of the connectors. At that point, the devotee stands still, motionless, free of emotional perturbations of the mind or intellectual ambivalence. In that state of existence, there is piece and sublime tranquility, which cannot be adequately described. It is experienced by each on their own accord through their own effort.

The oil lamp which illumines the idol remains still and motionless. The devotee also remains still and motionless. "Self-Control" illumines all aspects of body, mind, and intellect of the devotee.

The steady mind of a person in deep and sustained contemplation is like the steady (un-flickering) flame of the lamp at the altar   B.G. 6. 19.

While the above verse refers to a devotee, it is easy to see the connection of steady intellect, backed up by an emotionally neutral mind and well-controlled body functions ready to respond to any commands of the self in any of our efforts. This is the state of anyone at the highest performance in any field of endeavor. All successful professionals – surgeons, musicians, engineers, leaders, scientists, workers, - as well as parents, teachers, and students require the state of mind of such a devotee as a prerequisite for the highest level of accomplishment in their endeavor. The steady (un-flickering) flame of the lamp at the sanctum is merely a beacon of light for such possibilities and accomplishments in the life of any individual.

Science, God and Our Understanding

Theoretical physicist Stephen Hawking said in an interview published in a newspaper that he rejects the notion of heaven and hell. In Hawking's interview, he "emphasized the need to fulfill our potential on earth by making good use of our lives". Here is a little excerpt from the Q and A with the famed physicist:

You've said there is no reason to invoke God. Is our existence all down to luck?

Science predicts that many kinds of universe will be spontaneously created out of nothing. It is a matter of chance which we are in.

So here we are. What should we do?

We should seek the greatest value of our action.

You had a health scare and spent time in the hospital. What, if anything, do you fear about death?

I have lived with the prospect of an early death for the last 49 years. I'm not afraid of death, but I'm in no hurry to die. I have so much I want to do first.

I regard the brain as a computer which will stop working when its components fail. There is no heaven or afterlife for broken-down computers.

Science provides the capacity to predict within the limits of our observation, our analysis of data leading to our understanding of the pertinent laws of nature. Certainty of such predictions is high when the context or subject matter is limited or well-defined. One can predict with reasonable certainty whether an iron rod will or will not break under certain load; conditions under which an iron rod will or will not rust. One can predict with certainty if oil or water will wet the floor and why? Greater our capacity to observe, quantify and analyze the evidence and arrive at the inherent causality (laws of nature), the higher the capacity for prediction and accuracy. Despite large volumes of data, science finds its limits to "predict". Therefore, we cannot pinpoint each tornado or earthquake ahead of time. In the end, we do our best and accept the outcome as determined by the "laws of nature"! It is interesting to note that Stephen Hawking uses the words "prediction" and "matter of chance" in the above statement almost immediately after each other!

Everyone –scientists, philosophers, and theologians – all agree with the existence of the laws of nature. It is the description of nature and its laws by each that is different. Scientists accept the laws of nature as unique and pertinent to each set of problems or observations. Even among scientists, there are those – the pre-eminent ones like Stephen Hawking – who seek a unified understanding of many of the laws of nature. Philosophers describe the sum of all laws of nature as the consciousness or *Brahman*.

Theologians describe the laws of nature as the "invisible hands of God". See Figure 4.19.

Each of us is a scientist (governed by our observations and their rational analysis) and a philosopher (governed by reflection, analysis and inferences of common themes across seemingly different and divided subjects) and a theologian (governed by a deep and infallible sense of faith in a larger order or the God). Hence our statements from any one of these points of view should not be treated as "be all and end all". This would be like the right-hand fighting with the left hand. If the right eye and the left eye do not see the object in a coordinated manner, we call it a "vision problem". Perceived discrepancies between the scientific, philosophic, and theological points of view must be understood and accommodated for a holistic vision of life and nature at large.

Science is the process of rational analysis of observations. It sets no values and certainly, no ordering of values such as high and low or great and small. Theology sets values based on morals and codes of conduct. Philosophy provides coherence between the cognitive world of science and the theological world of faith.

Humans live in the material or cognitive world – the world of action and reaction. Science provides a framework for such a cognitive world. We also live in a world of emotions. This is a world of hope and fear, a world of love, compassion, generosity, caring, etc. Theology provides a logical framework and value systems to steer through this world of emotions. We also live in a world of thoughts, ideas, and contemplation – the intellectual world. This is the realm of philosophy. In common parlance, these three worlds are described as the realm of body, heart, and mind. This might be an oversimplification but serves to identify the three spheres of human existence. Can you imagine anyone normal that functions as a human without the body and its functions or emotions or thoughts? So, when Stephen Hawking states that *"I regard the brain as a computer which will stop working when its components fail, "* he describes the brain purely in terms of its body functions. We all know well that for many people, long before the failure of the kind he describes, the brain fails when it acts in an emotionless and cruel manner unless it is coached and mentored by theologians on right and wrong, on the moral values of life. In other words, the brain as a computer may fail due to software glitches long before the hardware fails! We also know of instances when the brain and its body functions perform well, but its thoughts are so out of whack (as if a virus has hacked it!) that it is drawn to an ideology that are destructive to that person as well as for large communities of people. This is the failure of the brain when it does not grapple with right and wrong from a philosophical point of view. This is like a computer that fails due to a faulty algorithm in its software!

Science, Philosophy and Theology may appear to be exclusive of each other for experts in these three fields. But they are mutually inclusive for a common man!

Is God With You?

At the end of our conversation, my friend said, "We know that all religions have such beautiful frameworks. They are simple and not so difficult to understand and comprehend. With all that, why is it most people are drawn into rituals which merely promote vanity, foolish reverence, and subordination to a few who are seen as the religious leaders?" While I do not wish to cast all religious leaders in such a negative light, one must admit blind rituals, adoration of religion and its leaders are very common.

I told my friend, "You are aware of the basic principles of Vedic Philosophy. You are also concerned about the pitfalls of foolish allegiance to rituals and their blind following. Then why don't you teach them to youngsters? Why don't you engage the next generation in meaningful discussions so that they can follow religious practices and rituals with clarity in their thought and a better sense of purpose"?

My friend told me how he attempts the same in his own way. To make his point, he described a story: Once there was a teacher with many students. He told all the students that God is within each of us as well as outside, everywhere. God is watching everything and all the time. After a few classes of repeated lessons on this theme, he did not offer them any food for a few days. Then one day, he gave enough food to each student and told them, "I know you are starving and ready to eat the food. You can all eat your food under one condition: Make sure nobody can see you when you are eating". The students ran away to far corners and hiding places and ate their food. When they returned, the teacher asked, "Have you all eaten your food?" Almost all of them replied "yes", except for one student who said, "No, sir. I have my food with me. I have not eaten it." While all the other students were shocked, this student continued, "Sir, you told us not to eat the food when someone is watching. You have also told us that God is watching all the time. Then how could I eat the food no matter where I hide?"

God is a point of reference to calibrate ourselves. God within each of us is reflected through the divine qualities in our actions. Such divinity within precludes vanity, greed, and foolish allegiance to rituals. Such divinity always shines. It has no hiding place. It is not dependent on education, academic excellence, or professional qualifications. Such divinity brings clarity for abstract concepts of love, compassion, forgiveness, kindness, helpfulness to the needy, etc. As a result, they are applied in real life with happiness within, bringing harmony all around.

My friend continued, "I tell my children God is within. You can go to the temple to worship or follow rituals as a matter of practice. They give you a certain way of conditioning your mind and maintaining a focus on the divinity inside of you. But do not lean on the rituals as a permanent crutch." My friend added, "These days whenever we leave on a family travel, with all children inside the car, I ask them, 'Is God safe and well positioned inside each of you?' When they say yes, we start our journey."

Following verses from *Bhaja Govindam* written in the 8th century AD, truly reflect the essence of the above conversation:

Oh, you man of foolish mind, offering your prayers to the Lord. What good will come of your meticulous observing of rituals while lacking in an understanding of the principles behind them? Verse 1.

There are those with long (and matted strands of) hair, others with a shaven head; some perform rituals of extreme pain (like starving) and others parading in religious robes. All these people, while proclaiming to preach religion and divinity, do not truly see the all-pervading Lord (Brahman). Sadly, all their efforts are disguises merely to make a living.   Verse 14

One may travel in pilgrimage to holy places, observe vows, practice rituals and perform charitable work. But all such efforts, while lacking in knowledge (and understanding that all rituals stand for certain principles leading to divinity in our daily life), do not liberate anyone, even in one hundred lives, according to all teachings.   *Verse 17.*

All religions and rituals teach us pathways to internalize the view that we as individuals are mere microcosms and part and parcel of the universe at large *(Thath Thwam* Asi)*;* anything and everything exists enabled by and as witness to the laws of nature *(Aham Brahma:* I am Brahman*).* Such knowledge and awareness promote objectivity which reflects as divine qualities in our actions, experiences and in our way of living.

Every effort to teach (and learn) scriptures must be to gain the true knowledge of "What is life? How it should be lived?" – in an objective manner fostering true inner peace as well as peace and harmony all around. This is the obligation of the students as much as it is an expectation for the teachers. With a genuine understanding and appreciation of the basic principles behind them, religion and rituals promote peace and harmony within, tolerance, inter-racial cohesion, inter-religious collaboration, etc.

God and Curry

Figure 5.3.

Curry is the hot spice that adds taste and flavor to Indian dishes. This is a prevalent notion, just as yoga is a form of exercise for physical fitness or meditation is a process to keep your mind calm. None of these generic descriptions of these terms accurately reflect their true meaning.

Curry is a generic name for a collection or mixture of spices. Mixture of spices used by Indian cooks is never the same. While there is always a basic theme, the spices used, and their proportions are generally left to the mood and creativity of the cook. This is what makes authentic Indian food far more unpredictable in its consistency for taste. While "curry" is used in various parts of India, the texture of the food and the taste of the same dish from many regions are different. This variety adds an additional dimension of deliciousness to Indian food.

On reflection, our understanding of God seems to be much like the understanding of curry. Everyone has a generic view of "God". Yet, each one of us have our own and unique view of God, conditioned by our knowledge, education, life experiences and introspection.

Everyone believes in God as a last resort, someone to look up to when all else fails. "God save the Queen" is the national anthem of Britain. Politicians take their oath to God when taking office "to protect and defend the constitution". Every religion invokes God in one form or another.

For some, God as the savior of last resort – when all else fails – is the beginning and end. Fear of God makes them behave in certain ways. Faith in God gives them hope to strive and pursue their activities in the face of looming uncertainties. In due course, God becomes their mystical superbeing. Concepts of heaven (as the place of God) and hell (as the place assigned to those cursed by God) dominate their thought and belief.

For some others, God is more of a goalpost, an ideal to strive for. They see God through divinity in their actions as well as in the action of others. For them, the divine qualities are enabled by traditions, and moral codes passed on through generations. Personal view of God as understood through religious teachings dominate their thought. When faced with changes in the society or natural order around them, they struggle to adapt to these changes.

Others try to learn and understand what God will do in daily life. They describe such manner of behavior as divinity. They try to understand when divinity comes into play in our actions and when divinity seems to dwindle. They learn that our opinions and judgement cloud our reasoning and analysis. Higher levels of reasoning and action that is in the best interest of all – objectivity – is seen as divinity. They also recognize that "reasoning", "action", "interest", etc., are all subjective. These are influenced by our limitations. In other words, they seek objectivity while conscious of the subjectivity of each of us as individuals.

Basic life processes – like breathing, digestion, assimilation, and sensory perceptions are the same for each of us (Objectivity). But each of us experiences or enjoys these processes differently (Subjectivity). We are aware that the laws of nature – governing the above human processes, as well as all other aspects of the universe – are truly invariant and hence objective. The sun that shines, the wind that blows, and the earth we sleep on are all the same for a king as well as for a poor nobody. Yet, each of us experiences them in our own personal or subjective manner. Those who reflect on all these marvels at this paradox.

Those who can accept this paradox as the way it is, describe the source of the paradox, its evidence, and effect as the laws of nature or "*Brahman*". Those who cannot accept the paradox – that the laws or forces of nature merely exist – seek a source or creator for these forces of nature and call that as God. Most of us can accept this invariant Brahman most of the time but need an authority figure "God", that governs our variability in action, feelings and thoughts, at least for a few moments!

God is a generic name for a collection of views and understanding in each of us. Even beyond that, the collection of views on God is never the same for the same person! The way one relates to God at moments of despair is different from the way one approaches God in the safety and comforts of life. While there is always a basic theme, the approaches used, and their proportions are generally dependent on the mood and circumstances of the individuals. This is what makes the role of God – as we relate to It – far more unpredictable.

Just as "curry" adds spice and flavor to the food, "God" adds a sense of purpose, direction, and frame of reference for our lives as individuals and as part of a larger order (the universe). Yet our understanding of God is very much personal.

Yearning for God – Two approaches!

Following is a quote from a book titled "They Lived with God: Life Stories of Some Devotees of Sri Ramakrishna". It is an excellent description of the longing for God.

"Yearning for God does not come until and unless a person has satisfied his cravings for mundane objects, renounced all attachment to lust and gold, and shunned worldly comforts and enjoyments like filth. How many people are restless for God-realization? People shed jugs full of tears for their wives, children, or money, but who weeps for God? He who longs for Him certainly will find Him. Cry to Him. Call on Him with a longing heart. You will see Him."

We weep and cry out for of fear for losing what we have! Attachments with our possession is seen as sources of stress, anxiety and unhappiness. Longing for God begins with non-attachment from all that is worldly, like relationships, material comforts, etc. As a counterbalance to this non-attachment from worldly objects, we need something else to hang on to. Religion and theology tell us that God, the all-pervasive, omnipresent, eternal, and objective source is the one to hang to. *"Anyone who longs for Him certainly will find Him"*.

Developing spiritual maturity is an individual responsibility. It is part of Spirituality in Practice. We can look at the above quote with an intent to further our spiritual maturity.

Let us reflect for a moment a person in family life, living in any community. His wife, children, or money – are they his sources of stress, anxiety and unhappiness? It is like blaming a stone by stating, "this stone tripped me, causing my injury, pain and suffering!"

Did the stone really trip you? Stone is an inert object incapable of moving or impacting anyone or anything. It requires my foot and its impact against the stone to trip me! Where did this motion of my foot in that direction at that moment come from? Because I did not see the stone before! My ignorant mind gave my foot a command to move in a certain direction resulting in my getting tripped, resulting in pain and injury. Any objective observer will know this simple truth.

Every aspect of our pain and suffering can be traced back to our mind and its attachment to something it knows and something else it does not know or believes to be true based on partial knowledge. When my mind is still – at peace, non-attached – things around me continue to happen, but "I" am non-attached. One can experience this non-attachment when your brain and its functions are sedated. In that state, the body feels no pain, even when it is cut by a surgeon's knife!

But can my mind remain unattached to anything and hence feel no pain or pleasure without my brain being anesthetized? Vedanta offers a simple approach for this. It is the exploration of the connectors and their roles.

Returning to our example of tripping on the stone, let us ask the question, "who really tripped me?" Not the stone alone, or my foot, my eyes looking elsewhere, my brain nor my mind. It is the way it happened where everything had a part. But collectively, it is part of nature. When I accept this view – *"na ithi bhavam"*: Not this attitude – we see all that is involved. Of course, my pleasure and pain come from many sources and reasons that include wife, children, money, etc. But, through sustained analysis and "Not this attitude" blame or responsibility shifts from anything or anyone specific to a collective view that it is all part of nature: *Sarvam Brahma Mayam.*

The more my mind is trained and focused to look at all that happens as part of nature, we are more objective and non-judgmental. We can see the full picture and proceed accordingly. We are at peace, calm and tranquil. We want to get united with the all-pervasive, Omnipresent, Eternal, and Objective source. Is there anyone like that? Can we get attached and emulate that person? Our longing and its intensity increases. Religion and theology tell us this void can be filled by God.

Philosophy tells us that as this longing to be relentlessly objective and to remain as part of nature increases, we see increasing divinity in our action and way of living. We live the life of God with increasing non-attachment and less perturbations, anguish and tumult in our daily life. That includes our life with wife, children and money!

Yearning for God through the religious path requires us to accept God as "someone else". We accept and worship that God! We surrender to that God, His mercy and blessings! Yearning for God through a reflective approach transforms us into better people (more Divine in our thoughts and way of life). We see God in us. We live the life of God through Divinity in daily life. We accept and adore wife, children and money as the extensions of God within, part of God's family (*Vasudeva Kudumbham*).

Perhaps they are not two separate pathways? Instead, they are two sides of a coin, integral and inseparable!

Brahmam Okate':
Everything Is Part of Nature!

The knowledge gained from Vedic Philosophy can be summarized in two statements:

- *Thath Thwam Asi* (You – the individual – and the Universe are integral in each other)

- *Sarvam Brahma Mayam* (Everything is *Brahman*)

The universe is the cognitive world of objects, emotions, and thoughts of which we are part of. Each of us – and everything we know of (and all that we do not know) – exist in this universe in one form or another as:

- Material objects

- Living beings

- Emotional human beings with our perceptions, thoughts, and feelings

- Analytical persons who understand and manage our physical body, emotions, and thoughts through self-control and objectivity

- With a conscious awareness of the above four states and hence in union with and respectful of the laws of nature (*Brahman*) that enable all these states of being!

Brahman may be recognized through the laws of nature (known to us and the unknown) that enable our existence. *Brahman* may also be recognized as the Lord we worship in recognition and awe of the marvel of the laws of nature.

The universality of nature (Everything is *Brahman*) is extolled, often in the form of poems or prayer songs. Below is the translation of one such poem from Telugu, one of the many regional languages of India. titled: *Brahmam Okate*': The individual self and the universal are one and the same

- *There are no differences of low and high. Brahman (the soul or the Lord inside all of us, the driving force behind everything) is one and the same.*
- *Every form of creation is one and the same because the indwelling spirit in every creature is one and the same.*
- *Be it a King or a Slave, everyone must sleep.*
- *Be it a nobleman or an uncultured rude person, the earth they stand on or lie down to sleep on is one and the same.*
- *The sensual pleasure is one and the same for angels or for insects and animals.*
- *The day and night are equal in duration for the rich as well as for the poor.*
- *One could afford to eat tasty food, and the other eats stale and wasted food. But for both the tongue and the sensory perception of taste are the same.*
- *An object of fragrance or an object of bad odor, the air that carries the smell is one and the same.*

- *Be it an elephant or a dog, the sun shines alike on both.*

- *The Lord who sits in judgment of the good deeds (Punya), as well as the bad or the sin (Papa), is one and the same.*

- *The laws of nature are the same even if their effect appears benevolent or violent.*

In the following, we illustrate the principle of *Brahmam Okate'* (laws of nature are universal) with few modern-day images:

Figure 5.4. Branches and roots are alike in their growth pattern. Branches seek the sunlight and grow upwards while roots seek water and nutrients and grow downwards

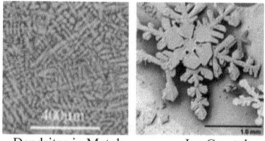

Dendrites in Metals   Ice Crystals

Figure 5.5. The growth pattern during solidification of hot molten metal is like the formation of cold ice crystals.

Figure 5.6. In a medina everyone shares the same narrow lane. It makes no difference if you are a child, mother, horse, or tourist!

Figure 5.7. Lucky cats sleep in the middle of the day, while the "unlucky" donkeys and the horse carry the load in a medina. They are all part of the same animal kingdom!

Altruism: Is It The Same As Un-Attached Active Engagement

Figure 5.8.

Every chapter of *Bhagavadgītā* offers some practical guidelines as well as some abstract concepts. In BG Chapter 12, unattached active engagement (*Karma Phala Thyagam*) is presented as the minimum required to acquire divinity. How can anyone engage in any activity without the desire for the outcomes?

Psychologist Abigail Marsh describes an incident early in her life in her TED talk "Why some people are more altruistic than others?". While driving on the highway, her car skidded and spun off the road and to the other side as she lost control. She was facing the oncoming traffic with a dead engine and was totally in despair. Another driver from a passing vehicle raced across the highway, running across lanes, daring the traffic, and pulled her out to safety. Without notice, he took off, continuing his travel. She wondered who this brave person was risking his life to save her life and yet left no trace of connecting with him. All she could do was acknowledge this altruistic person.

Abigail's experience is not far from my own experience. After my undergraduate education, I headed to the U.S. for studies at MIT. I had to travel by train from Chennai to Mumbai to catch a flight to London and onward to New York and ultimately to Boston. As our train pulled off the station at Chennai, I noticed that my briefcase was missing and every form of identification along with it. That included my passport, visa, and admission papers. Everything! As the train was moving, I and my father, who was accompanying me, could do nothing other than convey the news and the shock to my relatives still at the platform in the train station. To make the story short, when my relatives went home, they found a person waiting for them holding my bag! This stranger had seen the thief, a toddler holding my bag. He was trying to get change from passersby on a major road in Chennai at a location not far away from the train station. In those days, the $5 bill looked more like Rs. 5 notes, both green in color! Looking at the dollar bill, the stranger grew suspicious, grabbed the bag, and found all my details, including my personal address. He promptly proceeded to my home in Chennai and delivered the bag. He left, leaving no trace of who he was! To date, I have no information of this stranger who has defined my higher education, career, and even the course of the rest of my life without expecting or seeking anything in return. All I can do even now is to say "thank you" in public through this essay!

Why do some people help others at times and at extraordinary cost, risk, or sacrifice for their own self-interest? We call such actions "altruistic", which Abigail defines as: Voluntary, costly behavior motivated by the desire to help another individual. It is also self-less act motivated only to help others.

Psychologists describe human beings fall in a spectrum between those who cannot recognize the distress of others (Psychopaths) to those who can instinctively relate to the needs of others (altruists). One example of altruism in our daily life is people who donate their kidneys or other body parts during their lifetime to total strangers. According to Abigail's studies, which included about 2000 persons, when asked what motivated them to do such selfless acts, they invariably said, "nothing; it is not about me". They are altruistic for their own sake and not for any other reason! As one can see, unattached active engagement (*Karma Phala Thyagam)* is not all that abstract concept for these altruists!

Altruism may be noted in the specific acts of individuals and at specific times. Hence, psychologists may tend to develop a causal connection between certain aspects of our brain or economic wellbeing as the prerequisites for altruism. In many respects, this diminishes the role of a human being simply to a biological species. Human beings are more than mere biological species governed by tangible causality. They may not function only in response to specific means such as unique aspects of brain, economic conditions, etc. Selfless acts of charity and kindness are not limited to a few or based on their economic circumstances alone. Genuine love, empathy, compassion, and forgiveness are not bound by results or expectations of some needs to be fulfilled as the pre-requisite.

Conditioned by our minds and our actions over the years or during our lifetime, we believe that everything can be done only based on our needs. Through such a conditioned mind and self-limiting approach, we fail to see the true joy of life or the universality of opportunities to participate in. If we are truly part of nature – *Thath Thwam Asi* (You and the universe are integral in each other) – and not a self-limiting biological species, there are many evidence for us as examples of altruism: The sun does not shine to create light; it merely shines. Rain does not pour, or the wind blows for any specific reason other than it is just part of nature. The breeze in the springtime that spreads the fragrance that we enjoy unaware of the fragrance, or it being spread around or the enjoyment of such a sweet smell by others.

Let us continue to respect and admire the altruistic acts of others. But let us also condition our own mind to be altruistic – for unattached active engagement. It is not the ultimate accomplishment but the minimum expectation for Spirituality in practice, according to *Bhagavadgītā*. Caring for neighbors and elders, kindness to elders and strangers, a smile at someone, acts of charity, a donation to needy causes, and volunteering to help those in need (and in no way connected with us) are all examples of unattached active engagement. Even help and support for anyone known to us – starting from the near and dear in our families – such as raising our children or putting food on the table, can be done because they are the right thing to do and not because there is a personal connection or obligation for such actions. In other words, "duty" is the right thing to do without attachment and not an obligation with an expected end benefit.

May be altruism – unattached active engagement – is much closer to us than we realize? In that case, it can indeed be the minimum step towards Spirituality in practice.

- *Controlling your mind to develop an objective outlook is the best.* It is Jnana Yoga
- *Controlling your emotions though faith in the larger order (God) is next best.* It is Bhakthi Yoga
- *Carrying out all activities with a genuine commitment to your duty is acceptable as well.* It is Karma Yoga
- *If you are not able to do even that, at least forego the self-driven needs (attachment to the results).* Un-attached active engagement.   B.G. 12.12.

Repentance vs. Forgiving

Figure 5.9.

Relationship is a two-way street. The mother loves her child, and the child, in turn, is attached to the mother. The same goes for any parent and child, husband and wife, brothers, sisters, relatives, etc. In every case, there are two parties involved. When both persons involved in a relationship see eye to eye, there is harmony, friendship, collaboration, joy, and mutual benefit. Such relationships are ideal. Often, these relationships are based on give and take. It is a matter of accommodation.

A relationship that starts with no constraints, fears, and apprehensions – like that between the mother and the child or between two perfect strangers who like each other – become constrained and limited over time. The deep roots of good relationship become subverted in our false attempt to preserve and "protect" the superficial or surface-level connections. Like a river set in motion, relationships take their own course. To cultivate a "family" with meaningful relationships requires sustained effort. See the essay on "How large is your family?" It is like two ships in the dark ocean working together while using their respective search lights to steer clear of each other and co-exist (in the same channel of water).

When the relationship is strained, there will be attempts to restore it. People of goodwill can disagree, but to claim only one person is at fault is like twisting a dried wood further, not strengthening and restoring it. To revive the relationship requires internal reflection – soul searching – on two dimensions: Acknowledging the sources of strain and finding ways to overcome such strain.

Repentance is the evidence of acknowledgment of the source of strain; Forgiving is the step towards overcoming the strain.

Repentance and forgiveness are important aspects of prayers in any religion. May there be peace and harmony for all (*Sarve' Janaha Sukino' Bhavanthu*) is the prayer through which Hindus seek the blessing of the Lord and His forgiveness to all. Let there be the protection of the Lord (*Ishwaro' Rakshathu*) is the refrain through which Hindus seek strength for their forgiveness and comfort for those who need to repent. We find a similar approach for repentance and forgiveness in other religions.

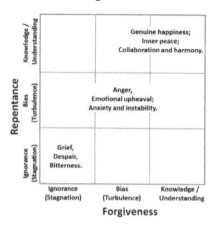

Figure 5.10. Repentance Vs. Forgiveness – stages.

Repentance and forgiveness are seen as a complimentary need in the Christian faith. One can repent for their failures and seek forgiveness through confession. One can also come to terms with the failure of others (external to the self) and seek forgiveness for them through prayer when repentance may or may not come from the other person. Through prayers, the worshiper finds his/her own reconciliation.

The inter-related nature of repentance and forgiving superimposed by the three connectors (ignorance, bias, and knowledge) is schematically illustrated in figure 5.10.

If we truly believe that anyone and the universe are one and the same (*Thath Thwam Asi*) and everything is governed by the laws of Nature (*Sarvam Brahma Mayam*), the pillars of Vedic philosophy, then how do we treat repentance and forgiveness? Let us look at the "objective" nature or the process behind these outcomes.

The offender and the person offended are droplets of the same body of water (*Thath Thwam Asi*) if the offensive action and its negative effect can be isolated. It is like removing a dirty cloth and placing it aside. This process of isolation and separation clarifies precisely what were the wrong actions and their effect. True acknowledgment and ownership of these actions and their effects are characterized as "Repentance". Decision to go beyond acknowledgment and move further is characterized as "Forgiveness". In this process, repentance and forgiveness are not centered on either individual. Instead, it is a collective outcome of the self-reflection of everyone involved on their own accord (*Yoga*). It is not limited to any one person.

The "spiritually refined person" (Yogi), with joy of internal contemplation, is peaceful and delighted within like an internal beacon of light, reaches unification with Brahman, and becomes Brahman themselves. B.G. 5.24

Meditation Simplified

Figure 5.11.

While traveling with a tour group, a fellow traveler and I started a conversation. The subject drifted from one to the other. At one point, my fellow traveler mentioned that despite her best efforts, she could not meditate. One could sense the deep disappointment in her. She said,

"My mind keeps constantly drifting. I feel very bad. I know that I can never meditate."

"Yes, your mind drifts from one thought to another, but so what? Aren't you still and quiet for the few moments between the thoughts?" I asked.

"Yes, that is true, but the teachers tell me that is not meditation. In fact, they say that through proper mediation, you reach a higher level of consciousness. I may never reach that state, I suppose," she replied.

I cannot sit still in one place and without thoughts of any kind for long durations. Maybe one can get there with practice, just like one can lift a heavy weight through years of practice and bodybuilding. But everyone need not be a wight-lifter! We can be contended with healthy living and a regular regimen of exercise and physical fitness.

Meditation is a practice towards a calm and contemplative mind available for us to reflect at any time on any subject we choose. It is an ability to quieten the mind such that it does not drift into thoughts on its own accord. Once the mind is focused on a subject of our choosing, how well we do with this reflection depends on our objectivity.

Meditation, like any activity, must be subject to the three connectors - *Guna* (knowledge, bas, and ignorance).

To control the mind and the thoughts that flow through our mind as an exercise without purpose is ignorance.

Attempting to meditate only because it will lead to a higher state is emotion-driven (bias) since we will not find satisfaction in this desire in our constant quest for such an elusive state of mind!

Reflecting on our thoughts that flow through our mind, their origins and how such a reflective mind can be used objectively and without attachment is the role and purpose of meditation.

A person is their own best friend through self-control. Being opposed to all that fosters self- control, a person remains an enemy for oneself. B.G. 6.6.

How does one reach this state of mind that treats every thought in an unattached and active manner, where dualities such as friend/foe, like/dislike, love/hate, etc. disappear?

We seek self-control through our actions (Karma Yoga), through our emotions and their dedication to a larger cause (Bhakthi Yoga), through the intentional engagement of our mind and thoughts that flow through our mind – Meditation – (Dhyana Yoga), through our knowledge (Buddhi Yoga), through an understanding of the invisible, eternal laws of nature and all that exists as the evidence enabled by these laws – Everything is *Brahman* (Jnana Yoga)...

The conscious choice and ability to control our mind and hence influence at will the thoughts that cross our mind is Meditation. It is not an endless exercise for mind control. It is a means to an end. The end is to reach a calm, contemplative, and objective state of mind. One approach is to negate every thought that comes to our mind. This can be done by simply focusing on one thought, such as repeating the same word or prayer song, or reflecting on neutral or impersonal scenery, such as the ocean waves.

An ascetic seated in a clean or purified place on a firm seat covered with deer skin and dried grass, placed on a level ground of moderate height, practices the process of self-control by a single-minded focus on restraining their thoughts and sense organs. B.G. 6. 11,12.

Let an ascetic free from fear, in constant pursuit of self-control, control the mind through their thoughts focused on Me (the Lord). The terms Laws of Nature, Lord, *Brahman* are used interchangeably to refer to the eternal, omnipresent enabler.

Such concentrated reflection is made further possible by the physical practice of holding the body, head, and neck in one line, motionless and the vision steady and unwavering and gazing at the tip of the nose. The ascetic who practices such self-control achieves an inner peace which leads to total renunciation (Nirvana), at which stage the ascetic is said to have reached a higher plane of existence (the state of union with the Lord). B.G. 6. 13 to 15.

The second approach is to challenge and inquire into every thought that crosses the mind at any time and place we choose. Instead of negating or erasing the thought, let us ask: What is this thought in my mind at this time? This process of self-inquiry or introspection has only one requirement – externalize the thought and all its attributes (e.g.): Imagine that you are seeking some favor of enormous impact. Let the mind wander to seek favor for you. Then seek the same favor for anyone close to you and continue the process. Pretty soon, your mind will exhaust this seeking of favor to all those close to you. Then add to the list those who are distant from you; the list gets exhausted soon. Then add to the list people, animals, plants, etc. Eventually, you will come to a point when the mind asks, "Why this person? Why this animal or why this object?" This is the point where you exercise self-control and say, "be inclusive and move on with the list." If you are genuine about this process of inclusion of all and exclusion of none, sooner than later, the mind will reach a state of calm and quiet exhaustion. Revel in that inner harmony.

Such a person sees no distinction between the loved ones, friend/enemy and is indifferent, uninfluenced, or neutral to all those who hate him and those who consider him as relative, noble and ignoble. Every one of this diversity of people is equal and accessible to an ascetic (Yogi). B.G. 6.9.

This process of self-inquiry can be practiced at any time and at any place. There are no time limits or number of thoughts to be controlled. The entire process may take only a few seconds. Revel in that calm, contented, and contemplative state of mind. That is meditation!

Let an ascetic be in constant practice of meditation as a means for self-control, and remain in quiet contemplation, thereby free from desires, belongings, or possessions.
B.G. 6.10

The two approaches of meditation: (a) Prayer or chanting and hence mind focused on a single thought and (b) Expanding our mind and thoughts to include all and exclude no one, are also described as a three-step process in Frontiers in Psychology –

Focused attention meditation (FAM): Mind focused on a chosen object or event, such as a candle flame or breathing. Through concentration on the chosen object or event, the mind is held in check from wandering.

Open monitoring meditation (OMM): During OMM, there is no object or event that the meditator has to focus on. The aim is to stay in the monitoring state, remaining attentive to any thought or experience that might arise, without selecting, judging, or focusing on anything.

Loving-kindness meditation (LKM): Meditators focus on developing love and compassion first for themselves and then gradually extend this love to ever more "unlikeable" others (e.g., from self to a friend, to someone one they do not know, to all living beings even the one they disliked).

Every Hindu worship starts with a focus on specific events or prayer services, much akin to FAM. This is followed by the lighting of the lamp and its offering (*Deepa Aradhana*) together with the prayer song noted in *Kathopanishad* (2.2.15) and also in *Bhagavadgītā* (15.6)

Transcend to that space where even the sun does not shine by itself, nor the moon or the stars, nor lightning, or even fire. All these bright objects shine by reflecting that

One. This whole Universe is illumined by That light (the Soul, Atman or Consciousness).

Through this prayer, the focus has moved past specific objects and activities to an abstract union with the soul (*Athman*), seen as the enabler of anything tangible and visible. Without selecting, judging, or focusing on anything, OMM can be noted here. The focus is on consciousness (inner self). At this point, the devotee – the worshiper – silently prays for the blessings of God. In an ideal prayer, the devotee moves gradually from seeking personal favors to seeking favors for family, for a broader cross-section of society, and into a seamless state of goodwill for all that knows no bounds. This largely mirrors the LKM mentioned above.

Dhyana, Chan, and Zen

Following is an excerpt from a book titled: "Zen and the Art of Motorcycle Maintenance – An inquiry into values" by Robert M. Pirsig, Page 177.

Logic presumes a separation of subject from object; therefore, logic is not final wisdom. The illusion of separation of the subject from the object is best removed by the elimination of physical, mental, and emotional activity. There are many disciplines for this. One of the most important is the Sanskrit "dhyana", pronounced in Chinese as "Chan" and again in Japanese as "Zen".

The above is a very insightful comment. It is indeed true that the subject "I" – the consciousness – remains in unison with the object "I" – the perception of who I am because of my experiences. The differences between the two – the subject (who I am) and the object (who I think I am) – exist if we do not understand the nature of the connection between the two. The analogy often cited is that of the lotus leaf (I – the consciousness), which lives and thrives in the body of water (I – the cognitive universe) and yet remains disconnected or untainted by the water. The living and growth of the lotus leaf in water, as well as its remaining untainted by the same body of water, are all governed by the laws of nature. Similarly, the perception and all experiences of the cognitive world are also governed by appropriate laws of nature. One who understands that everything exists merely as representations of the laws of nature begins to see that the subject and the object nature of "I" are merely a matter of perception. We have outlined in detail the connectors, the basis of all our experiences, and identify them in several of our earlier essays. This is the logic or reasoning for the anatomy of our experiences. One, who understands this connection in any aspect of our cognitive world, also sees the difference between the subject and the object only as the interplay of the three connectors (our knowledge, bias, and ignorance) pertinent to that subject matter. Such understanding of this connection removes the illusion of the subject "I" perceived as the object "I". This requires an intense focus or concentration on the connectors and how to decipher them. This is the goal of *"Dhyana"*, or internal reflection. It is best practiced as meditation, followed by reflection and contemplation. This is the discipline of *"Dhyana"*, referred to by the author in the above quote.

The above quote would also seem to suggest that through *"Dhyana"* we are seeking something that is other than "logic" or reasoning driven. It also seems to suggest that the goal of *Dhyana*, Chan, or Zen is to minimize all activities. This, in my view, seems to miss the main point.

Logic is a process of reasoning. Understanding the causal relations is the outcome. Once the outcome is realized, the process seems irrelevant. Once we have reached the destination, the journey – the process – may not be relevant anymore. Only in this manner of speaking would one say that *"logic is not the final wisdom"*.

Laws of nature are the connectors that link the subject with the object. In our exploration of the laws of nature, it is easier to focus on one experience at a time since our reasoning may be less clouded and our focus much sharper. Dhyana, Chan, or Zen is the process that facilitates such focus and concentration. The goal of Dhyana is not withdrawal, isolation, and the life of a recluse. This view may be completely counter to the reality and suggestions from the philosophy. Through seclusion and elimination of many activities (physical, mental, and intellectual), one could minimize the number of activities that create distractions. This helps to focus or concentrate on one thought or subject matter at a time.

Dhyana is a physical process that conditions your mind for a deep and sustained analysis – the logic – of "who am I?" Such introspection becomes easier by minimizing the number of activities we are engaged in. But, if one can infer for oneself even for a fraction of the moment that I am merely a product of the laws of nature, then one can instantly understand the indivisible nature of *"everything that enables "I""* and *"everything you perceive as "I""*. The oriental approaches of *Dhyana*, Chan, or Zen are means to facilitate this logical understanding of who we are and who we perceive we are, why congruence occurs when it does, and why divergences occur when they do. The practices of withdrawal, seclusion, and minimization of physical, mental, and emotional activities are more of a means to this end. They are not the end in themselves. Nor do they need to be thought of as necessary prerequisites.

This understanding of the basic principle – that the enabler (laws of nature) and the enabled (the cognitive world of objects, emotions, and thoughts) remain integral to each other – could occur instantly. Such realization may pertain to a given activity, a collection of activities, or as a lifelong principle. In every one of these situations, enlightened living is the outcome. It is stated that we recognize that reality only during those rare moments when we remove the veil of ignorance in our thought process.

What Is Next After "Yoga" And "Meditation" Session?

Loving Kindness Meditation (LKM):

You are somebody who can make anybody feel like somebody!

Figure 5.12.

Google search on why we meditate and/or practice Yoga converged on a few reasons:

Why do we meditate?

1. Relief from stress and anxiety (meditation mitigates the effects of the "fight-or-flight" response, decreasing the production of stress hormones such as cortisol and adrenaline)

2. Decreased blood pressure and hypertension

3. Lower cholesterol levels

4. More efficient oxygen use by the body

5. Increased production of the anti-aging hormone DHEA

6. Restful sleep

Why do we do Yoga?

1. Improves muscle tone, flexibility, strength, and stamina

2. Reduce stress and tension

3. Boost self-esteem

4. Improve concentration and creativity

5. Lower fat in our muscles.

6. Improve blood circulation

7. Stimulate the immune system

8. Create a sense of well-being and calm.

When you read them carefully, the above suggests that Yoga and meditation are efforts to improve the person in some form or other in terms of better physical fitness, better health, or lifestyle habits (restful sleep). How far along the three steps of meditation do you progress? Calming the mind and hence influencing the related body and mind functions are indeed fabulous. Hopefully, meditation and yoga practice will lead to a healthier and longer life. That may also depend on what one does after the meditation or yoga session.

Charged with an enhanced sense of the self after yoga or meditation sessions, one can be reflective, caring, kind, and genuinely focused on the welfare of everyone (i.e.) "Everything is OK". This is the effect of Loving Kindness Meditation. This internalizes the Vedic principle: *Thath Thwam Asi* (You and the Universe are integral in each other). In this state of mind, one truly enjoys life as part and parcel of the Laws of Nature (*Aham Brahma:* I am Brahman) – witness, observer, and participant in the role of the laws of nature. Objectivity (being non-judgmental) becomes second nature.

Meditation has been described in an earlier essay composed of three elements: Focused Attention Meditation, Open Monitoring Meditation and Loving-Kindness Meditation, Here are a few pointers to look for as we progress from FAM to OMM to LKM:

1. Look before you leap; always have the larger perspective in mind.

2. Think before you speak. What you say reflects the thoughts that preceded those words!

3. It is OK to be wrong if you are willing to accept it. Acceptance will be reflected in your next word or action!

4. Listen and reflect more than speak and interrupt.

5. Look farther than your nose and hear more than the noise!

6. Feel the pleasure and pain of others even before they express them; pain has a language that is not heard by the ear but felt by the heart!

7. Take risks to engage rather than withdraw for fear of self-incrimination.

8. Forgive the self and others rather than seeking forgiveness or acceptance from others.

9. Enjoy the good at hand rather than regret for the wishes not realized.

10. Practice detachment: it gives more time for your observation and analysis and more space for others.

11. We do everything for others to enjoy. But few realize this basic truth!

12. Life well lived is far better than a life long-lived! No one knows the end, but everyone knows the present!

The above are just a few simple pointers to check LKM in practice. If these are not the outcomes, one wonders what is the benefit of yoga and its arduous twitching of the body? If the above are not the outcomes, does one truly remain calm and tranquil after painstaking efforts for mind control through meditation?

Vedic Philosophy and the Knowledge Economy

This essay was published earlier in Prabuddha Bharatha, Jan. 2022 (annual issue).

Knowledge Economy and its Binary Nature:

Knowledge Economy (KE) in the 21st century can be defined as follows: *"Economy which is increasingly based on knowledge-intensive activities, creating a greater reliance on intellectual capital rather than physical inputs"*. Knowledge is an intangible asset. Yet aggregating and leveraging that for new and higher value addition is the driving force behind the Knowledge Economy. As human beings, we contribute our efforts to economic activities through our job, work, etc.

Through our:

- Knowledge and its use (A),
- Ability to collect and process information (B) and
- Through our physical effort (C).

While the use of information and labor are required in any job or career, the demand for value addition through knowledge and its use has been increasing in the Knowledge Economy. We can describe the value addition (VA) in the knowledge economy as: $VA = A / (B+C)$. It is schematically illustrated in Figure 5.13 where we observe two pathways for economic progress:

1.   Increase the contribution to knowledge content and its use: higher values for the numerator.

2.   Use knowledge-based solutions while reducing the effort expended in "information processing" and "physical" work: lower values for the denominator in the above equation.

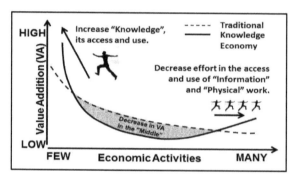

Figure 5.13. Knowledge Economy: Two pathways for higher Value Addition with a decline in Value Addition in a large segment of "Middle" level economic activities.

IT tools and their applications have catalyzed "Globalization" thanks to ready access to information, a large pool of low-cost labor, and all other global resources. Acceleration in the use of Digital Technology is now creating new knowledge-intensive fields and developments such as self-driving cars, genomics, data science, 3D and smart manufacturing, healthcare solutions, unmanned warehouses, and space travel, among others. These are enabled by a few highly talented and skilled "knowledge workers across the globe". Through this combined effect of digital technology, a large segment of the economic activities traditionally considered as the "middle" are now seen as adding lower value relative to activities in the above two extremes or pathways. This, in summary, is the "Knowledge Economy". This development is true for all enterprises, sectors of activity, or the national economy! In this KE, there is increasing demand for knowledge workers in a diminishingly smaller pool of well-paying jobs and careers. Workers who contribute only marginally to knowledge work are not considered very valuable. This shift is true for developing economies as well as advanced economies. This shift may be accelerated by growth in Artificial Intelligence (AI) and Robotics! This seismic shift in work, job opportunities, and economic activities in the KE will require a radical change in thinking and new knowledge-based skills for everyone.

Shift in thinking required in the Knowledge Economy:

Progression from physical labor to information work and moving into new knowledge-intensive work has been the pathway for economic progress for individuals as well as families for generations. In the KE, this orderly and seamless progression in opportunities seems to be broken. In the KE, only a few Knowledge workers in any company or in the population are well off measured in financial terms based on their high-value addition. At the same time, a large majority see their economic standards slipping away. This is not a sustainable situation for peace and harmony for all. While a few across the globe enjoy the benefits of industrial advancements, their impact on ecology and climate affects every person and all living and non-living material objects on earth. How do we rebalance this affluence and benefit for the few at the expense of the many? The required changes cannot come unless we shift from purely material comforts and financial measures to a holistic view of well-being for all. This is where the Vedic guidance - *Sarve' Janaaha Sukino' Bhavanthu*: May everyone live in peace and harmony - acquires profound and practical meaning. This mind shift is required in each of us as individuals and collectively as a community and society. This responsibility is even greater for knowledge workers who preferentially benefit more than others in the KE.

KE is empowered by instant access to information for everyone powered by digital news media, search engines, and social media. This empowerment, in turn, may populate negatives faster than positive stories, thoughts, and ideas. It requires a determined effort to fight off our subjective negative impulses, which in turn lead to isolation, self-selected groups, bias, bigotry, and depression. This attraction to negative news and the negative tendency is assessed to be more personal in nature rather than universal. It requires clarity and understanding in each of us on Subjectivity Vs. Objectivity. It also requires persistent clarity of thought and managing our mind to seek the truth all the time in all that we watch, read and absorb through an internet search and social media tools such as WhatsApp, FB, TV, Twitter, etc.

The above discussion, even while it is brief, raises some serious questions: What is true knowledge? Can that be universal and applicable in every field, even in the face of increasing "specialization"? How can we acquire that universal knowledge for success in the KE? What is Objectivity? How can objectivity and non-attachment be developed as protective armor and tools against the barriers imposed on us in the Knowledge Economy?

Universal lessons from Vedic Philosophy for the Knowledge Worker:

Every knowledge worker is a "professional" as well as a "philosopher" in a limited context. For example, every doctor or cardiac surgeon observes the patient unattached and objectively - without personal attachment to the patient - based on all available evidence. The next step – prescription of medicine and treatment or surgery - is what they are required to do (duty or *Dharma*). They perform that without any undue expectation for the results. Yes, the goal is to see that the patient gets better. But a good doctor/surgeon is not burdened by the outcome. The same is true for engineers, scientists, teachers, mechanics, accountants, supervisors, managers, authors, cooks, etc., in their respective professions. A carpenter chooses the best wood based on his knowledge (and the laws behind their use, such as strength, flexibility, durability, etc.). He is happy to sell the furniture he made and move on. He is not attached to each piece of furniture he makes obsessively! From the above, it is obvious that each knowledge worker at their best level of performance lives by the following guidance:

Do your duty the right thing to do based on your best understanding and objective analysis. It is the only thing left for you to do! Don't be fixated on the outcome. Yes, there is always a goal and purpose. But let the result, whatever it is, happen because of your performing your duty. Don't belabor on the possible impact of the results or the outcomes. You, the physical person, are not in total control of everything; have the mindset to be flexible and adaptable rather than rigid and inflexible; don't let the mind wander in fantasy or self-inflicted grief. Do not shy away from your association/ engagement from what you are supposed to do (i.e.) your duty.   *B.G. 2.47.*

If the goal for anyone in the KE should be to prepare oneself for jobs and careers which are knowledge-intensive, then it raises the question: What is the "true knowledge" required? Most people assume higher education as the answer! More education is believed to open the gateway to better, higher-paying jobs. Is college education by itself adequate to gain the "knowledge" required for sustainable jobs and career growth in the KE? Without clarity on this, workers and their employers are required to be innovative, entrepreneurial, work smarter, work harder; jump from job to Job, become global, seek higher education; be interdisciplinary, etc.

"Getting the job done" is valued highly at any time. KE requires this skill to define what is the job or solution that is new, that needs to get done, why it is important, what the knowledge required for that solution, etc. and then relentlessly work to make it happen. This is system thinking. This requires the knowledge worker to think holistically. When asked "2 + 2=?" one should never answer "4" instinctively and impulsively! Instead, probing into the question, why it has been asked, the details behind it, and the comprehensive solution relevant to it is needed! Then it requires transformational skills to execute that solution efficiently and collaboratively with everyone involved.

The system thinking and the related transformational skills described above mirror the knowledge and approach described in the Vedic Philosophy (summarized in Bhagavad Gita, Chapter 14):

• **Always take the time to reflect before engaging in any action.** This process of reflection and analysis is YOGA (Union with the Self). It requires:

• **Practice patience and perseverance to gather all observations** (lend a patient ear; listen carefully and with kindness, study, observe, and collect all data as much as possible).

• **Focus on the primary invisible driving force (the knowledge) behind the solution** (Experience and its disturbances tend to distract the self and others into the myriad of data and observations as well as from one ad-hoc target to the next endlessly).

• **Emphasize on the application of the "Science of Connectors"** – All our data and observations are the connections between the knowledge (the driving force) and everything external to it (the team, resources, analysis, signals, sensors) through the three connectors or ropes (*Guna*): Knowledge, Bias and Ignorance and their equilibrium states (*Gunathvam*): inertial, turbulence, and tranquility. *An inertial* state leads to procrastination. *Turbulence* leads to an unending series of actions without the ability to meet the ever-changing needs or demands. *Tranquility* leads to clarity on "Why?", a collective sense of purpose, as well as a common understanding of the laws (knowledge) governing the solution and an ability to arrive at it efficiently since the connection between the data and the knowledge (driving force), is clear to everyone!

• **Let your reflection lead to objectivity** (*Sagunathvam* - Seeking balance through the ever-present connectors (*Guna*) as best as one can) over subjectivity (*Gunathvam* - impulsive responses through tasks and actions, unwittingly choosing actions based on presumed knowledge, whims, bias, and ignorance).

• **"Externalize" the subject matter and analysis** -- Look at the subject matter, experience, and analysis in a detached and impersonal manner (i.e.) practice non-attachment!

Every knowledge worker, to be successful, needs to practice the above "philosophy" as a basic knowledge or foundation! Whenever we engage in this manner of reflection and analysis – through non-attachment, objectivity, and the science of connectors - we are freed of self-limiting issues and concerns. On the other hand, since the focus is directed toward the solution by the same pool of knowledge and understanding, work becomes a collective output of everyone and is not driven by personal attachments and preferences. Working with anyone becomes natural, even if they are far away and across the globe. There are no strangers, no specialists, no silos, no "other"!

"Science" has a pre-eminent role in the KE. It attempts to answer the "WHY?" question or the invisible governing forces that enable the phenomena of nature. Gravity, magnetism, electricity, buoyancy, life processes, optics, chemistry, biology, friction, nucleation, crystal growth, heat transfer, etc. are a very small list of infinite phenomena of nature known and unknown that we seek to use and exploit in the KE. Collectively they are all amenable to the definition of *Brahman:*

The invisible, omnipresent enabler recognized only through its effects (the enabled) (i.e.) That which enables the fire to burn, water to wet, wind to move, etc. They are all eternal and objective – invariant of time, place, etc.

Science is an attempt to understand the invisible enabler and find laws to better explain or understand their presence in the cognitive world.

Every knowledge worker is a specialist in the laws of nature pertinent to their field. Vedic Philosophy teaches us that the ideal person is an objective and relentless observer of *Brahman*: governing forces as evidenced by the invisible laws of nature and their visible effects. Knowledge workers have to internalize this thought since their work exists enabled by and as a witness to the invisible forces of nature and their influences, even though limited to their field of activity.

Knowledge workers have to be always open-minded and willing to change their knowledge and understanding based on new evidence and their objective analysis. They need to be always mindful of the injunction from Upanishad:

One, who thinks he knows Brahman, but he is not sure that he knows completely, truly knows Brahman.

Any subject learned with the above knowledge framework becomes far more comprehensive. Such education. knowledge and practice is useful to the professional in a wide variety of situations and opportunities. It allows the ability to open new doors when none seemed to exist before!

Practice-oriented Vedic Philosophy for the Knowledge Workers:

Barriers may exist in adapting the above universal knowledge from Vedic Philosophy. By treating "Religion" and "Philosophy" as synonymous, we may fail to see the role and practice of philosophy in aspects of our daily life outside the religious context. There is also a belief that philosophy and spirituality are for old age as they deal with topics for the afterlife! Vedic philosophy can be applied in every stage of life practiced with objectivity and non-attachment. Under ideal conditions, it aligns with divinity in action, reflecting the mindset as declared in the Vedic pronouncement *Thath Thwam Asi:* Inclusiveness for all and exclusive of none. This mindset requires a relentless focus on the larger context of life in contrast to the focus only on individuals, their tasks, and the actions surrounding them.

We may need early education on Vedic Philosophy, its practical relevance in all aspects of life, and sustained reinforcement through a lifelong learning process. A reflective mind rooted in Vedic Philosophy has to become a natural way of life for anyone independent of religion, age, proficiency in academic education, economic success, social standing, and affluence. Also, there may be no better substitute for self-education through reading, reflection, and practice with help from innumerable resources readily accessible to anyone in the KE.

It is not prudent to assess jobs and careers exclusively in financial terms and the material rewards. Maintaining a holistic perspective on life and work is always the desirable path. This includes the power of self-awareness and finding a limitless union with the universe at large. In the KE, this deliberately cultivated spiritual outlook and practice may be a direct and imminent need for every knowledge worker.

Sustained learning of the basics of Vedic Philosophy and its practice will help to explore our own inner thoughts and feelings and build an equilibrium or harmony within. It is said that a butterfly fluttering in Brazil can lead to a tsunami in Japan! It implies that even a very small perturbation in any of us can end up in chaos for the group, team, family, society, etc. The more we learn to address and help the hidden anxieties or worries in any of us, it is a great help without our knowledge for all of us! Conversely, anyone at peace and harmony interacting with others is like a seed that grows into a giant tree or a snowflake that gradually builds up into a snowball, including everyone and everything in the vicinity.

Practice-oriented Vedic Philosophy referred to in this section apply universally to everyone. But they are particularly needed for the Knowledge Workers who play an increasingly vital role in shaping the future of everyone and everything in the Knowledge Economy.

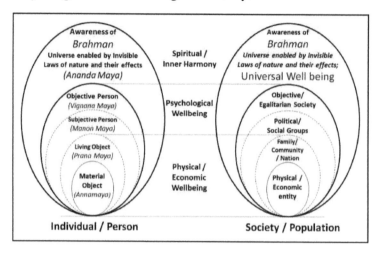

Figure 5.14. Five Layers (*Pancha Kosha*) applicable to each person and, by extension, to the society/population at large.

Knowledge Economy and Spirituality in practice:

According to Vedanta, each person exists in five interconnected layers or sheaths (*Pancha Kosha).* These five layers are illustrated in Figure 5. 14. These layers also align with the three dimensions as part of our existence: (a) Economic / Physical well-being, (b) Personality or Psychological well-being, and (c) Inner harmony or Spiritual well-being.

A large body of this essay has been devoted to clarifying the lessons from Vedic Philosophy that are pertinent for professionals seeking success and economic well-being in the KE. Understanding the role of the pertinent laws of nature and their deployment holistically as needed in a system is the true knowledge for any knowledge worker. The ability to accomplish the larger intended purpose objectively and without attachment is the true hallmark of any leading-edge knowledge worker. Vedic philosophy also teaches us the ability to look at our interconnectedness across all the five layers illustrated in Figure 5.14, in any and all aspects of life. This expansive view is an important asset for knowledge workers. Those who find a personal connection between the invisible laws of nature and their visible effects across the five layers in their field of work will also find it easier to extend such thinking to any other aspect of their life. Figure 5.15 also illustrates how these observations, and their application can be extended to the family, society, or nation at large. Enlightened Knowledge Workers will find ways to see the connection between the five layers in their personal work or life and how they translate into the five layers of the society or population at large.

Swami Vivekananda states, "Service to humanity is service to God". In the emerging bimodal KE, with a collapse in demand for the "middle", paying attention to fellow human beings may be more than mere service. It may be the true display of divinity and the spiritual core in everyone. Enlightened knowledge workers with Vedic Philosophy as their driving force can become transformative in many ways. They can start by looking at each knowledge solution, which enables their personal success also creates new economic opportunities for many more people and not merely as means to reduce employment in the name of efficiency and productivity. Charitable work and Corporate Social Responsibility (CSR) can become part of the spiritual evolution of knowledge workers when they think of themselves as a droplet of water in a large body of water (individuals indistinguishable from humanity at large). Enlightened knowledge workers can transform social media tools as enablers to propagate social harmony instead of polarization, bigotry, and bias. Climate crisis, eliminating hunger and poverty, clean water, energy, decent living conditions for all, reducing racial tensions, eliminating gender bias, and the many other challenges need not remain as crying calls limited to a few activists and their action groups. Instead, they could become the targets for new solutions for every knowledge worker in all organizations. If successful, expanding the knowledge in Vedic Philosophy for spiritual evolution and for wider impact may indeed be the lasting role of knowledge workers with their preferred status in the KE.

You Can Take A Horse To The Water But Cannot Make It Drink!

"You can take a horse to the water but cannot make it drink!" is a proverb familiar to many. It suggests that one cannot force or coerce others to do anything without their own intent or willingness. Reflection on such common statements lifts one above the cloud of confusion and challenges faced at times, despite one's best intentions and efforts.

Figure 5.15. Why doesn't this horse drink
the water in front of it?

Behind any proverb are lots of assumptions. In this case, for example, the horse is thirsty; it has been taken to a source of clean water in sufficient quantity; it has the freedom of movement, and not restrained, etc., and yet it refuses to drink! Our knowledge, bias, and ignorance in all these and many other matters will have an impact on the intended goal. Let us make a short list:

Is the horse thirsty?

Knowledge: Yes, this horse is fed water at this time daily by me, and it generally drinks water. Bias: The horse is expected to drink water at this time, and it knows that very well! Ignorance: Someone else has earlier fed water to this horse; nobody told me.

Is the water clean to drink?

Knowledge: Yes, the horse is fed this water daily by me, and it generally drinks. Bias: After all, it is a horse; should I feed it bottled water? Ignorance: What is the difference? Aren't all water the same?

Is the horse free and not restrained from drinking?

Knowledge: Yes, this horse is free and not restrained; It can drink easily; I check for this daily. Bias: A horse cannot be left unrestrained; I am responsible, and I will be blamed! Ignorance: Horses have a sense of anticipating danger better than humans. I didn't know that!

If our knowledge is dominant in all cases, we will check for the remaining bias and ignorance at play. We check around and learn that the horse has been fed water a little while ago by someone else. Or there was a snake nearby that the horse perceived as dangerous. Being unaware of the frightened look in the horse, sensing danger is ignorance. One could learn of these possibilities by observing the horse and its behavior. Blaming the horse as "unwilling to drink" is bias. Our thinking shifts from being judgmental – blaming the horse – to better understanding the cause or reason behind its behavior. The best course of action for the moment follows. That is karma or duty. Such reflection and analysis preceding any action is yoga.

It is easy to analyze and discuss a horse and its behavior toward drinking water. Even that requires breaking out of our impulse to action, jumping into an opinion or judgment. Action, doing something – blaming the horse as unwilling to drink – follows the judgment instinctively. It is a genuinely cultivated habit to be calm, contemplative, and reflective through any action in our daily life. To guide us through such challenges, the proverbs serve as a crutch, a walking stick – accepting reality as it is without bias and moving on.

But we must discard such support occasionally and challenge ourselves. Consider, for example, a family matter. Or it could be a matter of discussion at the workplace. After great reflection, you offer your views or opinion. You follow it up with an offer of some help that could be useful. If pursued further, your input could greatly impact the peace, harmony, and overall welfare of all. But your input is summarily rejected. What can you do? Simply say, "You can take a horse to the water but cannot make it drink!" and walk away? The above situation is not hypothetical. We are faced with it all the time: in communication with immediate family members; across families; communication in a project team; religious and political groups; social circles, etc.

Have you given sufficient reflection prior to offering your views or opinion? Have you relentlessly addressed your own bias and ignorance and minimized them before, during, and after sharing your opinion or suggestion? That reflects your objectivity. Are you rejecting the obvious clues or signals received? Are you unhappy with the outcome, even if it is partial? That reflects your attachment (Turbulence). Are you feeling helpless? That reflects your ignorance and its dominance (Inertia). Are you pleased with the outcome and willing to let things evolve, as the matter requires participation and engagement by others over time? Then you are Tranquil. Precisely which equilibrium state truly reflects my state of mind will be known only to myself. This requires me to be non-judgmental: distant from the situation, details, inference, communication, etc. This non-attachment with which I observe my state of mind in any instance is Objectivity.

The Sources of Anger

"I really don't want to get angry. In fact, I don't even realize it until after I get angry. This really upsets me!" These are words spoken by good people after serious reflection of their behavior. Such a sense of helplessness should be a matter of concern to all of us. Take a minute to reflect on the simple question, "Why do we get angry?" Invariably it is the outcome of:

— The reaction when the mind is unable to comprehend reality (of the laws of nature and their logical outcome).

— Our unwillingness to accept our own understanding (we clearly know why things are happening the way it is, but we wish it was different or we demand a different outcome);

— It is an expression of our commitment and determination to do the right thing (i.e.) the determination to carry out the required action appropriate for the moment.

One should develop clarity in understanding among these three sources of anger.

How do we recognize anger? Generally, anger is perceived through spoken words, physical actions, or emotions expressed through "body language". We have programmed visions of an angry person with abusive language. We can see the fiery tiger or cobra ready to pounce and attack! We can also envision the wounded animal, overpowered and hence angry and hurt but unable to do much. As soon as we see glimpses of such evidence in people, our mind jumps to the conclusion, "Aha! This person is angry". In other words, our mind races to the judgment or conclusion based on the observation. What is missing here is reflection and analysis.

We need to step back and ask the question: "Why would someone normal, by all accounts, show this evidence of anger? What are the inputs that are triggering these responses"? As soon as the mind moves away from judgment to analysis, the entire picture changes. We no longer see the angry individual. Instead, we see an individual tormented by certain information, opinions, unfulfilled expectations, lack of clarity in their reasoning, etc. Take the case of the raging bull in the bullfighting ring. We may not know the psychology (or the laws of the inner workings) of the bull's mind. But we know there is a predictable consistency in the bull's behavior. Sadly, the bull has been trained to charge at the red cloth, even if it leads to its cruel death in the end. We are all conditioned in our mind and its thinking like the bull in the ring.

Now, reverse the situation. You are the observer, and your body, mind, and intellect are being observed. Strangely, it takes less than a few seconds to see the causes of the reaction, called anger. You are no longer angry. You are merely the observer of your anger. That is really a strange experience indeed! We are like any spectator in the bull fighting arena. Such role-playing, where we become merely the observer – the audience – not the director, actor, or participant in any manner, is a powerful method to study the anger inside of us. Studying the anger of others, we are associated with is equally powerful. Such dispassionate analysis will come naturally only after some level of practice.

Every person can ascend the heights of enlightened living through self-control. Do not allow yourself to sink into despair and difficulty due to the absence of self-control. Thus, a person is their own best friend or worst enemy.

B.G. 6. 5

Through self-control, remain as your best friend. Through enmity for all that which supports self-control, do not descend to become your own enemy. *B.G. 6.8.*

Meditation is generally used to develop skills for internal reflection and self-control. Prayer, where we place the full faith and power in the hands of a larger order, followed by meditation, is frequently recommended in the scriptures as a process leading to internal reflection and analysis. Yoga, or conscious control of breathing (*Pranayama*) and other body functions, are also very helpful in this process.

Anger is the conflict between the intellect (which lays out the logic or the "What and Why" of the situation) and the mind (with its attachments unwilling to accept such logic and its clarity)! When we are mere observers of the evidence and the background reasons, we can also see this conflict vividly. Scriptures deal with this conflict in any number of ways. Following verse is very appropriate here:

There are three principal reasons for our destructive approach to life. These are:

- Passion or Extreme attachments to "pairs" of pleasure/pain, love/hate, happiness/sorrow, etc.

- Unbridled jealousy arising due to unfulfilled desires and their effects.

- Anger as a response to the insatiability of our wants and desires.

One should abandon these three sources of the destruction of a person that limit a person from their becoming enlightened. B.G. 16. 21.

This implies that the unyielding mind when it torments our intellect, we respond through our body (which we call as anger). Buddha has simplified this by stating, "Desire is the cause of sorrow".

The third source of anger is very intriguing. Based on our analysis of the evidence and after careful reflection, we conclude that certain outrage has been committed. The situation must be rectified. It is the call of duty at that moment. There is a certain determination to do the right thing and perseverance to accomplish the goal. It is a commitment or determination to channel our efforts to the required action. All of this can be perceived as anger by the observers. But it is the channeling of our energy from its dissipation through anger. It is the direction of our energy for a selfless goal. Following excerpts on anger from the book The Dhammapada by Eknath Eswaran are appropriate here:

"I have learnt through bitter experience the one supreme lesson: to conserve my anger. As heat conserved is transmuted into energy, even so, our anger controlled can be transmuted into a power that can move the world". –

Mahathma Gandhi

"Always a pragmatist, the Buddha even goes to the extent of saying that he would welcome an outburst of anger if it really could help bring an end to suffering. It is precisely because it does not help end suffering that he urges us to curb anger as its source". – Eknath Eswaran

"Anger is fire in the mind, burning up the forest of your merits and blessings. .... Guard your mind against anger" – Zen poet Han – Shan of Tang Dynasty, China.

"Mastery of the practice of non-anger ends in the precious capacity to return love for abuse, an ideal of all the world's major religions" – Eknath Eswaran,

Desire, Anger, And Passion – The Forces That We Need To Contend With

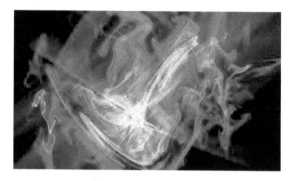

Figure 5. 16.

This essay is an extension to the previous on "Sources of anger". There are many incidences in which we witness acts of others and the anguish and grief they create for them. Yet we forget them soon, get into the rush of life, and repeat the same actions before we realize that we are also engulfed in grief and anguish through our own actions. According to the scriptures, any action, even without malice, but results in anguish and grief to others should be thought of as a sin (*Papam*). There seems to be an abundance of repeating the same mistake. One can wonder why? The same question is asked by Arjuna and answered by Lord Krishna in, *Bhagavadgītā* as noted below:

Why is a person compelled to commit acts leading to grief, death, and destruction (described as sin), even when they are unwilling based on earlier knowledge or reasoning and yet compelled by a force, as it were?   B.G. 3. 36

Desire (to exclusively meet one's personal needs at all costs), anger (as a consequence of unfulfilled desires), and passion (uncompromising affection) are the forces that are the outcome of turbulent/agitated nature (Rajasam) of a person. They lead them to the path of grief and destruction. These are the enemies of any person.   B.G. 3. 37*

Fire, the source of energy, is covered by smoke. Mirror gets covered by dust. The embryo is surrounded by the womb. Each are influenced by the object that envelop them. Similarly, the knowledge of an individual gets enveloped by the connectors (Guna) and hence influenced by their forces.   B.G. 3. 38

Knowledge or wisdom gets covered by un-relenting desire, the insatiable foe of the wise. The body and its functions through sense organs, the mind, and the intellect are the seats for these forces. Through these means, they obscure the knowledge and negatively influence the person. B.G. 3. 39, 40.

Therefore, through control of the instruments of body, mind, and intellect, destroy these forces: unbridled desire, anger, and passion. Otherwise, these forces take hold of both the knowledge and the ability for reasoned analysis and decision-making.   B.G. 3. 40

It is said that controlling the body and the sense organs is good. Having control over the mind is better. Controlling the intellect may be the best. The enlightened person controls all three and yet actively engages them without being affected by them. Such a person is the most superior.   B.G. 3. 42.

Thus, having become aware of the true nature of enlightened living, one who uses total self-control to manage oneself engages vigorously in efforts to destroy the enemy presenting itself in the form of desire.   *B.G. 3. 43*

Conscious awareness of desire, anger, and passion and their regulation must be practiced in any aspect of life. Such reflection and regulation in our daily life is an aspect of Spirituality in Practice.

Pressure Vs. Stress Vs. Relief!

Figure 5. 17.

I recently came across an article where the author states: "*Pressure is not stress. But pressure is converted to stress when you add one ingredient: rumination, the tendency to keep rethinking past or future events while attaching negative emotions to those thoughts. The corrective process starts with understanding that stress is caused not by other people or external events but by our reactions to them. In the workplace, many people blame their high anxiety levels on a boss, job, deadlines, or competing commitments for their time. But peers who face the same challenges respond without stress. There are executives who have high levels of pressure but low levels of stress, and vice versa.*

The author offers four steps to prevent the pressure getting converted into stress: 1. *Wake up*;   2.*Control your attention*; 3. *Put things in Perspective*   4. *Let go.*

In summary: Become aware of the reality of your life and its larger context, not constrained by the events and activities constituting the "Pressure". Then let go of the ruminating thoughts or negative effects of the events. Internalizing pressure leads to "stress" and its conversion into biological, physiological, and psychological responses and their negative consequences.

If one can accomplish the above steps easily, we may all have far few cases of anxiety, depression, and ulcer, all of which require medical intervention. Even without reaching such extremes, our unhappiness, anger, grief, and a general state of letdown are all reflections of the conversion of the pressures of life into personal stress.

Engineers design pressure vessels. The high pressure inside is contained by the stress in the container walls. To keep the vessel within its stress limits, designers also include a factor of safety and relief valves in their design. The three steps proposed above – wake up, control your attention, put things in perspective – are the pressure relief valves in life and its activities. The basics of philosophy provide the knowledge of the safety factors as well as the relief valve necessary in human aspects of life.

Life is not always a negative conversion of pressure into debilitating stress. It is also a process of accomplishments, kindness, compassion, sharing, and joy. It is conversion of the pressure we face to positive experience. To see both sides is "Spirituality in Practice". SiP is the relief valve we need to go from Stress and its ill effects to stress and its positive engagement for a larger and more full-filling nature of life.

Spirituality in Practice is an ascending ladder:

1. I am not okay — Ignorance (*Thamasam*) leads to grief, depression, and lack of direction.

2. I am not okay. You are okay; I am okay, you are not OK — Attachment and bias (*Rajasam*) leading to endless chain of activities due to incessant unfulfilled needs and a constant cycle of happiness and sorrow. It is a life of looking at the glass as half empty!

3. We are OK — Knowledge and understanding (*Sathvikam*) leading to an objective outlook and the difference between possible and attainable Vs. challenges and unattainable (at least for now). This is a life of looking at the glass as half full as often as possible.

We also know of three ways of connecting my SELF (inner person) to our perceptions, feelings, and thoughts. These connectors are knowledge, bias, and ignorance. The dominant connector among these three determines our perceived pressure and internalizing that as our stress.

Spirituality in Practice requires us to evolve to a larger frame of mind (i.e.): We are ALL okay (*Sagunathvam*). No amount of reading, teaching, or learning can lead to this state of self-realization. It is the fourth step: (i.e.) Let Go.

Scriptures and philosophy teach us a fifth or final state: Everything is nature (*Nirgunathvam*); everything is okay.

Internalizing the thought that everything is nature can be the result of a detailed analytical process or a simple matter of recognizing the self-evident truth (i.e.)

- I am part of nature; so is everything else! (*Thath Thwam Asi*)

- "I" am enabled by the laws of nature (I am *Brahman – Aham Brahma),* and I exist as evidence of the laws of nature. Everything else is also enabled by laws of nature and exists as evidence of such laws of nature!

Where everything is part of nature, pressure remains as much a part of nature as well as my response to it. There is nothing to internalize. There is nothing to experience as "stress". This transition (i.e.) We are all okay leading to Everything is OK can be learned. According to scholars, Meditation is a tool for learning and practicing this state of mind. It is a relief that is readily accessible to anyone who seeks it! (See earlier essay titled *Brahmam Okate')*. Now ask yourself: Where does your stress come from? What are your relief valves? How can you help someone, anyone, to relieve their stress?

Morality Is Paper Thin

We tell children that it is not proper to lie. They behave accordingly until they grow up and learn the benefits of being truthful on their own. They share this norm with their children, which continues through generations. Nowhere can one find a precise definition of a lie or truth. It is all subjective. Yet, conditioned by their morality everyone instinctively knows the difference between truth and lies. This knowledge comes from within. No amount of writing or codification can replace this personal knowledge on matters of morality.

We cheat occasionally and bend the truth. Over a period, such occasional deviations become the accepted norm. Some pay a heavy price for the small gains of others. But all of us as a society pay the price, but life goes on. In due course, the price of untruth becomes too high. Then communities define and promulgate laws to uphold the truth. One law and its simplicity are not adequate. Hence a collection of laws evolves, along with them justice system with lawyers and judges to implement and administer the laws. Yet, there are always lingering questions of truth and untruth, and the society struggles. The nature of truth comes from within. It is the soul of the society or community. It is the moral fiber that weaves the fabric of any civilized society. Scriptures provide the following guideline:

1. Follow the moral codes of conduct (laid out in the scriptures) when you don't know what to do in a situation.

2. If you cannot do that, follow what scholars/elders have done in the past.

3. If it is not possible, look at or consult scholars/elders living in your time.

4. If none of this is working, do what you honestly and objectively think is right, and that is the truth (*Sathyam*)

Besides the truth that we are willing to stand by, we also take vows that we promise to uphold. There are vows of marriage or the promise to uphold and defend professional ethics. The vows we take multiply as our role as leaders in society increases. Under the weight of all these vows, we struggle. It seems OK to slip up occasionally on a vow here or a promise there. Eloquence and arguments come in handy to defend our position when we choose to ignore the rules or violate our vows. They reach a crescendo when a U.S. President famously said, "It is the right thing to do if the President said so"! Yet, there is an inner voice, the moral compass, that is always telling us the difference between being honest (and keeping our vows) and being dishonest (or violating our vows).

Our behavior as individuals extends to the behavior of the community, which may be local, national, or global in scope. On occasions, nations (and their leaders) lie or bend the truth just as individuals do. Nations violate their vows just as individuals do. Such deviations in the past weaken the nation's moral fiber in the present and, ultimately, its ability to make critical decisions at crucial moments in the future.

Precisely how we uphold morality always starts as an individual decision. In due course, it evolves into a mosaic that holds together the social unit – the family, community, nation, or humanity – together. Morality represents the social conscience and hence a compass that serves well for society at large. Yet, morality has no force on its own since its enforcement power comes from something invisible and intangible (i.e.) the soul or conscience of all of us as individuals as part of the society or community. It is like a sheet of paper. Only when it is whole, it serves many purposes. When it is ripped or torn, it is cast aside into a pile of waste.

It is often easy to fall behind the wisdom of the three wise monkeys: "See no evil; Speak no evil; Hear no evil". Much of the rupture and degeneration of the moral fiber starts with this seemingly moral position. Yet inaction, when action is required, is also a moral failing.

Many Facets of Silence

"Silence is Truth. Silence is Bliss. Silence is Peace. Silence is Athman or Soul. To live in this Silence is the Goal. It is Moksha or liberation. It is the end of the endless cycles of birth and death.

Sri Ramana Maharishi was an embodiment of such Silence"

I read the above in an article written by Swami Tapovan Maharaj. It is a very appropriate description of the demeanor of someone who has truly attained the state of enlightened living such as Saint Ramana Maharishi. How does one attain this state of enlightened Silence?

To remain silent is merely an activity. *Bhagavadgītā* tells us that any activity can be perceived with respect to five aspects associated with that activity:

The objective: Is the silence an expression of agreement, disagreement, or a neutral frame of mind? What is the need to remain silent?

The person involved: Are we referring to the silence of the person who is expected to say something or the silence of the person who is anticipating something to be said, or the silence of the person who says something through the silence or the silence of the person far away, who has said something but never been heard by others?

The means: Is silence achieved by willful suppression of speech? Or is it achieved by suppressing the noise (such as by closing the ears or closing the mind)? Or is it a reflection of a mind actively engaged and yet at peace like the stillness of a deep body of water?

The circumstances: Is the silence one of awe and amazement? or is it a silence of grief? Or is it a silence of respect to the event (such as in a prayer hall) or the silence of training (such as in meditation), or is it a silence of discipline (such as in an examination hall or that of an army at standstill or a concert hall in the middle of a brilliant performance)?

The laws of nature or divine influence: Is it the silence of a still rock or a piece of wood? Is it the silence of a tiger ready to pounce? Is it the silence of an object in midair? Is it the silence of an ascetic? Is it the silence of an audience mesmerized by the performer and the performance? Is it the silence of the person in wonderment, just saved from a grave incident, as if by a miracle?

Many are the facets of silence.

Bhagavadgītā also tells us that any activity has three attributes: ignorance (or inertia), turbulence, and tranquility. Let us look at these attributes by taking just take one aspect of silence: The silence of the person expected to say something. Let this person be myself. I am expected to say something, but I say nothing. I am silent.

Am I silent because I don't know anything better to say or do? Am I ignorant of the fact that I am supposed to say something and empowered to speak? Am I inertial and unwilling to use the skills of thinking, speaking, reasoning, and influencing bestowed on me? I am overcome by Inertia?

Am I silent because I am fearful of speaking? Or am I angry and unwilling to speak? Am I proud and feel that the listeners are not worthy of my words? Overwhelmed by emotions and not mindful of the opportunity lost? Am I overcome by my desires and attachments - turbulence?

Am I silent because I have thought through the various facets and to the best of my knowledge, it is preferable to be silent. Hence, I am silent for the moment, but ready to speak up at the next moment if I need to. I am not hesitant to admit that I could be ignorant of some aspects, but open enough to receive inputs in any form as they come. I wish not to be overwhelmed by such inputs, but I am willing to admit that I could be overwhelmed. Maybe I am silent and tranquil, but I am vigilant. Silence for the moment is merely a reflection of my readiness to engage as required in the next moment?

Why did my mind wander into this analysis? Why not simply pick any aspect of silence and transcend to the highest and broadest level of existence – the abode of the Lord? How can I do that?

How about if I offer respectful prayers to the Saint? Reflect on the Silence of the saint as a form of prayer. Prayer for what? Pick anything. Prayer for the betterment of myself? My family? My friends? My colleagues? My neighbors? The community? for anyone and everyone? Let this limitless and expansive reflection gradually lead to prayer for all, exclude no one. This expansive internal outlook, like a large deep ocean, transcends into a calm, peaceful silence. I can hear myself, but I am not speaking.

Let the mind continue its respectful prayers for the Saint: calm, reflective, expansive, and all-inclusive. Let there be an inner glow that unites with the peace and the silence of the saint. Dwell in this silence for a few moments or as long as one can. This silence is truth, bliss, and peace. This Silence is You, the Soul, or *Athman*.

Go ahead and start thinking of all the above while dwelling in this Silence. Conduct all aspects of life while dwelling in this Silence. Let there be this constant union with this silence among the noise and clutter of the world of activities. This union is Moksha or liberation? This may be the blessing received for our prayers to the silent saint Ramana Maharishi.

Who Sets The Standards For Your Life?

Plants live, grow, and thrive or decay by the constraints – imposed upon them by the neighboring trees! The same goes for the animal kingdom. In this respect, we are no different from any of these species of nature. We have a need to live as part of the social order within a family, within a community, as citizens of the nation, and ultimately as part of the planet earth. All these accommodations and living within the social norms and expectations must be based on reasoned choices. It is important to reflect on the standards and rules we set on our own and the rules we impose on each other.

Do we raise our children to live a life of reasoning and conscious choices, or do we subjugate them to fulfill a series of expectations set by the parents and society to meet perceived standards? Do we set the climate of reasoning and logic in family matters, or do we let the preconceived notions of right and wrong rule the day? Do we speak up and engage when it matters at the workplace, in a social setting, and at public events, or do we merely stay quiet and dismissive to avoid "making the waves"? Do we relate to each other as friends and members of the community based on a common understanding of values, or do we just live a life of "going with the flow"?

Here is an anecdote:

"As the day went on, I spoke with the doctor, and I said, "Doctor, I'm not supposed to get a shock treatment today. Permission [has] been removed by my family," John Brock recalls. "The doctor looked at me and said, 'Get up on the table.' And I do remember a slam of the electricity through my head." Some years later, Brock looked back through his psychiatric records and found that his elder sister Kay had, in fact, retracted his family's consent to shock treatments.

"How did you get out?" his daughter Glenn asks.

"In a word, I lied," Brock explains. "I started studying television programs. I would just watch people and listen to how they interacted. I knew that to the degree that someone seemed normal — to the doctors, the nurses — they were more interested in thinking of that person as someone who could leave Bryce Hospital."

Jon Brock went on to get a Master of Public Administration, and today he works as a Peer Bridger, someone who helps current and former mental health patients with their recovery.

"Watching how you have lived your life makes me think that it is possible to fight through things and to live," Glenn tells her father. "I think it sort of made me brave."

http://www.npr.org/2011/03/25/134828647/father-moves-past-a-once-unforgiving-diagnosis

We learn from the above real-life story one simple truth: There are times we are forced to live a life considered "normal", as judged by "others" and their "standards". It is this need to live up to the expectations of others that create the complexities of life. For Mr. Brock, such expectations were imposed on him. Being a mentally disabled patient, he had little choice but to undergo electric shock therapy involuntarily and unwillingly. To escape from these shackles and hardships, Mr. Brock had to imitate others and thus live a life that appeared "normal" to the people to whom such normal mattered the most – the doctors and nurses.

For most of us, the constraints imposed on us are not as severe and shocking as the episode in the life of Mr. Brock. Yet, most of us must ask the simple question: Are there constraints imposed on me, or are they self-imposed? Is there a logical fit to these constraints, or are they merely a blind following to meet someone else's opinions and judgments? Such internal reflection is part of our spiritual evolution.

The duality (right/wrong, good/bad, like/dislike, love/hate, etc.) are created by our connectors (Knowledge, bias, and ignorance). Any person, who overcomes the constraints of such dualities, lives an enlightened life and the joy associated with it. The rest struggle through life with their attachments and the emotional pains associated with them. In this process, they miss the opportunity to realize the potential for a larger purpose in life and the joy associated with it   B.G. 15.10.

Having separated from pre-determined notions of duality and constantly dwelling in the permanence of contemplation, reasoning, reflection, analysis, and the conclusion derived from it, one reaches the goal of unification with the changeless state of existence. B.G. 15.5.

Those who can function with such enlightenment (Yogi) – with total self-control and unattached active participation– are able to enjoy life to its fullest extent (described as finding the Lord within oneself). The rest, even though striving to seek perfection, happiness, or the Lord's blessing (through prayers), do not attain such enlightenment.   B.G. 15.11.

Athithi Dhevo Bhava – May The Guest Transform Into God!

Figure 5. 18. Arrangement for Puja – Hindu Prayer Service.

One of the injunctions from the *Upanishad*: *Mathru Dhevo Bhava; Pithru Dhevo Bhava; Acharya Dhevo Bhava; Aththi Dhevo Bhava* (your mother, father, teacher, and guest exist as your God). This statement is often used to teach basic moral principles. This injunction can be followed merely as being respectful to our parents, elders, teachers, and guests. This can be thought of as Karma Yoga (The practice of self-control through your duty).

At times our reflective mind asks: "Why treat the parents, teacher, and guests as God? After all, they are also human beings like the rest of us? Also, why this special place for the guests?" It is this curiosity to learn and understand that is the basis of *Jnana Yoga* (The practice of self-control through reflection, knowledge, and understanding).

Any single word like "*Bhava*" can convey several messages. Two among them are: "exist" or "remain as" and "become" or "transform into". Hence the above injunction can also be understood as "your mother, father, teacher, and guest transform into God; become aware of this transformation"!

Guest implies someone in transition! Can you see the seamless existence of the same guest in all that is past, present, and future? Then you have a clear vision of God! In other words, the abstraction of God can be visualized through the many real entities (i.e.) the parents, teacher, and guests - all representing the past, present, and future respectively.

Athithi stands for one without a specified time or appointment. While it might sound odd for someone to show up without an appointment, reflect on this from the point of view of such a visitor. Who would want to show up without an appointment? Someone in real need who genuinely believes that you can meet such need willingly and without hesitation. Someone who knows you well enough to believe that you will recognize them and hence willing to go out of the way to receive them when they show up at your doorstep, without prior discussion, reservation, and confirmation? Rare indeed are such individuals. But, to the extent you can view all your guests with such a mindset, Godliness (Divinity) permeates in your thoughts and deeds.

Can you shed all self-imposed constraints and show up at someone's doorstep unannounced? This calls for genuine faith that you will be accepted. It also calls for faith that your actions and behavior in the present are not tainted by the experience from the past and that the arms of the host will be equally open without reservations. These are not hypothetical descriptions. When an individual and all their connections are truly unattached and actively engaged in the welfare of each other, the true meaning of guest (*Athithi*) is realized. May your next gathering be a source for such reflection and fostering the spirit of *Athithi Dhevo Bhava* in everyone!

Attachments inhibit us from doing what is right for the moment. We postpone or procrastinate what we wish to do now for a future time and date. Uncertainty of possible future needs prevents us from sharing what we have today for genuine and well-identified needs. The joy and genuine internal happiness of helping others in their need is lost through such attachments and indecisions. To minimize such possibilities, we have traditions such as Puja or worship services for the chosen deity.

In every Puja, we observe nearly the same process leading up to the transformation of the guest into God (*Athithi Dhevo Bhava*). Before a guest arrives, we clean up our home and prepare the assigned space. We prepare ourselves neat, clean, and well-dressed! We also make a promise or commitment to do our best in the care and attention to every detail of the needs of the guest. The preliminaries of the Puja follow exactly these steps!

Then as the guest arrives, we offer them a seat, resources to shower and dress up. We offer gifts and share a nice meal with them. These are also the same steps prescribed in the Puja for the God(s), our special guest(s) at the Puja. On occasions like the state visit of a dignitary, we observe speeches in praise of the special guest. This is also what we observe in most Pujas, through the chanting of 108 or 1008 names of the Lord, which describe His/Her valor and accomplishments.

This is the moment where the guest transforms into God (*Athithi Dhevo Bhava*). God is an entity from which we seek protection and comfort. God is also an entity that symbolizes the best of the ideals one seeks to be. God is also the representation of anything conceivable (and beyond conception) of which each of us is a minuscular part. The Puja transcends through these levels of understanding of God, first by seeking the blessings, then seeking guidance for the best one can be, and ultimately into a state of surrender recognizing the unification of the self with the larger order. *Thath Thwam Asi* (You and the universe are integral in each other).

At this point, the true wisdom of Vedic Philosophy is realized (i.e.) Everything exists merely enabled by and as a reflection of the infinite, eternal, intangible laws of nature, visible only through their effect. This universal presence (*Brahman*) is true knowledge. *Sarvam Brahma Mayam*. Such knowledge is to be inferred and cannot be seen or transferred in any other fashion. It is the transformation. To reinforce this, the following verse from *Kathopanishad* is chanted at the end of the Puja as part of the offering of the light (*Deepa Aradhana*):

The sun does not furnish the light there, the moon, the stars, or these flashes of lightning in the cloud. How can the light of this fire illuminate thy light? The SELF (Brahman) shines, and all else shines as a result. Everything in the universe reflects but That light. Kathopanishad 5.15.

The Certainty Of Ignorance

Self-realization at its very basic level, is the exploration of our knowledge, bias, and ignorance and their interplay. All forms of education, reflection, meditation, rituals and religious practices, social rules, friendship, counseling, etc., are all means we use to focus our mind on these connectors to better understand and relate to the world around us. Each of these connectors becomes evident when the other two are diminished! The dominance of one connector over others can also be identified through self-reflection before, during, or after the events leading up to our experience.

Each connector is unique in its impact. For example, it is futile to desperately want to increase our knowledge! The more we study or learn about a subject matter, our ignorance about those subjects gradually decreases. The more we reflect and explore the alternatives and the causal relations behind that subject, without any attachment, our bias in understanding of that subject matter decreases. As our ignorance and bias decrease, in due course it leads to our better understanding of the subject matter. As a result, we are better informed or become more "Knowledgeable"! My effort is not to become an "expert", but "expertise" evolves because of declining ignorance and bias about the subject!

The more I empty the pot of its ignorance and bias it appears that the pot gets filled with knowledge. Outcome of its impact is the only way we know about knowledge and its abundance.

Bias, however, is more of a "balancing" act. I am not totally ignorant, but I am not sufficiently informed. In this situation, I have to make a choice, a trade-off. While all events are due to the course of nature, some are to my liking (and I am happy), and some are not (and I am unhappy). It is the duality (like/dislike), and my attachment to one over the other that leads to my bias.

The most fascinating is the degree of certainty when I am totally ignorant! I am reversing my car, with absolute certainty, until I bang the rear of my car against the garage door that has not been opened. The moment my car hits the door, my ignorance (that the garage door is not open) has vanished. Now, as my ignorance has vanished, I have become better informed! I am more knowledgeable!

This certainty of ignorance also has its strange consequences. It is almost impossible to argue with anyone who is ignorant of a subject matter.

Through lack of understanding, the reasoning or wisdom which leads one to conclude inappropriate activities as appropriate and everything else in reverse, such reasoning is described as out of ignorance. B.G. 18.32

One of my colleagues frequently reminded me of his father's advice: "Don't argue with a fool since there are two in the room by then"! It appears that only through facilitation and engagement leading to pertinent knowledge that certainty of ignorance be replaced. But, the certainty which covers-up ignorance creates huge barriers to our engagement of knowledge that challenges the ignorance. As an example, the more certain I believe that I am an "expert", the more ignorant I will become on that subject matter! My expertise needs to be tested constantly through engagement and willingness to learn. A person of knowledge never believes that he is an "expert" with the degree of certainty that someone else of lesser knowledge feels.

If I find myself in a situation where everyone speaks only kind words and compliments and do not wish to be critical or offer ideas or alternatives, then I feel that the certainty of ignorance may be playing havoc for my own good! By creating a climate where only compliments are welcome, we also create a situation where our ignorance grows like the mushroom (shielded away from the warm glow of reasoning, logic, and debate). Failure is not the outcome of ignorance. Unwillingness to challenge ourselves and allow others and circumstances to challenge us may indeed be a sure sign of the certainty of ignorance and the failure it leads to!

Success and popularity have their role in promoting the certainty of ignorance. This is illustrated in an ancient Sanskrit poem:

"Oh, King! It is easier to find people who will always speak nice and kind words to you. It is difficult indeed to find people who would either listen to or speak harsh but necessary words of wisdom at the appropriate time".

Above poem suggests that "the more successful, powerful and influential you are, less likely that people are going to tell you directly on matters you are ignorant about"!

Sadly, ignorance cannot diminish on one's own accord! It requires external inputs, stimuli, engagement, and experimentation. There is a tendency to avoid helping others to get over their ignorance in the pretext of being nice to each other, not to be too critical or "let me mind my own business"! These are indeed tradeoffs – the bias – we need to deal with. Sometimes one may need to be proactive, and at other times we may need to let the course of nature play it out. But consistent avoidance may reflect the certainty of our own ignorance!

Ignorance Vs. Denied Knowledge

When a tree falls in the forest, and nobody is there to hear it, does the falling tree really make any noise? Through inference, we can suppose that there would have been noise. But until we physically hear the fall or a recording of such noise, how can one be sure? One could argue legitimately there was no noise!

Consider a pothole on the road. Ignorance of the pothole can lead to serious accidents. A warning sign (knowledge) alerts the driver that prevents and avoids such accidents. But what happens when the warning sign is removed or missing? In this situation, ignorance is the result of denied knowledge.

Figure 5.19. Warning sign removed: Denied knowledge?

Before we accuse someone of ignorance, we may need to look into the knowledge that has been denied. Objectively speaking, if someone had the necessary knowledge, their choices and hence their experience will be totally different. So, if there is a desire to help someone else out of ignorance, would it be better to focus on the denied knowledge? Teaching, preaching, and mentoring are all approaches for removing ignorance. Those who strive for this lofty goal – the teachers (*Guru*) – are held in high esteem. Maybe their primary role should be to explore the denied knowledge?

Denied knowledge has many practical implications as well. You say something in a conversation. You hear a comment back. You are surprised at the response and the reaction. Ignorance would lead to an instant counter-response. But if you take a moment to reflect on the first response, you may become aware of some additional information unknown to you. Integrating this new knowledge before responding would be objective. Willful ignoring of the new knowledge would be biased or turbulent. To remain unaware of this new knowledge would be denied knowledge. It is like removing a warning sign or ignoring it?

Being "in the moment" truly implies a conscious awareness and search for the denied knowledge. It is like using a radar or sensor. It requires a personal effort to seek out new knowledge. It is also a matter of open mind, being available when an opportunity presents itself with new knowledge.

In addition to being self-awareness, denied knowledge can also be a matter of social responsibility. Denied knowledge forces the poor and underprivileged to remain that way. Bigotry and racism are part of life for many when they are not exposed to the realities of their practices and assumptions. Religion promotes rituals. But denied knowledge of the meaning behind the rituals fosters segregation and isolation into religious sects and subsets. Leadership is required to shine a light on this ignorance.

Figure 5. 20. Parrot trapped in an open cage - denied knowledge due to the conditioning of mind.

There is a story in the life of Adi Sankara, 7th Century Indian Saint and Philosopher. When he opened the cage, the parrot living in it for years would not fly away. He says,

"While there is wide open space and you have the capacity to fly away, you can not avail of it conditioned by your mind".

Denied knowledge we suffer from is the conditioning of the mind on our own and through the influence of others.

Everyone is familiar with the "elephant in the room" syndrome. Everyone in the room has partial knowledge of the "elephant". When this knowledge is integrated, objective outcome will evolve. Such an outcome will be acceptable to all those who are also objective (with their enhanced knowledge). It will not be acceptable for those with a highly biased (turbulent) mindset. But isn't it denied knowledge when nobody wants to speak up and expose their share of knowledge?

Denied knowledge permeates almost every facet of our society: at the workplace, within the family, among friends, etc. Overcoming the fear of engagement is required to break this cycle. Let us remember not to accuse anyone of ignorance. We need to merely engage in the service of eliminating their denied knowledge!

Where Is The Stop Sign When You Are Flying In The Sky?

You are driving along, and you come upon a stop sign. It is a point of decision – you turn right, left, or proceed straight forward. All of us make such decisions as part of our life journey all the time. Nobody stood still forever at a stop sign! But while you are flying in the sky, you have no choice to stop. You have to keep moving. There are also no discrete choices. You can gradually change your course, but there can be no sudden or discrete events or choices.

These are two conditions imposed on us by nature: You can stop and go at will on the land, but you must be in constant motion to travel through the sky. The bird cannot stop in midair, nor a plane in flight. Even the helicopter that hovers in the air may appear to be still for short periods of time only if its propellers keep moving!

Figure 5. 21   Birds and Planes do not have stop signs!

In a macro scale, the earth, the sun, the moon, and the planets cannot stop their constant motion. At a micro level, our heart cannot stop its function from beginning to end. The discrete points where the heart starts and stops, we call them as birth and death!

What does all this mean?

There are times in life when we feel like we are in constant motion with no end in sight. Consider the situation where one is confronted with some serious personal tragedy. These are times of flight, with no place to rest and recover. Also, consider yourself as a passenger on a long journey. For that matter, we consider life itself as a long journey with a constant stream of events, most of which are beyond our control for one reason or another. In all these situations, the rational mind, when it is genuinely objective, can find the cause and effect of all the happenings, feelings, emotions, and outcomes. Consistently rational and objective mind is a hypothetical and ideal state of mind. Our goal is to reach that state of mind. But there are times when such an ideal seems far away. In those moments, we still need to control and govern our emotional mind. It is like deciding at the stop sign. This is when faith or implicit belief in a larger force or God is helpful.

A large majority of religious writings emphasize faith to control our emotional mind. Traditions, rituals, and religious practices codify and formalize methods to promote such faith. Calm and reflective mind, in turn, becomes rational and analytical, leading to objectivity in our actions, like deciding at a stop sign. What appears to be an unrelenting grief becomes a discrete event with the next steps to follow as directed by the rational mind. But it requires a deliberate shift in our thinking from an emotional and subjective state to a rational and objective perspective. Belief in God or faith alone will not get you past that place. It requires a deliberate engagement of the mind to be reflective and the willful decision and actions that follow.

However, one cannot prescribe rational thinking to an emotional mind. It requires guidance and persuasion. It is like the work of the pilot and the flight crew to guide the passengers – who are truly helpless – while flying through turbulent weather. The godmen and those who preach religion, and the counselors who offer coping skills must keep in mind that their role is not to prescribe endless rituals and action plans. Instead, it must be a process to help those under stress slowly grow out of the relentless grip of their emotional upheaval. The end goal must be reliance on their own rational mind – the ability to discriminate between Subjectivity and Objectivity.

Arjuna: *The proper course is not at all clear to me. ..... My heart is filled with compassion; my mind is confused between the right and the wrong. I am suffering from a sense of guilt as I struggle to execute my duty. With all this anguish, I approach you. Please take me as your disciple and teach me the proper course of action.* B. G. 2. 6, 7.

Lord Krishna: *When your wisdom overcomes the confusion in your mind, you shall become objective and less under the influence of subjective feelings like grief, sorrow, anxiety, etc. Even though your intelligence is confused as it is through your worldly learning, you shall attain enlightenment or insight if you remain focused in contemplation. When one casts off all desires that enter the mind, then such a person is satisfied in all aspects within themselves. Such a person of an undeterred mind is unaffected by sorrow.* B. G. 2. 52, 53.

Despite their best efforts, the turbulent and energetic senses (impulsive forces of sense organs and their effects) of a person constantly influence their mind, as it were, by a force of compulsion. With their senses under control, their wisdom is unwavering. Having such control of your senses, remain firm in your devotion to me (i.e.) to the cause of self-control and un-attached active engagement. B.G. 2. 60, 61.

Above verses provide us meaningful guidelines, like making a decision at a stop sign, even when the life seems like a flight, with no where to rest and no stop signs to force our decision!

Success: A Matter Of Clarity Between "Needs" And "Wants"!

For many success is like trying to stomp on one's own shadow. It is like waiting for the waves to subside while sitting on the beach. It never seems accomplished. Why is this? Our wants are endless if we let them be that way. When one is clear on what the need is, one can set a goal or criteria to measure when that need is fulfilled. When you achieve that goal, you are a success! Don't look for success if you have not clarified in your mind what is your "need" to start with. Most people have a need to fulfill, to accomplish something, and prove something can be done, and they go after that relentlessly. When they do, in some cases, it shows up as lots of money. The success, in this case, is not a lot of money but a clear objective – a "need" – to be satisfied. Good health, family, friends, accomplishments in a profession, at school, good neighbors, and respect in the community; one can go on listing the needs in many dimensions in which we can perceive success if we choose to look in those directions.

"Wants", on the other hand, are different from needs. Want is like a wish list, while need is something to be accomplished here and now! Very often, we don't see success since we are confused between the want and the need. For example, consider a successful professional, recognized by their peers and colleagues, making lot of money, with a good family life. Now, the want is: Get the next higher position in the company, which has been eluding them for the past few years. Is this person a success or not?

If we are consumed by our "wants", we will never feel ourselves a success, no matter how much of our needs are already met. One who has worked hard, and for whom most of the needs have been met. could feel miserable chasing that next "want" and hence feel that "I am not a success". I am not suggesting that you should not have any goals for tomorrow. Go for it. But be clear in your mind if it is a need or a want? Need is all that is already met or must be met soon. "Want" is an elusive goal with its constantly shifting goal post. To recognize if your needs are met or not, you need to learn to "smell the roses" on hand. Take stock of what you already have. Be sure you are putting to use all that you already have wisely. Never stop smelling the roses on hand and feel good about it! Even those who feel most miserable due to lack of perceived success have their own rose to smell. Too often, we let the rose we have on hand wilt and die as we chase the one that may be merely a shadow of the rose in our own hands. Success is the feeling at heart to enjoy and cherish what we have on hand while putting the mind to work on the next unfilled need.

Why do we not cherish what we already have and feel good about it while setting our sight on the next goal? Is it the ignorance of our own true worth in a comprehensive manner – about our body, living person, and the enabling soul? This ignorance, unawareness of ourselves, also keeps us unaware of our success. Is our emotional turmoil confusing us between the "need" and the "want"? Is it our intellect and its failure that prevents us from realizing our true worth and value as reflected in our sense of inner joy and contentment?

Ignorance of own self-worth, leads a person to become unstable, unreliable, indiscriminate, unrelenting, obstinate, deceitful, malicious, lazy, dejected and a procrastinator.
BG. 18. 28.

Turbulent nature is seen as lacking in clarity between needs and wants. It is passionate, driven by the excessive desire for the results (fruits of all actions), harmful, impure, with extremes of happiness and sorrow. BG. 18. 27

Self-control leads to a free or balanced state of mind, liberation from all attachments, clarity between needs and wants. Endowed with consistency and enthusiasm, one remains steady in the face of success and failure. BG. 18. 26.

When the Spotlight Shines

One contestant is eliminated in each episode as determined by a team of judges on a reality show on TV. The last one standing is crowned as the winner! At the end of one episode, one of the judges said, "Many contestants may have all the talents to make it to the finals. But each must perform when the spotlight is on you. Otherwise, you are still in the dark and in the shadows!" The harsh reality is that those who do not perform when the spotlight is on are dismissed unceremoniously. Fortunately, real life is far kinder than these reality shows!

There is a proverb that states, "Everyone gets a few minutes of fame." That is true only when you are ready to perform when the spotlight is on. Why is it that many with lots of talents do not step up to the plate or, when they do, they are not able to perform to their full potential? This is the perennial question faced by teachers, coaches, elders, or leaders of any kind. What is it that makes one shine through when the spotlight is on and thus perform to the full potential, despite all odds? This is the question addressed effectively by everyone who is successful in anything. When the spotlight is on, one could pull all the stops and burst forth, being cheered on by others. There could be revulsion and withdrawal in rising to the occasion. Real life is a spectrum between these extremes.

Commitment, courage, and faith are essential ingredients to perform well when the spotlight is on. Spirituality in practice is helping others shine when the spotlight is on them. This could be through help to identify inherent talents, identify the moment when the spotlight is on them, and facilitate their ability to shine through at those moments! Epics are full of examples or metaphors as guidelines for this in our daily life.

In the story of Baghawath Geetha, Arjuna, the hero, finds himself in the spotlight when he faces his archenemies on the battlefield. Just as the war is about to begin, he drops his weapons and pleads with Krishna (Lord also serving as chariot driver) that he is not ready to fight and that he should be excused! This is often described as "emotional frenzy of Arjuna on the battlefield."

Another perspective of this metaphor could be that Arjuna was not a coward nor panic-stricken. Even at the precipice of a crisis, he was courageous enough to ask the question, "Why this war? Why this action? What is right? What is wrong? Why?"; he was also committed to finding the answers before proceeding further; at the same time, he also had the faith and conviction that answers to his questions do exist, and he can find them through his process of inquiry and/or that he can get those answers from someone else with the necessary wisdom (i.e., Krishna). In other words, when the spotlight was on, Arjuna was ready to perform, with courage, commitment, and faith in self-inquiry as the pre-requisites, even if his behavior would seem to suggest otherwise!

Emphasis on self-control is essential for effective performance, especially when you are under the spotlight. No one will know for sure how Arjuna truly felt in the scriptural episode. But, everyone of us can pursue reflection and analysis preceding any action, when the spot light shines on us.

Every moment of life is an opportunity to be in the spotlight. The ability to smile, say a kind word, or offer a helping hand to a total stranger are all moments when we grab the spotlight. These are also the moments when the spirituality in us shines through. Offering help at moments of distress, objective counsel, or a pleasant conversation with someone with no expectations whatsoever are all acts of spirituality when we let the spotlight shine on us.

Content and the Context

Just before the Thanksgiving holiday, one of my friends said, "During Thanksgiving, when all the family is gathered together, I want to explain what I would like to be written in my obituary."

"What a morbid thought?" flashed through my mind. Why would anyone want to talk about his obituary at a joyous occasion – the family gathering during a holiday break? Even before I could finish my thought, my friend chimed in, "The family members think that is a morbid thing to do or say at that time. What do you think?"

Thoughts, ideas, actions, and events are all the content. How the thoughts are expressed, how we go about executing the action, or how we frame the ideas are all influenced by the context. While the content may be the same, how we relate to them is a function of the context!

If the words of something said about me come from someone I respect or admire, I take the words with great value. I feel good about the words expressed. The same words are received with apprehension if they are expressed by someone I am not well disposed to or someone I am suspicious of! I would rather be left alone than be praised by someone who is not high up in my esteem. You get the idea:

Content alone is not important. It must be blended, in tune with the context, and achieve the right impact. This simple truth is missed by most of us some of the time and by some of us most of the time!

When there is a discord between the content and the context, we usually feel that as a negative experience. Whenever you are angry, upset, or disturbed, ask yourself, "Are you bothered by the content or the context in which it is delivered?" Our objectivity is always the highest when we focus more on the content and look at it independent of the context. With such objectivity, every situation is an opportunity for observation and learning. We become less influenced by context and better informed by the content. When the Content and Context are in harmony, there is a resonance, a feeling of joy and elation.

I asked my friend, "What is it that you want to be written in your obituary?" He wanted an emphasis on some principles that he lives by. He wanted everyone to benefit from those principles. Then I asked him, "What is more important to you: How did you find these principles useful and may be of use for others' benefit? Or do you merely want them to remember you by those principles?"

"Of course, I want them to benefit in their life. It really does not matter if they remember me or not!" I was perplexed. "I thought you wanted to share your obituary?" I said. "Forget about that. I will tell them what I have in mind: the principles for life and why they are important and how they will be of use to them." "That sounds like a perfect Thanksgiving Day message. Go for it." I said. Focus on the content helped him to fit the context.

Content and context co-exist all the time. The content is most often concrete and firm. The context is subject to variation with time, the people involved, and the circumstances. Reflecting on both – content and context – and their inter-relationship is an aspect of Spirituality in Practice. Next time you are elated or perplexed, step back and ask the questions: Content and context – are they both clear to me? If not, why not? Am I at odds with the content or the context? Or am I disposed favorably to both, which makes me feel happy? In some instances, the context can be changed relatively easily. In other cases, it may need a longer-term effort. In some cases, it may be a lifelong struggle! But, once you know the nature of the content and context, you become more at ease with the situation and better informed on your next step! That is also part of "self-realization."

Framework For "Good" Choices

There are so many other things we face in life, such as, should I buy a house, sell a house, continue in my current job, relocate to another place to live? We find ourselves in a situation of "no good choices" in many of these seemingly difficult matters! Reflecting on choices and how they are made is more than an academic curiosity!

In any decision-making process, we reflect, analyze the data or observations on hand, and conclude. Such conclusion, in effect is the choice we make on the subject at hand, which may lead to specific action steps. We could also decide to defer or postpone an intended action. We observe, gather data, analyze, and conclude, leading to further action or seeking more data or observations... life goes on... We could also be whimsical and make decisions only based on our biases, opinion, or desires. One could also remain stuck and procrastinate. Instinctively we know that we wish to avoid the latter two choices.

When we say, "we have no good choices," we have to acknowledge that the quality (good or bad) of our choices depends strongly on the quality of our data and analysis; this analytical process of engaging in any activity is complex indeed!

First, we can ask the question, what is the playing field, scope, or subject matter pertaining to which we are required to make the choices? Too often, we don't even know the purpose or the playing field. "You can't get there unless you know for sure where you want to go?"

Who is the person making the choices? Are you responsible for making the choices, or are you merely a means or tool in the decision-making process? The larger and more complex the problem, the clarity of who is the decision maker or the process or hierarchy of decision-making is often not so clear.

Frequently, we get worked up when we are engaged and committed in the process and tend to forget that we are merely agents, tools, or the means in the data gathering or analysis towards the decision-making process. This detached outlook on our role brings a lot of clarity on the context, role/functions of the tools at our disposal, and their effectiveness.

After all, these are understood; there is an intangible and yet permanent, eternal aspect to all our activities. No matter what we choose to do or however much we wish it would be otherwise, it is impossible to violate the laws of nature! These are the intangible and yet permanent aspects of all aspects of our life. The entire purpose of education in any field is intended to fathom the mysteries of the laws of nature in that field! There are limits to our understanding of the laws of nature in any field. When we cannot comprehend or relate to them, we find it easier to accept them as influenced by a larger power. Theologians would describe this as the "divine influence."

In any decision-making process, five components are involved as described above: The subject matter, the decision maker, tools or means, context/role or function of these tools, and the laws of nature or divine influence. A greater understanding of these five components makes a choice and alternatives more comprehensible. The choice based on such objective reasoning is neither good nor bad but merely appropriate under a given set of circumstances afforded by these five aspects for decision making.

It is stated that there are five aspects necessary for the culmination of any activity: the field of activity; the person or agent responsible for the activity; the means or tools available for such activity; the effects/context/role or functions of the tools and the laws of nature or the divine influence.

Whatever activity a person carries out, these are the five aspects or considerations behind all such activities. This being the case, anyone who believes – due to their limited reasoning – that they are solely responsible does not see the full picture.　　　*BG. 18. – 13, 14, 15, 16.*

Aspects of "Help"

Helping others is a natural part of living, though it may appear natural only for humans. A wounded animal in the herd is cared for by the rest. Plants grow in ways that sustain each other through a well-balanced eco-system. There is a poem in the literature in Tamil language that captures this spirit of help, an aspect of nature:

The water that is channeled to irrigate the rice field also feeds the green grass on its path, just as the rain showers the needy along with everyone else! — Naladiar

Who should I help? Generally, this question is answered by "I help those who can help me in return." At minimum, I wish to be acknowledged for the help I offer. Here are two poems the Tamil literature that offer different perspectives!

Those who genuinely appreciate the help received, will consider it as huge even if it is minuscular in nature.

– Thirukural.

Do not despair if your help is acknowledged or not! The water fed to the roots of the coconut tree shows up as sweet coconut water at far heights at the top of the slender and tall coconut tree. — Naladiar

Help is not as always a matter of significance to those that offer help as to those who receive and benefit from such help. Help may not always be visible in its immediate impact. On the other hand, doing the right thing for the moment, to the best of one's ability, without expectations may be the best form of help. In this case, the help is not seen as a favor to someone else. Instead, help is seen as the duty to be carried out at any moment as the situation warrants. This manner of helping others does not carry the baggage of obligation for those who receive the help, nor does it create expectations on those who "help" now and feel bitter later if their expectations are not fulfilled.

Offering help through social service and volunteering appears easier to do since the expectations – return of favor – is minimal. It requires generosity – an open heart – to help those whom we do not know or may never see or meet in person. Helping those in need in our immediate circles, like the elders in the family, disabled children, and the sick become a chore and a burden in due course. Accepting help or seeking help among friends may be avoided due to a fear of being perceived as "dependent". Good people with noble intentions often struggle with these aspects of helping each other. Much of this stress can be diminished on the helper as well as those who need help if "help" can be seen as the strict and rigorous execution of one's duty!

Carry out the course of action properly for the moment (Karma), not to their consequences or effects (results). Your motive should not be the results of your action, nor should you remain attached to avoidance of your duty B.G. 2. 47

What is "duty" and how to execute them relentlessly is an essential aspect of Spirituality in Practice! The following episode illustrates this principle vividly:

There was an unexpected complication during one of my international travels. The visa needed was not in order. A very good friend jumped in and helped me to cut through the red tape, which otherwise would have ruined much of my travel plans! I was immensely thankful to my friend for this help in need. He quietly asked me, "Do you take a shower every day?"

Much surprised at this question, I answered, "Yes."

Then he asked me, "Do you thank the soap after your shower?"

I replied, "Not really!"

My friend continued, "Then why do you thank me so much? Just as it is natural for the soap to clean you in your time of need, it is my duty to follow up as needed. My efforts might or might not have paid off. You may or may not have been helped. All I could do was my duty."

The Burden of Relationship

There was an intellectual debate: "Family, Relatives or Friends – who is the most important?" There were three teams of scholars, each arguing their case. "What else can substitute the mother's love"? argued the team adoring the family. "In good and bad times, the family is held together thanks to the care and support that comes from the relatives. It is always a kind uncle or aunt who picks up and provides loving care necessary for the success of a child under difficult circumstances" argued the team for relatives. "You are judged by the friends you keep, not your family or relatives," retorted the scholar speaking for the third team. As is usual in most of these debates, there was no clear winner. There are personal experiences in any one's life where we need to rely on family, relatives, and friends simultaneously. Invariably a crisis calls for such collective support.

Non-attachment is prescribed as the basic requirement for evolution in everyone's life.

Renouncing all activities arising out of desire or attachments is called as self-control. Renouncing the effects or outcomes of all activities is called liberation or non-attached participation. B.G. 18.2.

Family, relatives, and friends each create a pathway for attachment! This connection or attachment is essential to create a sense of identity "I". Breaking away from this platform through non-attachment is stated as the requisite for spirituality to evolve! This conundrum is what I find as the burden of a relationship. No one can escape from this burden!

Think of a child that you parent with utmost love and affection. But the child will never grow up to full potential unless you let go of the child at some point. Maturity requires the bird to fly out of its nest and soar to new heights. "I brought up this child, and now I let go of this child to grow into a man or woman to his/her full potential," would be the commitment of a parent with non-attachment.

Family and relatives provide a nurturing climate for one to grow. They provide a safety net and a sense of security. But, like the plants in a garden, each person in the family is different. Some are good, some bad depending on the time, subject, and perspective. One can never be always objective and equal to everyone unless one develops a sense of non-attachment to all relatives. Everyone belongs to the family, but no one is more important or less. Everyone plays a role like a team of ball players on the field. But every team player must be treated equally for the team to win or succeed. A person with such a viewpoint invariably evolves into the coach or leader of the family. If there is not at least one person with such a perspective of non-attachment, invariably, the family struggles with feuds, rivalries, dysfunction, and conflicts. As more members of the family evolve in their non-attachment, surprisingly, there is greater cohesion and harmony across all members of the family! In all this, one should be clear between non-attachment and selfish isolation and withdrawal for personal gains. One should also be clear between non-attachment and the objectivity that arises because of our views and actions vs. subjective opinions, preferences, and actions. This struggle between non-attachment and bondage or the desire to isolate from connections for personal/selfish reasons could make one at times fret and wish there were no family or relatives at all. This is the burden of relationships!

Finally, we come to friends. We do not have a choice on who the family members or relatives are? But friends happen through personal choice! Non-attachment with someone you have chosen to be attached with sounds absurd at first sight! Let us think about it for a moment. Your friend is engaged in an activity or behavior that is not constructive to the self. What would you do? Close a blind eye and pretend like it did not happen. Confront the friend and seek for a change?

Work with the friend until the matter is resolved with a constructive outcome. What happens if there is no change, or it takes too long and very slowly? Would you persevere or drop the friend and move on? How much would you persevere and stick with the process of change? Would it be equal or more in intent and commitment if it were a family member or relative vs. a friend? All of these are not easy questions to answer. Yet, non-attachment brings clarity and a better ability to answer these questions. In the end, through non-attachment, we find a totally new meaning for the proverb, "A friend in need is a friend indeed!" The need met may be larger than mere physical acts of kindness!

In fact, non-attachment is the common factor required in all our relationships. Through non-attachment, the differences and boundaries that exist separating people as family, relatives, and friends gradually vanish. A basket of flowers may have roses, carnations, mums, and lotus. Yet through non-attachment, we see all of them as flowers with a pageantry of colors, smell, and beauty. Next time you offer a flower bouquet to a friend or relative or when you offer a flower garland during worship, think of non-attachment! It is the beginning of spirituality in practice which gradually melts away the burden of relationships.

On Selfishness

Why should I not be selfish? Though it is provocative, it is also a genuine and honest question. Many of us think of such questions but tend to shy away from asking them or probing further for the answers. Raising such questions with comfort is an essential part of any learning process.

We tend to distance ourselves from words like "selfish" and tend to pretend that we are not selfish. Unknown to us, in some matters, one may indeed be selfish. But we look at the world around us and its response to our selfishness and blame, "Why is the world treating me this way?"

Following are a few quotes on Selfishness (with some help from a google search!):

"To be successful, you must be selfish, or else you never achieve. And once you get to your highest level, then you have to be unselfish. Stay reachable. Stay in touch. Don't isolate." — Michael Jordan

"Money doesn't change men; it merely unmasks them. If a man is naturally selfish or arrogant or greedy, the money brings that out, that's all." —- Henry Ford

"It is to be regretted that the rich and powerful too often bend the acts of government to their own selfish purposes." — Andrew Jackson

The above quotes raise several questions: Does it mean you can be ruthlessly selfish until you become great, famous, and successful like MJ? Since money exposes my selfishness, it may be better not to acquire more, at least not until I get control of my selfishness, which means never. I should expect nothing but a corrupt government, bent and shaped to the will of the rich and powerful, driven by their selfish motives. When one becomes rich and famous at any cost, and then such wealth unmasks the inherent selfishness, and in the process, also gets control of the power in the government? One shudders to think of the consequences!

Understanding "selfishness" is essential before answering the questions of why or why not to be selfish. To box or confine us by our pre-conceived limits is "selfishness". Such limits work against the laws of nature and create undesirable effects. A plant shaded by another plant from sunlight finds a way to grow in another direction to catch the sunlight necessary for its growth. That is the way nature works. That is not selfishness. In this process, both the plants grow and thrive! The outcome of nature is to let everything thrive in harmony with everything else!

People can choose. We can grow while providing space for others nearby, resulting in collective growth. This is in accordance with nature's way. Our choices counter to nature's way are self-centered and selfish!

Understanding "Selfishness" is a part of governing one's own self. It is a gradual and evolutionary process. We learn about selfishness through a set of "dos and don'ts" as a child. When you are a toddler, "what is selfish?" is determined by a set of rules given to you by your parents, teachers, nanny, other elders, etc. Rarely does a toddler challenge the parents and ask, "Why should I share my candies with my friends?" On rare occasions when such a challenge is raised, either the child is forced into submission or branded as a selfish brat! These are the rare opportunities for learning in childhood. If they are missed, later on they come out as the genuine question: Why should I not be selfish?

When one is young (K – 12 and later on as a UG student), you are taught the rules of the road – the do's and don'ts – in any number of ways. The questions of what is selfish or not, why and why not, gets taken care of through these rules learned early on! You merely do what comes naturally and appropriately under these rules! This process of self-governance is called Karma Yoga.

As we grow older, we have situations when "You can feel within yourself a discomfort, and an uncertainty, a feeling of conflict between right and wrong". The discomfort is often resolved by resorting to the "rules of the road" mentioned earlier. It also requires faith and commitment that we are all part of a larger order. Self-governance through faith is called Bhakthi Yoga. The question of "Why should I not be selfish?" does not arise for those who are at ease with the view that "Under God's eyes all are equal and deserve good and bad equally".

The true joy of life [is] being used for a purpose recognized by yourself as a mighty one ... being thoroughly worn out before you are thrown to the scrap heap ... being a force of nature instead of a feverish, selfish clod of ailments and grievances. " — Bernard Shaw

"As a Buddhist monk, my concern extends to all members of the human family and, indeed, to all sentient beings who suffer. I believe all suffering is caused by ignorance. People inflict pain on others in the selfish pursuit of their own happiness or satisfaction." — Dalai Lama

Then there are the limited few situations where the "rules of the road" or a desire to feel at ease within oneself are not adequate. There is a burning urge to learn and understand "What is selfishness? Why and why not be selfish?" At this point, the analysis becomes reflective and intense. We resort to looking at "selfishness" as an activity and its components. We recognize that every activity of any kind has three attributes associated with it: Knowledge, Ignorance, and the Bias imposed on them. This reflection is the process of self-governance (*Jnana Yoga*). This analytical process requires commitment, patience, and perseverance. It is not for one who raises the question ad-hoc or seeks casual answers.

We rely on all three avenues – *Karma Yoga, Bhakthi Yoga,* and *Jnana Yoga* – interchangeably and almost involuntarily. For one who understands all these, the entire world (and life as a whole) is merely a theater in which we participate in all the activities under these three roles (*Karma, Bhakthi, and Jnana*) through the three attributes (*Guna*). One who understands all these and practices them as a part of living transforms into an "enlightened person"! It is the essence of *Bhagavadgītā.*

Old Age And Caring For Elders

IIT – Madras is a prestigious academic institution located in the heart of Chennai, India. Such a sprawling campus built in an area that might have been a forest at one time is amazing. The suburban growth around the campus has made it a green oasis in a heavily populated urban metropolis. Much of the vegetation on this campus are tall and well-grown trees, like Neem and Banyan trees, among others. Despite the oppressive summer heat, my early morning walks on this campus have been a soul-cleansing exercise. A few sights that caught my attention while walking during my visit here and the thoughts that followed are summarized below:

Trees are like people. They grow from seeds, spring up, and develop branches. They do good in their own way when they are alive such as through their sprawling canopy offering shade, flowers, fruits, etc. With the passage of time, they lose their vitality at their roots or in the trunk and eventually die. Some trees are used even after they perish as firewood, lumber for construction, furniture, etc. So too, are the wealth and knowledge of many people used well after they are gone!

We see the signs of old age very visible in many people. I was reminded of it when I saw this pair of neem trees. See Figure 15. 23. One tree reflects years of growth and struggle. The tree continues to survive with only one large branch and another weak branch. In contrast, we see a relatively young

Figure 5. 22.   Old Neem Tree (left) Vs. Young Neem tree (right) with its luscious growth: Images of old age Vs. youth?

neem tree with its branches spreading in all directions and covering a wide area underneath. Neem trees survive solely on the strength of their trunks. They can survive harsh summers with very little water. So do many people who endure their old age largely based on their personal tenacity and strength.

Banyan is the national tree of India. It is unique in that it sprouts new roots from the branches. As it grows older and even if its trunk weakens with time, its branches are supported by a new network of roots that act like the trunk of the tree. At some point, it is difficult to recognize the original trunk among the myriad new roots supporting the tree. There are many families where such an invisible merging of the old with the new seems natural. Generally, we find such support in large traditional families. We also see such support structure among friends with shared values and coherent purpose in life. As families grow apart and nuclear families have evolved with very few children, such intrinsic support for the elders seems to be the challenge of the day.

Figure 5. 23. Banyan tree with its trunk replaced by its sprawling roots (left). Another group of Banyan trees merged into one through the supporting roots (right)

Next to it, I saw a section where banyan trees adjacent to each other have grown with their roots (growing off the branches) in a way that several trees have merged into one! I could not believe this versatility in nature. I went around several times looking into this collection of trees to see if I could isolate the trees from each other. I could not. Maybe it is nature's way of suggesting new models that can evolve where seemingly different families (trees) may find ways to support each other, and their elders collectively and not merely attempt the same constrained within their own physical and social confines. One could think of such an arrangement may be possible within families with similar backgrounds and cultures, like trees from the same species.

As I was walking along, I came across the next scene. Palm trees are distinctly different from Banyan trees. Palm trees have no branches. They grow straight up with few leaves only at the very top. Single or isolated palm trees cannot survive the forces of wind for too long. Yet, here was an old palm tree right in the middle of the thick growth of a banyan trees. It was like a person or family isolated and left alone yet protected well by the close-knit alliance with another family. Another model to care of elders in our society?

Figure 5. 24. Distinctly different species of trees co-exist!

Nature is a limitless teacher when we take the time to look around.

Big Dog; Little Dog

I was sitting in a park in the town center of Puerto Varas, Chile, on a beautiful Fall day. Puerto Varas is a small town on the shores of lake El llanquihue (pronounced Jong-Ki-Way), with the majestic Mount Osorno volcano on the other side of the lake. I have learned that there are 95 active volcanoes in the world, of which six are in this region!

Figure 5. 25. Mount Osorno, Chile.

After many days of travels in Chile with its diverse geology – from desert to lakes, from mountains to green valleys - it was time to sit quiet and take in all the experiences and reflect, an effort to live in the moment, one might say. I picked up a cup of coffee and an empanada and brought them to the park. Empanada is a typical dish from Chile, much like a turnover filled with cheese or vegetables, or meat. It can be fried or baked. After much effort, I had learned to ask for and get a vegetable empanada (empanada verdure; sin carne). It was time to sit down and enjoy my vegetable empanada along with a cup of coffee.

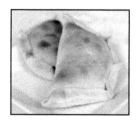

Figure 5.26. Empanada.

Empanada can be small or reasonably big. One in my hand was of the larger variety. I decided to split it and save one half to eat later. Just as I settled down to enjoy the snack, a small dog showed up looking straight at my face or, more accurately, at the food in my hand. Clearly, the little dog was eyeing for some food. There are lots of stray dogs in Chile, and no one seems to mind them. Our tour guide had mentioned something about these dogs earlier in the morning. She said she had three dogs as pets, all of which she had adopted from the street. Only one of them has a collar since that dog tends to get lost. The other two stray wherever they wish but promptly return home for food and shelter!

I offered my second half of the empanada to the little dog by carefully placing it on the ground. Now I proceeded to eat my half, thinking the little dog would proceed to eat its share.

Instead, the little dog continued to stare at me. Even my modest coaxing of the dog didn't seem to move it to eat the food in front of it.

Figure. 5. 27. Big Dog and Little Dog.

Suddenly, a rather large dog showed up. In one quick swoop, it picked up all of the food on the ground. Having realized its lost chance, the little dog tried to scrape up the floor with hardly any food left. It was really a strange feeling to see this. By now, I had eaten some of my share and threw the quarter or so left in my hand towards the smaller dog and it promptly jumped forward and picked it up before the big dog could even get a chance to get near it. In a short while, both the dogs ran away, probably looking for their next opportunity.

The big dog and the little one are no different from two people. We all vie for material objects and anything else we like. Opportunities come and go like the morsels of empanadas. Some opportunities work out, and others don't. It is but part of nature to seek out opportunities. It is also part of nature to compete for opportunities. One may even compete, unaware of others waiting for the same (like the big dog). One may not take advantage of the opportunities in front of us (like the hesitant little dog).

With all these thoughts sweeping through my mind, I finished my coffee and went to my hotel room. A little later, as I strolled out of the hotel for another walk across the park, I saw these two dogs again, this time in a playful act jumping over each other! There was no animosity or visible signs of dislike between the two! My thoughts earlier of competition between the two dogs seemed imaginary, limited only to my mind!

Maybe competition and collaboration are also parts of nature. While all of these exist – little dog, big dog, seeking opportunities, getting some, losing some — it is our mind and how it perceives one vs. another – satisfaction, disappointment, competition – that creates all the perturbations in our mind.

An enlightened person lives "Without the sense of self as the only one responsible or source of the event – ego"; "Even minded with respect to happiness and sorrow"

B.G. 12.13

Overcoming the "Drum Major Instinct"

Dr. Martin Luther King Jr. delivered many powerful sermons as pastor at the Ebenezer Baptist Church. One of these sermons was delivered on February 4, 1968. Dr. King states, "*Deep down within all of us is an instinct. It is a kind of drum major instinct – a desire to be out front, a desire to lead a parade, a desire to be first. And it is something that runs a whole gamut of life…. We all want to be important, to surpass others, to achieve distinction, to lead the parade…. this desire for attention, this desire for distinction is the major impulse, the basic drive of human life – this drum major instinc*t."

Dr. King provides in his speech many examples of the evidence of the drum major instinct in our daily life. He also points out some of the pernicious outcomes of this instinct. Following are a few excerpts:

Nobody is unhappy when they are praised, even if they know they don't deserve it. The only people unhappy about praise are when that praise is going too much toward somebody else. But everybody likes to be praised because of this drum major instinct… It often causes us to live above our means… It causes us to live our life outdoing the Joneses… There comes a time when the drum major instinct becomes destructive… if it is not harnessed, it becomes a very dangerous, pernicious instinct…. It causes one's personality distorted… It leads to snobbish exclusivism. This is the danger of social clubs and fraternities… The drum major instinct can lead to exclusivism in one's thinking. ….

Because he has some economic security, he's a little better than the person who does not have it. It leads to tragic racial prejudice.

Do you feel a sense of inner satisfaction for all that you have accomplished, or do you feel a letdown because someone has not recognized you, or do you think that you have not done better than Mr. or Mrs. Jones or someone has not satisfied your drum major instinct? Do you recognize others for their genuine role, accomplishments, and contributions, or are do you merely feed their drum major instinct? Are you willing to share your genuine thoughts and emotions, or are you merely speaking to be visible to satisfy your drum major instinct?

As we grow older, we find it impossible to tally the score between what is genuinely deserved vs. all those that are recognized. This could lead to a tendency to shy away from what is right and seek out the activities that are visible and satisfy our drum major instinct. We may fail to educate the children for learning and new knowledge. Instead, we may seek education that brings glory through certificates, awards, and recognition exclusively. We may fail to recognize failure as a steppingstone for success. Instead, we may hide our failures and highlight only what we see as success. The never-ending drum major instinct impels us to be engaged in an unending chain of activities. Pausing for a while and "smelling the rose" is given up in our rush for the next role as a drum major.

Drum major instinct arises out of ego: a self-image that promotes the "I am responsible for" attitude. *Bhagavadgītā* summarizes the role of ego – drum major instinct – in action:

Turbulence or agitated activity is rooted in excessive desires (Drum major instinct), due to our attachments with worldly needs. The tendency for these agitated activities binds a person to an endless chain of activities.   B.G. 14.7

When agitated activity prevails, a person is drawn into greed or desires of endless nature, driven by an intense need for recognition, initiation of innumerable activities, unease, and longing.   B.G. 14.12

At a time of crisis, the increased level of agitated activity leads a person to a further relentless chain of activities.   B.G. 14.15.

Virtuous acts arise from tranquility and clarity of purpose. The result of the agitated activity is sorrow. Inertia and procrastination are the fruits of ignorance. B.G. 14.16.

No one would be free of the drum major instinct. Dr. King recognizes this unenviable reality. He suggests that if drum major instinct is unavoidable, then let such instinct be focused on larger themes that uplift society.

"Yes, if you want to say that I was a drum major, say that I was drum major for justice and peace; I was drum major for righteousness. And all the other shallow things will not matter. I won't have any money to leave behind. I won't have the fine and luxurious things of life to leave behind. But I just want to leave a committed life behind."

What Can We Learn From Nature?

Upanishad: *Thath Thwam Asi* (You and the Universe are integral in each other). Since we are part of nature, everything we know is already contained in nature. When we become aware of it, we become informed or knowledgeable.

There are circumstances when our life appears to be torn apart into pieces. This may be due to a loss of a loved one. Or you are accused of something you are not remotely connected with. An ailment of serious magnitude threatens ominous outcomes. Peace and stability are challenged through floods, war, or other calamities. Progress in life does not seem to match the effort and/or skills. At times like these, I find it comforting to look around. We find remarkable evidence of resilience, survival, and growth against all odds. Following are a few examples from the plant kingdom, a random collection from my travels. They serve to reassure us that despite all adversities, there will be a different and hopefully better outcome. Such reassurance keeps our energy and motivation high to seek the higher ground, like the eternal blossoming of flowers of all shapes and colors. There are also evidences that defy our expectations. They remind us that life need not be what we define it to be in our minds. It can have myriads of diversity. It is all part of nature. The images below can be our voices from nature to seek out such alternatives. They can be the symbols for the change that we can be part of.

Figure. 5. 28.

White sands desert in New Mexico is a lonely dry place with hardly any rain. Desert grass and wild flowering plant grow in these sand dunes. They give us hope for positive outcomes in highly unexpected and adverse circumstances.

Figure. 5. 29.

Sometimes aspects of life may seem to be out of place or not in order. Maybe it is part of nature, just as these roots form a trunk of a tree or a palm tree with many branches.

Figure. 5. 30.

Trees die, but the trunk survives: Sometimes people perish, but their legacy lives on. The trunk grows sturdy, stunted by constant pruning. But small shoots find their way to grow out of their thick barks and the distorted and knotted surface: For many people, despite huge struggle and hardships, there is a ray of hope within a lifetime.

Figure. 5. 31.

Some flowers grow and thrive in water and yet remain unattached. Others survive and bloom even when there is no water to be seen nearby.

Figure. 5. 32.

Flowers come in many shapes and with many features. They come in a wide array of colors. While each flower has features and belongs to a species, we instantly recognize all of them as "flowers". Their very image conjures up thoughts of vibrant energy, growth, and harmony.

While we look at nature and its remarkable diversity, we can also ask, "What can I do to work with the forces of nature towards a benign and positive outcome? How can I help others meet their needs like a flower blooming in a barren desert? What can I do to help in a situation and for people that appear to be abnormal or disabled to become normal and empowered with their own potential and possibilities?" All of these are pathways for Spirituality in Practice.

What I Learned During A Nature Walk!

I had an opportunity for a peaceful walk on a bright sunny morning. As my walk continued, I arrived at a winding river with lush greenery everywhere. I continued my stroll along the banks of the river. With each passing scene, my mind raced through thoughts that linked life events as parallels to nature's images.

The river flow seemed still, and the surroundings serene. Most of the time, life seems still and serene; everything in its place, well balanced. Yet, there is a change only moments later. Neither the flow of the river nor the journey of life ever stops or remains still.

Figure. 5. 33.

The calm flow of the river was interrupted by a sudden change in the terrain. There was a man-made dam to channel the water flow. The dam across the river covered only part of the flow. The rest had an uninterrupted flow down the ledge and, along with that, the turbulence it created. The stark contrast between the still flow of the river earlier and its turbulence only moments later was so visual. It was right in front of your eyes as if nature was telling us something.

Figure. 5. 34.

Life that seems to be in a steady flow gets jolted occasionally. There are turbulences and perturbations created by manmade choices – sometimes self-initiated and other times imposed on us like the dam across the river. We are challenged. Just like the flow of the river over the dam, these moments also shall pass. But to gain that confidence requires us to remember that events in life are also events of nature. *Thath Thwam Asi* – You and the universe are integral in each other.

The water caught at the corner of the ledge sees the most turbulence. There is no difference between the water droplets in the middle of the river and that in the corner of the ledge. They just happen to be there.

Figure. 5. 35.

Many times, in life, we can reflect and analyze why certain situations are the way they are. But it may be equally important to accept the reality as it is and do the right thing to move along, just as the river flows as a coherent stream or turbulent white water as the situation warrants. The flow of water continues, and so does the journey of life.

The calm flow of water and the severe turbulent white waters are less common than a river that combines both. More frequently, life seems to be a blend of smooth flow and challenges to be faced. The stillness of a totally calm river is experienced only by a few and for short periods of time.

Figure. 5. 36.

When the stone and rocks are far below, the river flow seems to be smooth and calm. When the impediments are small and well below the surface, life's journey seems smooth and well-balanced.

I turned back. As my walk ended, I came to the place where I had started. A flock of Geese were merrily swimming in the still water. Were they aware of the steep fall ahead, or were they merely happy to stay in the body of water that was nearly still and peaceful?

Figure. 5. 37.

The geese, the water, the ledge, the rocks, the turbulence, and the greenery, the many things we do in life, and the journey of life are all parts of nature.

Thath Thwam Asi – You and the universe are integral to each other.

Adversity and Faith In Nature

To be fortunate can be defined as the outcome that beats the odds. The fact that our body functions well, despite the myriad of parts and complexity of their functions, is to be truly a matter of awe. The number of possible reasons for which anything going wrong is larger than the limited set of conditions under which everything can go right. This is the good fortune bestowed on us. It is truly a miracle of nature. Our body must operate within a narrow window of temperature. The heart and its complex functions, the lung, muscles, nerves, skeleton, and brain... all must function ceaselessly within a narrow set of limits. Yet, everything works in harmony, like a complex and well-oiled machine, and we generally have a good life!

Despite these great fortunate circumstances, we are occasionally destabilized. Maybe the body parts do not function the way they are supposed to. Maybe emotional comfort and stability is challenged. Our knowledge and wisdom are shaken up due to events and information unknown to us. We may never know certain information and hence ponder about them lifelong. For most of us, these are not enduring circumstances compared to a lifetime. Many of these are short-duration events. Yet these experiences dominate our thinking and challenge our faith in our good fortune. These thoughts steer us away from the reality of how much we are better off than being worse off!

The other day as I was walking along the street in my neighborhood, out of nowhere, I saw this limb growing on a large tree. The limb was a fresh shoot, but it was growing squarely on a large flat surface created where a rather large tree limb had been neatly sawn away. To be sure that I absorbed the full impact of what I had seen, I took a second look, much closer than before (Figure 15. 38).

Figure 5. 38. Resilience of nature

This resilience of nature is truly marvelous. Evidence of this resilience and tenacity in this fresh growth in the tree truly surprised me. I became aware of the needless worry we go through when we face adversity. If I am part of nature and if nature is so resilient, what is there for me to worry about? The laws of nature are eternal. A broken limb, a lost cause, a financial setback, an indignity from unexpected quarters –

aren't they all like the huge branch sawn off the old tree? Just as a new shoot grows off a trunk where a huge branch had been slashed off it, nature will find a way to rejuvenate itself. The outcome may take time. In the beginning, the outcome may be small and insignificant, but nature will find a way. I may be unaware or ignorant of the laws of nature at work. Instead of getting affected and agitated by the events or happenings, I need to keep my commitment and faith in the laws of nature, explore them as they unfold, and foster the right climate for these laws to take root.

When I move away from that conviction that I am truly part of nature and fall into a false sense of belief – that I am something other than nature – then all the worries and concerns that shroud my thinking take hold. It is in those moments one needs to shake the traps of disbelief and return to the unrelenting faith that we are all part of nature. Perhaps this is the meaning of the following verses?

The Lord (laws of nature) dwells in the heart of all things and all beings. Through the power or influence of the Lord, all beings participate in their life and activities like the components of a large complex machine. B.G. 18.61

It is by Surrendering unto Him (through total and unrelenting acceptance of the role of the laws of nature) and through His grace (through the play of the laws of nature, which are eternal and omnipresent) one transcends to a place of eternal peace. B.G.18.62.

When Does One Become An Adult – Aging Vs. Maturing?

I heard the following from someone in their mid-fifties: *"In effect I changed, I transformed, and I had become an adult. Things that mattered a lot, things which seemed very important and personal and significant, no longer seemed to be that big a deal anymore"*!

What does being an adult really mean? When does one become truly an adult? Do we ever become adults in the true sense of the word? Does it need a life-changing experience to become an adult? What happens to those whose life is smooth sailing, without any serious or consequential experiences?

Each of us can relate to our childhood. These are the tender young ages when one is cared for. All the needs are attended to if one is lucky to have the right situation and circumstances. The child can get what it wants since there is someone with the means to provide them. There is the comfort pillow, the teddy bear or the favorite blanket, or the toy that one can hug. With such simple comforts and in the protective custody of the caregiver, life looks complete, secure, and comfortable. But what happens to those children who are not in such a fortunate set of circumstances? They learn to cope with limited options, choices, and comforts.

They learn to make tradeoffs between what they need and what they can get. They learn to make choices between what is legitimately available to them and what they can aspire for. They learn to set goals, persevere, and accomplish their goals. Their needs and adversities help them to build their character. In this sense, do these children become adults at an earlier age?

In due course, it appears that everyone must face the same music! Very few – certainly not many – can continue to enjoy the benefits and comforts provided for them by others. Each is required to put in their due efforts to earn that. Once again, the lessons of life would appear to be to make the tradeoffs, set goals, persevere, and ultimately find inner comfort with what one can accomplish and what one can acquire. At some point, success is measured by getting what we want, while happiness appears to be wanting what we get. Becoming an adult could have much more to do with developing a sense of inner equilibrium in a world of limited options. This inner comfort reflects in our sense of who we are, our relationship with others, and our respect for the value system in many aspects of the world we live in. Becoming an adult would appear to have little to do with age but more to do with the diversity of experiences. It seems to have more to do with the many intangibles, which reflects in our ability to cope with diversities – diverse situations, economic conditions, cultures, and people...

What happens if someone grows up in privileged economic conditions, a stable social climate, and limited exposure to a diversity of any kind? Perhaps in such circumstances – for the fortunate few (very few?) – perspective on who we are and what matters the most in life may be shaped by sudden and unexpected deviation from such a stable climate. In such cases, life-altering experiences appear to be the catalyst for the transition to "becoming an adult". Does it imply that there could be a few, who may grow to their ripe old age, but never become "adults"?

Implicitly we assume aging, being an adult, and maturity as interchangeable. Is that true? Once I received a birthday card that read, *"Aging is inevitable; Maturing is optional"*. The card is priceless, just as the close relationships and the warmth and joy they add to life! It was a well-chosen card and set me thinking about aging and maturing. I have also received another birthday message that reads, "Wishing you the very best as you journey around the sun once more in the coming year"! How true it is! All of us are objects of nature. As part and parcel of planet earth, we continue our journey around the sun precisely once a year! It is this journey around the sun that we identify as "aging"! In this respect, all of us and everything we know age with time. It is natural! There is no choice in that. It is inevitable.

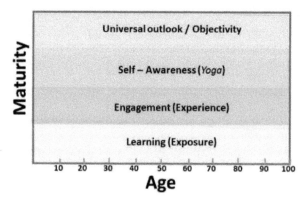

Figure 5. 39. Aging Vs, Maturing

What is maturing? Is it optional? Why? That depends on the meaning and our understanding of the term: maturing.

Maturing occurs in four layers, irrespective of our age. (Figure 5. 39). Reflective management of the mind – maturing – can occur at any age, at any time, and with respect to any event or situation. Maturing indeed is a choice while we age and grow old inevitably!

A fruit-bearing plant grows from its seed. It is considered "mature" when it yields a good crop of fruits rewarding the farmer worthy of his efforts. Hence in some regard, "maturity" is a matter of benefits derived or delivered as a natural course of events. But it is also a matter of perspective or judgment. Excessive use of pesticides and chemicals, which are ecologically unfriendly for society at large, may be seen as immature practices of a farmer, even with the high yielding "mature tree". The fruit-bearing trees that grow in the wild are not seen as "mature" even if they bear lots of fruits. They will be described merely as "old growth". This human-centered view may contrast with the joy and satisfaction of all the animals in the wild nourished by the fruits of the mature wild tree. To be recognized as "mature", both the provider and the beneficiaries must be visible and compatible. In Bhaja Govindam Verse 5, Adi Sankara warns us on this subjective view of "maturity":

As long as you are seen as a productive member of the family, you are wanted and welcomed. When you become merely old and unable to contribute, no one wants to speak even a word with you!

"Maturity" need not be limited to material things (like the trees yielding fruits in our analogy). We are endowed with our body, mind, and intellect. Maturity can be witnessed through our actions, emotions/feelings, as well as through our thoughts and ideas. In every case seeking the outcomes of the larger common good is a measure of maturity. Maturity can span a wide range of means (physical, emotional, and/or intellectual), outcomes as well as beneficiaries. Maturity can also be seen as the ability to deploy our mind through our thoughts to control our emotions or feelings while recognizing their interconnected nature. This kind of maturity can evolve with age (and hence time), but it can also come at any age from our objective outlook gained through self-control. One can be mature and useful even at a very young age through our mind and its control towards empathy and wisdom of value to others.

As part of nature, we exist in five parallel layers: Material objects, living objects, individuals with emotions, the ability for rational or objective analysis, and one with enlightened or universal perspective. We see guidance in the scriptures on the role of our mind and its control. This is understood as a measure of maturity:

Katha Upanishad: *The notions of age, death, and birth are determined by the state of mind.*

Buddha: *Learn to control your mind. Everything you experience is determined by the conditioning of your mind!*

Adi Sankara: *Learn to focus your mind on the enlightened view of the Universe (i.e.) everything is enabled by the same laws of nature, described in totality as Brahman.*

How Old Are You?

It is in the most unexpected moments you get the lessons on the true nature of life, its beauty, and joy. Such an experience occurred one evening. "Do you think it might rain soon?" asked the person I had just passed as I walked along the sidewalk. The sky was partly overcast.

"I don't think so," I replied. "Where are you coming from"? I asked, continuing our conversation.

"I have been to the nearby farmer's market," came the reply. This frail-looking woman with an arched back could have been in her late eighties. She was sporting a backpack on her shoulders.

"How far along do you have to go?" I asked.

"Not very far," she replied and then explained to me her plan to walk nearly a mile further in the neighborhood, part of the road along a steep hill.

"Do you need a ride?" I asked.

"Oh! No," replied the woman, "I am on my walk, and I will do just fine!"

I was about to ask her, "How old are you?" Before I could ask, she added, "Usually, I ride my bike. Today, I just decided to walk!" I could not believe my ears. Her energy and enthusiasm were that of a much younger person. I felt it was not appropriate to find out how old she was or even think along those lines. Her age really did not matter. Her spirit and enthusiasm for life are far younger than her looks would suggest.

No sooner than I parted company with this youthful soul, I saw a family of Canadian Geese in the nearby yard. It was just another group of birds resting while on their long journey southwards. It was not the case with my young at heart acquaintance. She was visibly excited at the sight of these birds and engaged in a cheerful conversation with them for a few seconds before she continued her walk. I truly witnessed a lesson on being in union with nature. For someone in that spirit, youth is eternal!

How Large Is Your Family?

With whom do you have the most comfort with?

For a child, it would be with the mother. There is a special bond between the mother and the child. The child may kick, scream, and throw temper tantrums. Yet, mother is patient and persuasive in working with her child and molding him into a better person. Then there is that unconditional smile from the child in the most unexpected moment that melts the mother's heart.

We are very comfortable with parents, siblings, relatives, spouses, a community of friends, etc. Of course, in this age of social media, our comfort level seems to expand with many strangers hardly known in person or in physical proximity. We feel profoundly close and familiar with them and share much of our personal details! The more you are at ease with someone, the easier it is to speak and communicate with them. Is that what a family is all about?

Is that what happens in real life? As our expectations, our fear of antagonizing someone close to us, or the fear of losing the relationship increases, our freedom to be comfortable with each other diminishes with time! Fortunately, this downward spiral does not extend to the mother and the child. But, as the child grows into youth and young adult, the comfort of being free with each other diminishes. There is a fear of "offending" each other more than the freedom to engage each other. We see this in family circles. At times, there is a greater sense of freedom to be candid with friends more than with the relatives. Opinions are expressed and argued more readily with strangers and outsiders than within the "family" members. We see this in the workplace as well. There is a preference to "put up and shut up" rather than "rock the boat". It is easier to bring an outsider – the consultant – to air the laundry rather than a willingness to bring them out internally for discussion and resolution.

As the freedom and comfort with each other grows with time, there is a sense of liberation and a greater level of in the relationship. The purpose of a relationship is not superficial but a deep sense of commitment to a shared common cause. Great public speakers connect with larger audiences primarily because of the shared commitment to the cause or causes between the speaker and the audience.

Why does a relationship that starts with no constraints, fears, and apprehensions – like that between the mother and the child or between two perfect strangers – become constrained and limited over time? Is it due to a fear of losing what we already have? It is often said that only when we are afraid of losing something of value that fear sets in and imposes constraints on our freedom of thought, freedom in our expressions, and our willingness to take risks and speak our minds. The deep roots of a good relationship – like that among family members or friends – become subverted in our false attempt to preserve and "protect" the superficial or surface-level connections. Like a river set in motion, relationships take their own course. To cultivate a "family" with meaningful relationships requires sustained effort. It is like the constant effort required to channel the flow and harness the energy of the river.

Perhaps it is wrong to ask the question, "How large is your family?" Instead, it may be better to ask, "How well do you know your 'family' and what are you doing to nurture it to grow larger and stronger?" When the deep roots of interconnectedness grow with time, the family gets larger as a full-grown tree.

How Many Do You Touch In Your Life: One, Fifty Thousand, Or Half A Million?

Mr. Keith Lockhart, the conductor of the famed Boston Symphony Orchestra, was once asked: "How do you stay focused and not get distracted by someone in the audience?" Mr. Lockhart replied: "You have to keep your purpose in mind. You are not playing the concert only for the lone person with the strange hat, but you are playing for the whole audience."

Then he was asked, "How do you play for the half a million people in the audience?" He replied, "Whether you play for fifty thousand or half a million, it is all the same. You cannot see much farther than fifty thousand people in the audience!"

The above seems to be an appropriate summary of the larger principle on how to conduct one's life! Almost all of us live to please someone else. The pleasure may come from direct feedback, such as the clapping of the audience as an expression of their appreciation of the fine music. The pleasure may also come from the indirect but instinctive understanding that the music is being listened to, enjoyed, and thus appreciated. The direct as well as the more subtle and nuanced recognition happens not only for music but in every facet of life.

How does one conduct the activities of life? Clearly, it is a performance to please a certain audience. It may be to please the children, parents, siblings, spouse, or someone near and dear. These are like the lone individual with the funny hat! They are easily identifiable and can be recognized readily as the audience in our theater of life. But we need to keep in mind the larger purpose in life, to serve the needs of a larger community. Of course, the person with the strange hat is also part of that larger audience.

There is a subtle difference between playing music and the conduct of life. In playing music, the rules are clear. The man with the strange hat has the same understanding of the rules of music as does every other person in the audience. But, in life, such rules and understanding may not be clear. Hence clarifying such rules are the essential first step to creating good music in the theater of life. Let us also keep in mind that no one becomes a maestro simply by a mere wish. It takes years of hard work and practice. Spirituality in Practice is a worthy process to refine such rules of music in life.

How large a community should we serve? What should be our goal or target? As Mr. Lockhart points out, after some size, it does not really matter. As we move away from the person with the strange hat to a larger audience, the emphasis shifts from specific tasks to meet larger goals and principles. For a poet, alphabets and words do have their place, but the emphasis shifts to larger themes, ideas, and emotions. For scientists, specifics of experiments are critical, but they take their due place and become part of an orderly arrangement in the thoughts, reasoning, and understanding of the phenomena of nature. For the conductor, the music transforms from words and poems and their collection to a seamless experience that binds everyone together. In this transformative process, the size of the audience or the size of the community we serve, after some modest size, does not really seem to matter. Each of us has the capacity to touch the lives of many and a few more, just like the maestro is recognized by the larger audiences he performs to.

Bishma Complex

Figure 5. 40. Bishma in his death bed of arrows after a very
long life that spanned many generations!

Epics are stories that convey the life and history of a time
in the past. They are described as "*Ithihasa*" meaning the
way it was. Ramayana and Mahabharata are two well-known
epics from Hindu literature.

The story of Ramayana is used to tell the way Rama
conducted his life from childhood till he ascended the throne
as a king with strict adherence to the discrimination between
right and wrong. While no one can be perfect, including
Rama (considered as the human incarnation of the Lord), the
story of Ramayana describes the challenges faced by anyone
as he/she searches for right vs. wrong in every step of life.

Mahabharata is a much more elaborate story with many
more characters, their strengths, and weaknesses. It reflects

the complex canopy we call "life" which includes the self, family, friends, community, and society at large. The central theme of Mahabharata is *Bhagavadgītā* – the conversation between the warrior Arjuna and his friend (who doubles as the charioteer) Krishna, considered as another human incarnation of the Lord. The conversation in the middle of the battlefield is metaphoric to the reflection on life and the battles to be faced by every one of us. The reflective and conscientious Arjuna wonders "if he should fight and why?" with the potential for a huge calamity and loss of life to follow, even though, as a warrior, it is his duty to follow orders and fight as required. Krishna uses this conversation to explain to Arjuna (and by inference each of us) answers to several questions such as: Who is "I"? What is "duty"?, What is "life"?, What is "Objectivity?", How a life of subjective experiences leads to all our perturbations? How it can be transformed into a life of objective tranquility? What is spirituality? etc. The essays in this book cover many of these questions and their answers from Vedic Philosophy.

Both these epics – Ramayana and Mahabharata – also provide an array of characters whose behavior, choices, and way of life can be analyzed. They are very rich sources of learning. One key character in Mahabharata is Bishma. His role is writ large in every aspect of this complex story.

Bishma displayed many virtues throughout his life: At a very young age, he took a vow to never become a king so that his father could have another child who could become the king. He also took a vow never to marry so that there would be no threat to the kingdom from his own children, thus preserving the valor of his earlier oath. For this noble act, he was rewarded with a long life that would not end even as many generations passed by. In a sense, this boon of long life ended up as a curse as well! His long life forced him to perform many acts considered as "duty" in a narrow sense. He participated in aggression to gain brides for his half-brother so that his dynasty could continue. In the process, he destroyed the tender love of a young woman without being aware of it. He stood by many evil acts of his clan, who were now ruling the kingdom, even though he felt they were wrong as well as incompetent to serve as rulers. Yet, he assumed the power as the general to lead his clan into a war, even though his heart was not for it and his clan was mostly unscrupulous and conniving at best. Finally, on his death bed, lying on a bed of arrows, he recites the thousand names in the glory of the Lord, which is recited in prayer even today by devout Hindus.

When blessed with long life, it also brings with it challenges and complexities that need to be addressed objectively. Response to events largely based on subjective preferences dominated by attachment and bias (*Rajasam*) and unaware of this implicit bias (ignorance or *Thamasam*) can lead to untold disruptions and tumult. Such behavior of the family elder brings harm not only for the elder but for the entire family (as illustrated in Mahabharata). We refer to this behavior by elders in the family and the impact it has as "Bishma Complex".

All our actions from childhood to old age will have good and bad aspects attached to them. Others look up to the elders in the family, community, or society for guidance. Behavior and decisions of family elders could be conditioned by lessons learned, tempered with judgment and reasoning that reflect objectivity? Or they could be driven by attachments and personal pet peeves, which lead to more anxiety and upheaval, as was the case in most of Bishma's life? Blind loyalty to traditional values (e.g., family, religion, nationalism, etc.) could dominate the larger common good (across families, religions, and nations)? These are not hypothetical questions.

In the past few decades, economic prosperity has spread through globalization. As a result, there are many families that have grown out of poverty into better education, employment, immigration, and migration leading to more favorable circumstances. As economic standards and affluence improve, the elders who pushed the boundaries for better economic growth in their youth may need to find new dimensions and challenges to pursue for their younger generations. At some point, one needs to realize that money and power is not everything. Having struggled with these for many years, transitioning to broader themes of love, kindness, and affection for all may not be easy. The politics of climate change, religious intolerance, and leaning towards the extreme right or left are all indications of blind loyalty. They may also be evidence that the older generation as a voting block insist on their blind allegiance to a narrow set of values and personal interests. In this regard, the Bishma Complex may be more real and present today than a fictional interpretation from an ancient epic.

The best effort of every person sets the standard for those who follow him/her. B.G. 3. 21.

Old age and the opportunities it provides, if they are not used wisely, can lead to harm and hardship over generations. On the other hand, practiced with objectivity and wisdom, old age creates unique opportunities for leadership, leading to peace and harmony over generations. The balancing act between these two alternatives may be described as "Bishma Complex"?

Family

"Why do we have such large temples and churches and mosques?" a stranger asked. *"To see the limits of us as individuals in our size" came the answer.*

"Why do we have such a large body of literature and scriptures?" a stranger asked. *"To recognize the limits of what we know" came the answer.*

"Why do we have such high mountains and deep oceans?" a stranger asked. *"To visualize the grandeur of nature" came the answer.*

"Why do we have such divisions like nations, communities, and religions?" a stranger asked. *"To accommodate our limits in size, our limits to know, and limits in our ability to see the grandeur of nature" came the answer.*

"I am small, limited in my knowledge and vision, and limited in my ability to see the grandeur of the large temples, the larger themes of the scriptures, and the largeness of nature," said the stranger. *"Yes, you are. That is why you are the individual with your specific name, size, age, background, and all other limitations. Your details are known to a few, and they know you well. They are your family," came the answer.*

"No, I am more than that. I know many friends outside of my family; I am part of a larger community. I have traveled farther, learned better, and can see issues connecting across nations and religions," said the stranger. *"Yes, you are. That is why you are part of a family that is larger than your father, mother, and siblings. You are part of a larger family known to you, and you alone,"* came the answer.

"How do I define my family?" asked the stranger. *"You define the family the way you choose to define it,"* came the answer.

"My family could be as small as I choose or as large as I wish?" asked the stranger. *"Yes,"* came the answer.

"What connects a family – a desire and commitment to love and allow to be loved?" asked the stranger. *"Yes,"* came the answer.

"What is love – a bondage for the shared common good?" asked the stranger. *"Yes,"* came the answer.

"Larger the reach of my love, the larger my commitment for the shared common good, larger is my family?" asked the stranger. *"Yes,"* came the answer.

"My family, its size – depends on my understanding of what is love, how to extend my love farther and let others who are far away love me?" asked the stranger. *"Yes," came the answer.*

"You have expanded my mind greatly. You have liberated me from the shackles of my limitations. You have enabled me to become limitless and large. I can see the whole universe as my family. Please confirm to me. Am I correct?" asked the stranger. *"Yes," came the answer.*

"Thank you. Thank you very much. My joy is limitless. I am eternally grateful to you. By the way, who are you?" asked the stranger.

"I am your reasoning, your knowledge, your teachings in the scriptures, your God in your temple, your father, your mother, your siblings and friends, and everything that has enabled you to be who you are. I am the limitless "You" in you, your family at large," came the answer.

What Should You Do, When You See A Turtle On The Sidewalk?

There is a medium-sized pond near our house. In the middle of the overgrown and thickly populated developments, the pond is protected by a nice trail for a nature walk. A small section of the pond abuts the main road. The sidewalk protects the pond and its natural settings for this small section. As I hurried along for a brisk walk along the sidewalk, my eyes caught the sign of an unusually large object, like a large stone. The closer I got to it, I saw a live turtle with its head projecting up, with its eyes fully open, and its tail wagging! After a quick glimpse, I walked past this live turtle. But slowly, my mind started churning, and the question kept coming back to my mind: What should you do when you see a turtle on the sidewalk?

I might have walked about fifty yards past the spot where I had spotted the turtle. This is not something usual. I have walked along this sidewalk scores of times. Never had I seen any turtle, let alone one of this size. Was it really a turtle? Was it really a live turtle? I had to be sure. I turned back and walked up to the spot. Yes, it was indeed a live turtle! It must have strayed past its normal habitat. It was close to the road, with substantial traffic during the day, even though the road was relatively quiet, with no one in sight at that moment. Now that I am convinced that my eyes were not fooling me, the question returned to mind: What should you do when you see a turtle on the sidewalk?

Not much. It is all part of nature. After this conclusion, I turned back and resumed my normal walk. But my mind kept churning. Clearly, the turtle is out-of-place. It does not belong here. When you are in a place where you do not belong, it may be by chance; it may be for reasons or circumstances beyond your control, or it may be a deliberate and will full choice. Do we know why we are at a given place at a given time? Our understanding of the anatomy of our experience comes in very handy to get a better handle on why we are at a given place at a given moment.

It appears that the lonely turtle, reasonably well-grown and hence belonging to this area, has somehow strayed off its course. Its continued presence on the sidewalk may be OK, but further straying into the road could be harmful. What should you do when you see a turtle on the sidewalk? My logic and reasoning suggested that I should coax this turtle into safety by guiding it into the nearby marshland and into the water in the pond. Despite such reasoning, I decided to turn back and continue my walk. One can always explain why we do certain things after the fact. But self-control is the ability to explain your decision before you take it. At this moment, I had acted as if by impulse rather than by choice.

Whenever your action is not based on reasoned choice, you can always feel the call of your inner voice. My mind was not at ease. I kept looking back to see if any other early morning walker would see or stumble on the turtle. I kept looking for someone in front whom I could caution and urge into action. But none could be seen in either direction. My thoughts turned to the many disabled and homeless, who find themselves on the sidewalk because they are lost or have strayed away. I have passed by so many, just as I have strolled past this turtle on the sidewalk. Maybe I should pay more attention to such situations in the future. I was also reminded of the situations where I had stood up when it mattered to those who felt like they were out of place. I also remembered the situations where others have stood by me to be sure that I did not feel out of place. The mind is a powerful instrument. It can gather so many thoughts and process them so quickly! But today, I had not followed the course of action required for that moment!

But who decides where anyone or anything belongs? I have never seen any turtles in this area. Is this a turtle that has strayed far away from its home? Even though I have walked around the pond many times, I decided to walk the trail one more time today. This will give me a chance to loop around and get back to the turtle and send it to safety. As I strolled along, I picked up a stick fallen off from an oak tree. I trimmed it for a length of about four feet, long enough to be used as a tool in case I needed one to push the turtle away into its safety. As my walk continued, I saw a couple walking their two pet dogs. The stick in my hand was not a welcome sight for these dogs! Now I was the person in a place where I did not belong, at least according to these dogs!

"Have you seen the turtle on the sidewalk?" I asked the couple, attempting to explain the reason for my carrying the stick. The man replied, "I have not seen it. But I have seen many turtles in this walking trail", with a hand gesture that suggested the size of the turtles, much larger than the one I had seen earlier! "What?" I asked myself since I had never seen a single turtle in this area until today. Maybe the turtle I saw is very much native to this pond and its shores?

I quickly rushed to the spot after walking around the pond in full circle. It must have been about thirty minutes since I first sighted the turtle. Much to my amazement, I did not see the turtle there anymore. I looked cautiously on the road for any signs of roadkill, but none was seen. It was clear that the turtle must have continued its stroll and, hopefully, for its safety as well. I felt relieved. I went home.

We are all part of nature. Opportunities present themselves to do the right thing. If we act promptly, we avail ourselves of such opportunities. But nature is not relying on anyone to engage in its course. Nature merely exists. Engagement in any action, especially appropriate action, as called upon by the moment, is purely a matter of choice.

No one but me had seen this turtle at this place during these morning hours. It will be my experience, known only to me! Hence the relief experienced with the belief that the turtle has moved to a safer place pertains to me and no one else! I was also beginning to doubt myself. Did I really see that live turtle on the sidewalk? All our experiences are real when they occur. Before or after, they are all a matter of perception!

No One Stood Still Forever
At The Stop Sign!

Have you ever felt like, "It looks like there is no end in sight for this"? If you did, you would not be alone. All of us face this feeling of uncertainty, the feeling that the situation we are in has no end in sight. That is when I would urge you to look around. Have you ever seen anyone who stood still forever at the stop sign? There is always a movement, a change.

It is a fascinating pastime to watch the people near the stop sign. Most often, there is a certain hesitation at the beginning, an uncertainty. But in short order, there is a determination, a will to find a way. This may result in following the rules with a clear and safe opportunity to cross the road. It may be a case of taking a risk to cross the road, despite heavy traffic. There may be a decision to abandon crossing the road at this point and move further along the road until a safer or alternate option is identified. But no one stands still forever at the stop sign!

Every time I step on the treadmill at the gym. I get this feeling, "Oh, my God, I need to go through this for the next thirty minutes." But, as each minute passes by, it is that much less to the endpoint, the finish line. The more you persevere, with a clear end in sight, you no longer feel like you are standing still forever. All that matters is to take the first step. There is a Chinese proverb that states, "The journey for thousand miles starts with a single step."

The feeling of "standing still forever" also has something to do with how much our mind is engaged in something that is appealing to us. There is as much a need to keep the mind engaged as it is to keep the body engaged to avoid the feeling of standing still forever. You are on a long flight. May be a fourteen-hour flight from Chicago to Tokyo. Initially, there is a lot of excitement. Then, after a few hours, you hit this mental roadblock if you are not busy doing something. If you had a rush job to do and you are plugging away in your computer, it looks like the time passes rather quickly. Or else, you are tired and able to sleep through the flight; again, there is no feeling of standing still forever. I am not one for watching movies on the flight, except on those rare occasions when I cannot do absolutely anything else. The occasional interruptions for meals and snacks in these long flights, I am sure, are also set up to get you through this need to do something to keep your mind engaged. Otherwise, you feel like there is no end in sight!

You are at the end of the flight, waiting to be picked up at the airport. You are looking for your car, maybe the ride from someone close to you, or may be the taxi or limo booked ahead of time. When you do this all the time, it is almost a routine. There is no emotional engagement in it. A few minutes, one way or another does not seem to matter.

The feeling that "one stands still forever" is an experience, just as any other experience we come across in our life. It is a matter of perception through our body (physical activity), mind (emotional engagement), and intellect (that engages our brain to do something). Just like any other experience, this feeling is also discreet, even though it appears to be eternal, during the moments when we go through the experience. In all those times where nothing seems to move or change, it is easier to push through it by reminding ourselves that nobody stood still forever at the stop sign. This sense of certainty – that change is inevitable – gives us hope and determination to look for alternatives or persevere to the end with the option on hand.

Knowledge, Happiness, And Food Habits

Knowledge:

"Knowledge" pertains to the intuitive as well as an explicit understanding of the laws of nature at work. For instance, once we understand the principles of electric discharge across charged particles, we can relate to the same phenomena if it occurs as a lightning at a high altitude among rain clouds or in a glass jar in a laboratory experiment. It might even as a spark due to static charge on a silk cloth. Laws of nature are permanent, eternal, and invariant of time, place, or circumstances. Their remarkable consistency is a matter of wonderment in itself! Such knowledge also leads us to the recognition of the consistency or the common principles at work in all situations, which on the surface, appear to be distinct and different.

Just as one can acquires the knowledge of physical laws – like the principles of electric discharge – through analysis, inference, and experimentation, one can also acquire an understanding of the common principles on any subject matter or situation. Hence life itself becomes a space for observation all the time! Such an observer is not affected by the situation or circumstances positively or negatively. But the joy of observation, comprehension, and understanding the common principles at work prevails forever!

As we observe and comprehend each law of nature, we begin to see that laws of nature exist irrespective of time, situation and circumstances. They do exist, whether we know them or not, whether we understand them or not! Each of us can also begin to see that our mere existence and our ability to search for these laws of nature are also governed by certain other laws! When we recognize the laws of nature at work, we can use them wisely. When we do not recognize or understand them, we are humble and modest to have faith that such laws do indeed exist. This knowledge leads to the understanding of the oneness of the universe or the comprehension that "I" as an individual am nothing more than the microcosm of the universe at large (*Thath Thwam Asi*) co-existing under the eternal and omnipresent and omnipotent Laws of Nature (and their metaphoric enabler – God).

Through tranquility, reflection, and self-control, one acquires the KNOWLEDGE through which one can perceive the same and changeless presence in all beings of the world; they also lead to the recognition of the undivided presence in all divided aspects. B.G. 18. 20.

The Knowledge which, through reasons of attachments, leads to separation or division and hence sees many severally divided existences in all beings, places, things, etc., arises out of Bias (leading to turbulence or agitated nature) of a person.   *B.G. 18. 21.*

The Knowledge that leads to unalterable attachment to one activity, object, or effect as if it were the whole of life, ignoring the true realities and narrowness of its scope, is declared to be Ignorance or illusion.   *B.G. 18. 22.*

Happiness:

That experience which appears in the beginning like poison and transforms into nectar in the end, that pleasure of transformation is declared as belonging to HAPPINESS (and its effect through tranquility). Such happiness arises out of the purity or clarity (through self-control) of one's own mind and its power of reasoning.   *B.G. 18. 37.*

That happiness, which arises through contact with the objects of nature and sense organs, which at the beginning is like nectar but slowly turns into poison (disliked and in disfavor due to its inability to satisfy the continued and increasing needs, wants, and desires), such happiness is described as belonging to bias (and its effects through turbulence, agitation or passion, desires and wants)

      B.G.18. 38.

That pleasure which at the beginning as well as in its continuance is deceitful to one's own self and leads to sleep, sloppiness, and lack of direction – such happiness is declared as that arising out of ignorance.   *B.G. 18. 39.*

Food habits:

Simple truths about our food and eating habits are captured in the verses below:

The dominance of knowledge (and understanding of the role of food in nourishing and sustaining our well-being) leads well cooked (lightly salted, lightly greased, wholesome) food, which promotes long life, good health, vitality, and strength. B.G. 17. 8.

Bias (or partial knowledge overwhelmed by our attachments) leads to choices of food of extreme nature (such as extremely bitter, sour, salty, excessively hot, sharp, of a strong odor and taste), leading to pain, sickness, and sorrow. B.G. 17. 9.

Ignorance (on the role of food for our wellbeing) leads one to choose to live with stale, taste less, and unhygienic foods. B.G. 17. 10.

It is important to note that in all of the verses quoted above, the basic principles for food habits are applicable irrespective of food options (Vegetarian, non-vegetarian, Kosher, etc.), place of living, country or ethnic origin, family life or monastic, etc.

The examples cited above also show that it is possible to look at any topic or any aspect of our life from the point of view of looking for the connectors and their roles. Such a view is not clouded by differences and details that we generally tend to perceive. It is such progression in our viewpoint that is described above as the knowledge *"through which one can perceive the same and changeless presence in all beings of the world: perception of the undivided presence in all divided aspects"*. This is the ultimate value and power of the anatomy of our experiences!

Life – A Collection of Discrete Events?

Following is a quote that I read a while ago:

"Thoughts are discrete, like the scenes in a movie. When we see the movie, we get the impression the image of a continuous flow, a chain of events all connected to each other. Yet, they are produced as individual scenes; each with many takes and re-takes, compiled and edited before the movie is released. Our thoughts are like the scenes or the takes and re-takes in a movie setting. Over the course of time – what we call as life – we come to believe that all these scenes are part of a continuum. Anyone watching the movie can readily relate to the scenes, the actors, and the possible take and re-take of the many shots. It is possible to look at our life like that as well".

Even though there are many takes and re-takes of a given scene, the editor uses only one of them or some segments of each in the final edit. Even though we have many experiences in life, we do indeed select a few and de-select the rest to weave the movie or our life story. Here is a simple example: Think of anyone you have known for over twenty or thirty years. That is a long time! There would have been many events that would have occurred in this long span of time. Some events would even have repeated many times, such as sitting together for dinner each evening with a family member or saying hello each morning at the workplace to a colleague of a long time. Yet, when we remember this person, it would be for a collection of few moments. Each of these moments remembered will be for something either extremely positive or extremely negative. All the rest are discarded as the cut tapes that have fallen in the trash bin near the editor's desk! Very few, if any, remember the entire series of events or experiences and thus develop a composite of all our experiences. If we do, maybe we will find that all our life stories are nearly identical!

How do we select the shots among the many to create our life story? Like the movie editor, we have a storyline in our mind. Sometimes the storyline evolves with time. At other times they are cast well ahead in the early part of our life. Everything that fits this storyline we keep, and the rest we tend to edit them out. In due course, such story line, its development, and editing become identified as "individual" or "personality". If we recognize the commonality of the process of such development of the storyline, then all differences among us as individuals disappear. We find ourselves as part of the same species – human beings – with the same process of building our life stories. We begin to see ourselves as part and parcel of the larger universe, co-existing with everything known to us as well as the unknown.

We can be engaged in life and shed tears or have a healthy laughter just as we do when we watch a movie. But, as soon as we leave the theater, the movie and its storyline are distinct and separate from us. To look at life in a dispassionate manner, just like watching a movie, we need the ability to recognize the picture in each frame. Then we can enjoy life, just as we can enjoy the movie. The movie viewing experience can make us one with the storyline of the movie. But we see the separation as soon as we step out of the movie theater. Such ability to observe our own life is part of non-attachment and Self-Realization.

Every scene or footage in each take and re-take in our life is what we call as "experience". Our thoughts are the record and recollection of our experiences. Like the movie film, we can look for our experience as the pictures in each frame, the collection of pictures in each footage or each reel, and ultimately in the final film. As an analogy with Digital Rewind, we also have our minds replay a few scenes frequently. But, just like any recorded medium, our mind can re-wind and re-play only that which has been already recorded (i.e.) our experience. But it cannot create a scene that is not recorded or yet to be filmed! Any fear, anxiety, or jubilation into the future is merely the creative imagination of our mind?

Meditating and the Ocean Waves!

Waves are composed of action, relentless, non-stop, 24 hours a day, 7 days a week, almost eternal. These waves and their churning noise on an island beach have been there and will continue forever. So are our actions through our body, mind, and intellect! We have to acknowledge that most of the body and its functions, along with our mind (and the emotions) and the intellect (and the thoughts), begin with our birth and end with death, unlike the eternal ocean waves! Body as a material object and its change or decay into other forms will continue forever like the stones in the ocean front, which are gradually eroded, crushed, and pulverized into sand over time! The residual effect of our emotions and thoughts may also endure, but their effects are less traceable except for a few connected to each other!

Waves continue their relentless motion. Their sway and intensity change with wind conditions and directions. Some waves reach the shores calm and subdue and return their water back to the deep ocean. Other waves are violent and hit the shores with great vigor and thunderous noise.

Calm waves or their splashing counterparts can be seen only moments apart, at the same place based on the energy and intensity of the waves (Figure 5. 41). They are also

Figure 5. 41. Severe and moderate waves only moments apart!

governed by the resistance they face based on the topography of the beach. Large sandy beaches foster slow and gradual waves, which recede the same way. Rocky beach and turbulent waves contrast with that (Figure 5. 42).

Figure 5. 42. Calm, Intense, and Severe Waves based on the beach and its topography.

Our emotions and reactions to events may be described as Tranquility, Turbulence, or Inertia (*Sathvikam, Rajasam, and Thamasam – Gunathvam*). They are subjective, each unique and dependent on the impelling forces (like the wind currents) and the reactive influences (like the beach and its topography). Do we have the capacity to manage each wave or even focus on all of them? Of course not. Each wave is unique and, to a large extent, independent of others. But we don't remain fixated on each wave while sitting at the oceanfront! So are also our emotions. Are we able to set aside each emotion as an independent event and not carry the burden of pleasure or pain of accumulated experiences? Is this part of our meditation?

At a larger level, we can recognize each wave as a response of the body of water influenced by impelling forces and beach conditions. We see calm and manageable waves on the sandy beach and turbulent and unmanageable waves at the rocky beach. We also see changes if the beach is shallow and gradual or a deep cliff! We can see a larger pattern in the waves across all of the oceans, beach topography, or wind conditions. Our "experiences" are also like that. There are common observable patterns in all our experiences. Many experiences, in the beginning, appear independent, different, and divergent. Through sustained observations and reasoning, we can see commonality or emerging themes across many experiences. Is this the Objectivity that we develop (*Sagunathvam*) as an outcome of our meditation?

There is no ocean on earth without waves. These waves are everywhere – at the shallow beach as well as in the middle across the wide span of the ocean. It is unmistakable evidence of the constant impinging of the wind on the ocean water everywhere. It is a natural phenomenon. All our experiences are also the common natural phenomena like the ocean waves!

We can see waves even in places where there might appear to be no waves at first sight! A closer look at the sandy surface below and its patterns suggest that such striations on the surface could contribute to the waves in the water that flows over it! The waves, in turn, could also contribute to the surface-level perturbations on the sand below. In due course, each influences the other. Are our experiences (waves) the undercurrent of influence from our body, mind, and intellect? How do these experiences, in turn, shape the function and influence our body, mind and

Figure 5. 43. Waves in the mid-ocean and subtle waves
on a shallow shore

intellect. Can we step back and look at this symbiosis instead of getting immersed in the experiences? Is this stepping away for reflection, a deep dive into the cause and effect of our experiences, part of meditation?

We can relate to only a limited extent, the expanse of waves and their occurrence everywhere. Even this simple phenomenon of nature is way beyond our total comprehension. Then what can be said of the infinite laws of nature and their indescribable limitless phenomena (*Nirgunathvam*)? They create and facilitate all that we have come to learn about our life, the universe, and existence. Is this what we are to infer from the dictum "*Sarvam Brahma Mayam*" – everything is *Brahman?*

6. Conclusion

Our life is an interdependent existence in three conditions: Physical or Material; Emotional or Social and Spiritual or Intellectual. Every one of us exists in all these three conditions from the moment of our birth. Life is a balanced outlook across all three conditions as illustrated in the front cover of the book, a balancing act like standing on a stool with three legs.

We make our best effort to take care of our physical body and its health. Our mind reflects the proper function of our brain as a physical organ. Through our mind and hence our knowledge, we learn to deploy and benefit from the governing forces – the "Spirit" or laws of nature – for our good health and physical wellbeing.

Emotional or Social wellbeing is the way we live as part of the family, community, or society at large. All our feelings of like/dislike, happiness/sorrow, rich/poor, friends/foe, etc. are the result of our need to live together with others. Our mind plays a critical role here as well. Managing our emotions and feelings is largely a matter of how we use our brain to think Objectively vs. personal centered or Subjective outlook. Our objectivity is enhanced when our emotions are managed as a response to the "Spirit" (governing forces or laws of nature at play.)

Physiology and medical sciences are being perfected to ever increasing details to improve and manage our Physical wellbeing. Psychology, religion, self-development, and related fields play their roles in our emotional and social wellbeing. However, conditioned by our thoughts we do well or poorly in our physical and emotional wellbeing. Our knowledge, bias, and ignorance are the connectors behind all our thoughts. Through these connectors our mind is tranquil, turbulent, or inertial. This intellectual condition of the mind and its reflection of the prevailing laws of nature is the Spiritual wellbeing. It promotes "peace of mind" and "harmony within". It also promotes a cohesiveness of who we are and how we relate to everything around us. They in turn enhance our wellbeing in all three aspects of our life.

Following is an excerpt from a talk given by his holiness Dalai Lama at the Tibetan Children's Village, on 16th Dec. 2011:

Though there has been great economic progress across the globe, there is still something that seems to be missing. Modern human knowledge has expanded greatly, yet there are many among the learned who create trouble. Our knowledge is put to destructive use because our mind remains untamed. It is only now people are seeing the destructive role of Information and Technology and are paying attention to the issue of peace and wellbeing of the mind. There is also a new interest in the issues of wellbeing in the society and families.

Taking medicines to treat the illness is not enough. If one's mind is peaceful and happy, then elements of the body come into balance. Even though two people may suffer from the same disease and under same physical conditions, the person with peaceful state of mind recuperates faster.

When we say "peace of mind" we do not picture someone with an idle mind sitting still, doing nothing. This is neither peace nor happiness. For real peace of mind, one should remain at peace even in the middle of turmoil. We must face our turmoil, keep our peace of mind and work our way out. This is what we should do. This is definitely achievable".

We hope readers will find enough materials and inspiration from this book and all its essays to find the meaning, purpose, and outcome to be gained from the above words of wisdom of his holiness. There is increasing emphasis on Yoga and meditation practices to tame our mind. Self-development is a popular subject of study for many these days. We do hope that the contents of this book channel the readers for better and more effective use of their Yoga practices, meditation sessions as well as self-development initiatives.

Vedanta (essence of Vedic Philosophy) states that "Spirituality" is a way of life where our actions, emotions and thoughts are centered on the "Spirit", the driving force of nature or enabler, collectively known as "*Brahman*". They are invisible, becoming visible only through their effects – our cognitive universe. They are always objective, reliable in their cause and effect, invariant of time, place, circumstances, etc. Hence the knowledge of the driving forces – the spirit, *Brahman* - provides a clarity on all that is physical, the objectivity needed to manage all our emotions and an ability to condition our mind and hence our thoughts such that we remain at peace within and with everything all around.

Swami Chinmayananda has said "*Do not go to the mountain peaks seeking meditation; seek the "peaks" in your meditation*". This book on Spirituality in Practice is a modest effort and a knowledge source for such practice orientated education on Spirituality.

Om Tat Sat brahmArpanam astu
Om shAnti, shAnti, shAntih
May all that we do be dedicated to total self-control
and Unattached active engagement!
Peace! Peace! Peace!

7. Glossary of Sanskrit Words

Word or Phrase used in the Manuscript	International Alphabet of Sanskrit Transliteration	Meaning	Word or Phrase in Devanagari Script
AUM	oṃ	The symbol that represents Brahman	🕉
Aham Brahma Asmi	ahaṃ brahmāsmi	I am Brahman	अहं ब्रह्मास्मि
AhamKaram	ahaṅkāraṃ	I am responsible; "ego"	अहङ्कारं
Ahimsa	ahiṃsā	Non-violence	अहिंसा
Akarma	akarma	Inaction	अकर्म
Astu	astu	So be it.	अस्तु
Athithi Dhevo Bhava	athiti devo bhava	Treat the guest as God	अथिति देवो भव
Athman	ātman	Soul	आत्मन्
Baghawath Geetha	bhagavadgītā	The Song of the Lord	भगवद्गीता
Bhakthi	bhakti	Faith	भक्ति
Bhava	bhava	exists	भव
Bhikshu Gita	bhikṣu gītā	One of many Gitas (poems of wisdom)	भिक्षु गीता
Brahmam Okate		Brahman is one (Telugu Phrase)	
Brahman	brahman	Singular term to represent all the eneblers and the enabled in the Universe.	ब्रह्मन्
Brhadaranyaka Upanishad	bṛhadāraṇyaka upaniṣad	One of the many Upanishad (Scriptures found as philosophic treatise as sections inside the Vedas)	बृहदारण्यक उपनिषद्
Deepa Aradhana	dīpārādhanā	Offering of light as a form of prayer	दीपाराधना
Deham	dehaṃ	Body, the visible evidence of a person	देहं
Dehinam	dehinaṃ	Soul, the enabler, the invisible evidence of a person	देहिनं
Dharma	dharma	Righteousness; the way the nature works on its own accord	धर्म
dhyana	dhyāna	Meditation	ध्यान

Word or Phrase used in the Manuscript	International Alphabet of Sanskrit Transliteration	Meaning	Word or Phrase in Devanagari Script
Guna	guṇa	Feature or Characteristics; Sources of all our experiences.	गुण
Gunathvam	guṇatvam	Equilibrium states that are identifiable with our experiences or their sources.	गुणत्वं
Guru	guru	Teacher	गुरु
Kalidasa	kālidāsa	A well known Sanskrit poet	कालिदास
Katha Upanishad	kaṭhopaniṣad	One of the many Upanishad (Scriptures found as philosophic treatise as sections inside the Vedas)	कठोपनिषद्
Mahatma	mahātmā	Great Soul	महात्मा
Maya	māyā	Illusion	माया
Moksha	mokṣa	Liberation	मोक्ष
na ithi bhavam	na iti bhāvaṃ	"Not this" attitude or outlook; Evidence of non-attachment	न इति भावं
Nirgunathvanam	nirguṇatvam	Without "guna" or identifiable features or charecteristics; hence without any experience to associate with; Evidence of true renunciation.	निर्गुणत्वं
Nirvana	nirvāṇa	Liberated state	निर्वाण
Papam	pāpam	Sin	पापं
Paramathma	paramātman	Supreme soul	परमात्मन्
Punyam	puṇyam	Divine acts	पुण्यं
Sagunathvanam	saguṇatvam	Balanced in outlook	सगुणत्वं
Sanyasa	samnyāsa	state of renunciation	संन्यास
Sathvikam	sāttvikam	Tranquility	सात्त्विकम्
Rajasam	rājasam	Turbulence	राजसम्
Thamasam	tāmasam	Inertial	तामसं

Word or Phrase used in the Manuscript	International Alphabet of Sanskrit Transliteration	Meaning	Word or Phrase in Devanagari Script
Uddhava Gita	uddhavagītā	One of many Gitas (poems of wisdom)	उद्धवगीता
Upadhi	upādhi	Condition; layer of our existence	उपाधि
Vairagya Shatakam	vairāgyaśatakam	One of the many scriptural poems composedd by Saint Adi Sankara	वैराग्यशतकम्
Vasana	vāsanā	Experience	वासना
Vasudeva Kudumbham	vasudhaiva kuṭumbakam	Universal family; Divine presence everywhere and in everything	वसुधैव कुटुम्बकम्
Vedanta	vedānta	The end or essence of Vedic Knowledge	वेदान्त
Vivekachudamani	vivekacūḍāmaṇi	One of the many scriptural poems composedd by Saint Adi	विवेकचूडामणि
Yagna	yajña	Any act of true non-attachment; Traditional offering or prayers to the Lord	यज्ञ
Yagnopaveetham	yajñopavītam	The protective shiled while performing Yagna; traditional rope with a knot worn across the chest as a religious symbol.	यज्ञोपवीतं
Yuj	yuja	to be in union with	युज
Karma	karma	Action; Activity	कर्म
Kamya Karma	kāmya karma	Action with a purpose or desire	काम्य कर्म
Naimitya Karma	naimitta karma	Action with a specific intent or goal	नैमित्त कर्म
Prarabdha Karma	prārabdha karma	Action as the result of the effect from previous life	प्रारब्ध कर्म
Sanchita Karma	saṃcita karma	Action as the result od accumulated effects of previous actions.	संचित कर्म
Nishkama Karma	niṣkāma karma	Action without any desire or attachment	निष्काम कर्म
Karman Eva Adhikarasthe, Maa Paleshu	karmaṇyevādhikāraste mā phaleṣu	You have a right to perform your duty - action as called upon under the righteous course; not for the end results.	कर्मण्येवाधिकारस्ते मा फलेषु

Word or Phrase used in the Manuscript	International Alphabet of Sanskrit Transliteration	Meaning	Word or Phrase in Devanagari Script
Yoga	yoga	Action or activity that brings one in union with the soul or inner person.	योग
Karma Yoga	karma yoga	Union with the self through action	कर्म योग
Bhakthi Yoga	bhakti yoga	Union with the self through faith or devotion	भक्ति योग
Jnana Yoga	jñāna yoga	Union with the self through reflection and analysis	ज्ञान योग
Dhyana Yoga	dhyāna yoga	Union with the self through meditation	ध्यान योग
Hatha Yoga	haṭha yoga	Union with the self through physical activities	हठ योग
Thri Guna Vibhaga Yoga	traigunya vibhāga yoga	Union with the self through the exploration of the three equilibriums states - the basis for all our experiences.	त्रैगुण्य विभाग योग
Sanyasa Yoga	samnyāsa yoga	Union with the self through renunciation	संन्यास योग
Maha Vaakyas	mahā vākya	Grand Pronouncements	महा वाक्य
Prajnanam Brahma	prajñānam brahma	Consciousness is Brahman	प्रज्ञानं ब्रह्म
Thath Thwam Asi	tat tvam asi	You and the Universe are integral In each other.	तत् त्वम् असि
Sarve' Jhana Sukino Bhavanthu	sarve jana sukhino bhavantu	May everyone remain in peace and harmony.	सर्वे जन सुखिनो भवन्तु
Aham Brahma	aham brahma	I am Brahman	अहं ब्रह्म
Aham Brahmasmi	aham brahmāsmi	I remain as Brahman	अहं ब्रह्मास्मि
Brahmavit Brahmaiva Bavathi	brahmavid brahmaiva bhavati	One with the knowledge of Brahman remains as Brahman.	ब्रह्मविद् ब्रह्मैव भवति
Anna Maya	anna maya	Material state or condition	अन्न मय
Prana Maya	prāna maya	Living state or condition	मनो मय
Manon Maya	mano maya	Emotional state or condition	प्राण मय
Vignana Maya	vijñāna maya	Analytical state or condition	विज्ञान मय
Ananda Maya	ānanda maya	State or Condition of bliss	आनन्द मय

Blank Page – for Reader's Notes.

Blank Page – for Reader's Notes.